"Through the story of one pioneering woman, a portrait of a statewide debate emerges. Only a few pages into [it]…and the reader, even with decades of study in the field of Maine history, is learning new, exciting information available nowhere else…The author, Whitehouse's great-granddaughter, is never sentimental, for this is a true work of scholarship."

—WILLIAM DAVID BARRY, Maine historian
Portland Press Herald

VOTING DOWN THE ROSE

Voting Down the Rose

Florence Brooks Whitehouse

&

Maine's Fight for Woman Suffrage

Anne B. Gass

To my aunt, Priscilla Whitehouse Rand,
who started me on this journey.

and

To my mother, Anne Whitehouse Gass,
who encouraged me every step of the way.

Preface

...I have no quarrel with you—but henceforth,
This you must know; the world is mine, as yours,
The pulsing strength and passion and heart of it;
The work I set my hand to, women's work,
Because I set my hand to it.

Florence Brooks Whitehouse [i]

With these ringing words, Florence Brooks Whitehouse concluded her speech before the Maine House Committee on the Judiciary. It was February 1917, and the nine men on the Committee were hearing testimony on a resolve to extend voting rights to women. Never had the Committee's proceedings received such public scrutiny; every available seat in the Hall of Representatives was taken, with extra chairs wedged into the remaining floor space and onlookers perched on the windowsills. Each side had brought its most prominent and persuasive speakers to argue its case. The pro-suffrage forces demanded voting rights as a matter of justice and political expediency, and produced 5,000 pledges from Mainers supporting the measure. The anti-suffrage forces opposed burdening women with this added responsibility, arguing that society was better served by keeping women in the home and out of political affairs. The audience clapped and cheered as speakers on both sides scored points in the debate.

Maine suffragists were seeking the distinction of being the first state east of the Mississippi to win full suffrage for women. Nearly forty years of toil had brought them closer to this goal than ever before, though some of the most heated battles of the movement were still to come. While suffragists believed their victory was inevitable, the citizens of Maine, as in the rest of the country, remained divided on the question. At the core of the struggle were questions that are still debated today: What is womanhood? Who defines it? What is woman's role in society?

The suffrage movement was led by brilliant and courageous women, and history deservedly remembers national leaders such as Elizabeth Cady Stanton, Susan B. Anthony, Carrie Chapman Catt, Anna Howard Shaw, and Alice Paul. Yet a thorough review of the suffrage literature shows that acts of sacrifice and personal courage were repeated through every level of the organizations, all the way down to the individual members. The national organizations were certainly critical to the eventual victory, but the battle for woman suffrage was waged in every drawing room, town, county, and state across the country. That story is not often told; most of the histories that exist focus on the actions of the national leaders, with the city or state level leaders merely a sidebar.

Florence Brooks Whitehouse was my great-grandmother, and yet I knew virtually nothing about her until I was in my late thirties. I first learned the extent of her activities when browsing through her papers, which my aunt had given to the Maine Historical Society. In the hushed silence of the reading room, I drew on the clumsy cotton gloves patrons must wear to protect fragile documents and began opening files at random. Florence had known she was saving history; the yellowed and crumbling newspaper clippings, for example, often had the newspaper name and date scrawled across the top. It intrigued me that history she thought worth saving was not something our society remembered much; as a child my history books (in the few sentences they spared for this subject) seemed to suggest that men graciously granted women the vote after a few big marches in Washington. A black-and-white photo of marching women clad in long white dresses usually accompanied the text in my books, but the camera lens focused from above the crowd at such a distance that the marchers' individual features were blurred.

I had heard that my great-grandmother had been one of those nameless, faceless women but the manila file bulging with newspaper clippings fairly screamed at me to understand that there was so much more to the story. Setting aside the clippings, I drew from the box another file marked "Correspondence" and in short order came across a copy of a telegram Florence had sent to

Senator Andrieus A. Jones of New Mexico, asking him to act on a suffrage measure.[ii] Why was Florence, who lived in Portland, Maine, writing to a United States Senator from New Mexico? Baffled but intrigued, I read on until I came to another telegram Florence had received from National Woman's Party Headquarters, which read:

> PERPETUAL WATCH FIRES TO BURN PRESIDENT'S SPEECHES IN FRONT OF WHITE HOUSE BEGAN THIS AFTERNOON FOUR WOMEN ARRESTED ALICE PAUL EDITH AINGE JULIA EMERY HAZEL HUNKINS WERE TOLD TO APPEAR FOR TRIAL LATER FIRE LIGHTED WITH WOOD FROM INDEPENDENCE SQUARE FIRE STILL CONTINUES GIVE PUBLICITY [iii]

The telegram had been sent at 5:12 a.m. Here was some drama, I thought. Burning the president's speeches in front of the White House! Women (whoever they were) arrested! And Florence was charged with publicizing these events in Maine. Later in the file was a letter from Lucy Burns, pleading with Florence to come to Washington, DC to picket in front of the White House.[iv] Who was Lucy Burns, and why was it so important to her that Florence come and picket? How did Florence respond to this plea?

I was hooked. From that point on, I read extensively about suffrage history, reviewed Florence's papers page by page, and researched other collections until I understood what happened and the part Florence played. In Maine the work was carried out by a relatively small group of women and men, typically from prominent families, who were linked by social and business ties. They attended the same churches, were actively involved in Maine's progressive movement, and were members of the same cultural and political committees. They shared a common set of values that, while supporting education and voting rights for women, also narrowly defined rules of behavior and social decorum. In the final years of the struggle, their combined power and influence helped win broader political support for suffrage.

Thus, when Florence and a handful of others elected to pursue a different and more controversial path to winning suffrage, the shock wave traveled beyond the movement to the core of their daily lives. In allying themselves with strategies regarded as militant and radical, Florence and her supporters challenged social norms of womanly behavior. As a consequence, they risked not just the success of the suffrage campaign but their social standing and their friendships with people who remained in the mainstream movement.

From 1914 on, Florence was in the forefront of Maine's efforts to win equal suffrage, working initially with the National American Woman Suffrage Association (NAWSA) *(see Figure 1)*. She later founded and chaired the Maine branch of the Congressional Union (which became the National Woman's Party), the group that pioneered picketing the White House in the suffrage fight. Despite the abundant public record that exists demonstrating her leadership, the scant histories written about Maine suffrage pointedly ignore her contributions.[v] This is likely because they were written by mainstream suffragists who wished to downplay the activities of their more radical colleagues.

Suffrage activities were just one aspect of Florence's accomplished and varied career. An early feminist, Florence would be impressive were she active today; viewed against the backdrop of her own time and the restrictions then placed on women, her accomplishments are remarkable. She was a published author, a playwright, and a painter, and was known for her leadership in civic affairs. During WW I she served as the public relations coordinator for the local Red Cross. She was a staunch advocate for peace who nonetheless sent two sons to fight in WW I and supported the war effort through the Red Cross and other means. She remained active in civic affairs in the years following passage of the federal suffrage amendment, serving as Maine's chairman for the Women's Committee for World Disarmament, continuing her work with the National Woman's Party (NWP), and representing women on the board of the Maine Chamber of Commerce and Agricultural League, among many other activities.

This book explores in detail the previously untold story of Maine's battle to win equal suffrage for women. It begins in 1913, when Florence first joined the struggle, and follows the campaign through the ratification of the Federal Amendment in 1920. The story relies on a wide range of original documents, including Florence's papers at the Maine Historical Society, newspaper articles, and the collections of the NWP and NAWSA held at the Library of Congress. Suffrage research conducted by other historians also sheds light on this exciting period in history.

At its most basic, this is simply the story of Maine's involvement in the suffrage campaign during the particularly tumultuous final years, how Maine occupied the national stage at pivotal points in the final years of the battle, and Florence's role in bringing the struggle to a close. This book also sheds light on how the clash in strategy at the national level, between the NWP and NAWSA, divided loyalties at the state level and hampered the effectiveness of organizing efforts. This was especially true in 1917 during Maine's only statewide referendum campaign for full suffrage.

Finally, this book examines the nature of leadership, comparing Alice Paul and the NWP's single-minded focus on winning suffrage to the more accommodating approach of NAWSA, as well as to the more varied allegiances of local suffragists like Florence who were answerable to the demands of home, family, and community. Demands on local suffragists became even more intense once the United States entered World War I. Ultimately, all three forms of leadership were needed to push the Federal Amendment through a balky Congress and get it ratified by Maine and 35 other states.

The book's title is drawn from an exchange of poetry between Florence and an anti-suffragist, which a local newspaper referred to as "The War of the Flowers" (this can be found in Chapter II.) The rose was the symbol of the of the anti-suffragists, while the pro-suffrage forces chose the jonquil. Florence used "While voting DOWN the rose" as a refrain in her poem, and it seemed a fitting title for a book about her successful efforts to win political and social freedom for women.

FIGURE 1   Florence Brooks Whitehouse
Women of Protest: Photographs from the Records of the National Woman's
Party, Manuscript Division, Library of Congress, Washington, D.C.

1 Maine's Newest Suffragist

It all started, Florence would remember later, when the topic of one of Mrs. Morrill Hamlin's Monday afternoon lectures had been woman suffrage, and Mrs. Hamlin took the anti-suffrage ("anti") point of view. Florence and several of the other subscribers had disagreed with Mrs. Hamlin but could not marshal the arguments to oppose her.

A group of women had gathered in the music room of Portland's Congress Square Hotel, as was their custom on Monday afternoons, to listen to another of Mrs. Hamlin's "Current Topics" lectures. It was one of a series she offered to women by subscription, and during the winter and spring of 1913, many took advantage of the opportunity to hear Mrs. Hamlin's views on subjects as diverse as European politics, "Pure Food and the High Cost of Living," South American republics, and the Monroe Doctrine.[1] A well-informed and engaging speaker in her own right, Mrs. Hamlin was also the daughter of Lot Morrill, one of Maine's most distinguished politicians. He had been elected governor in 1858, but left that position in 1861 to fill out Hannibal Hamlin's term in the US Senate when he became Lincoln's vice president. Morrill's own Senate career had lasted until 1876, after which he had served as secretary of the treasury under President Grant. Coming from a prominent political family gave Mrs. Hamlin's views added cachet.

Yet on this day, when Mrs. Hamlin trotted out the usual arguments against woman suffrage, Florence felt a great dissonance. She learned from Mrs. Hamlin that women did not want to vote, they would not use the vote if they had it, and they had too much to handle running their households as it was. Women were not well-suited to voting, she argued; they were too frail for the rough and tumble of politics. Besides, if they needed a measure passed, they could simply ask their men to vote for it. Women had no need to vote because everything they required was provided for them.

Mrs. Hamlin's arguments were not new, but for some reason they rankled Florence in a way they never had before. Under her modish hat, perched on carefully dressed light-brown curls, Florence's bright-blue eyes fairly blazed with indignation. Looking around the room, she would have seen intelligent, well-educated, capable women who were at least interested enough in current events to attend Mrs. Hamlin's lecture series. They all sought to improve society through involvement in a variety of women's clubs, civic groups, and the Women's Christian Temperance Union (WCTU). They chaired committees, led efforts to improve conditions for the poor, campaigned for educational and legal reforms, and won praise from the men with whom they worked shoulder to shoulder on these issues. And how on earth could Mrs. Hamlin, whose skills as a lecturer kept her on tour throughout New England, keep a straight face as she presented herself as unworthy of the franchise?

Florence and some other like-minded women argued with her, but Mrs. Hamlin was a skilled debater who had marshaled her facts beforehand, and there was no getting around her. Florence finally admitted, "I am not convinced, but I cannot argue with you, for I do not know enough. Still, I feel that you are wrong." Unwilling to leave it at that, Florence volunteered to read up on suffrage and come back in six months for a debate. Mrs. Hamlin accepted the challenge.

****

What prompted Florence, at this point in her life, to delve into suffrage? As she walked home along Congress Street, the lights from shop windows pooled on the sidewalks and the trolley cars rumbled past carrying riders home from work. She was a middle-aged married woman and the mother of three fine sons. She moved easily through Maine's highest social circles. Her husband had encouraged her writing career, which enabled her to publish two novels with Little Brown and Company, as well as numerous short stories. With the glaring exception of being denied the right to vote, she had suffered relatively little from the laws governing how women were treated.

In truth, she had always pursued her interests with determination and focus. Florence Brooks was born in 1869 into a prosperous and socially prominent family in Maine's state capital, Augusta. Her father was Samuel Spencer Brooks, a businessman whose various enterprises were sufficient to maintain his large family in substantial comfort. He started out in groceries with his older brother and later dabbled in furniture and shipbuilding, but from 1885 on, he focused primarily on his wholesale and retail hardware business at 251 Water Street in Augusta.[2] The Brooks family lived in a spacious and elegant house at 7 Spruce Street, on the eastern bank of the Kennebec River. Florence was the fourth of five children and the family's first girl.

In the years after the Civil War ended, Augusta became a bustling, thriving city sprawling across both sides of the Kennebec River. The Kennebec gave it life, powering its factories and connecting Augusta to the sea and to foreign ports. Factories churned out cotton cloth, lumber, railroad cars, furniture, and flour, shipping them to market by rail or by boat.[3] Water power also supported an active publishing empire. Typical of the dramatic expansion of the press in the second half of the 19th century, Augusta was home to several daily newspapers as well as weekly and monthly journals devoted to literature and politics.[4]

The Brooks family maintained friendships with many leading people, including politicians, judges, writers, newspaper publishers, and other business owners. Mr. and Mrs. Brooks supported education for all their children. As a child Florence attended Augusta public schools, later enrolling at St. Catherine's Hall, a private finishing school affiliated with the Episcopal Church.[5] She then spent several winters studying music, languages, drawing, and painting under "the best masters" in Boston. It is not clear why she chose this route rather than attending college, which growing numbers of young women were doing and which must have been an option for her. She may have preferred the freedom she enjoyed in Boston, where she could focus on the subjects that interested her. In the summers, she returned to Maine to her family's cottage on Squirrel Island, a middle-class summer colony off of Boothbay Harbor. The Brookses were one of the original families to buy into the island in 1871, and from the outset Squirrel was unique, establishing rules that set it apart from towns on the mainland. Its early members were firmly committed to temperance, and though Maine had enacted prohibition some years earlier, Squirrel's early settlers found the law easier to enforce. Apart from strict prohibition, life was more relaxed and there was freedom to stroll the island paths, play tennis and baseball, paint, and sail. The families were all affluent and well-educated people, and included business and political leaders such as the Stanley brothers, who invented the Stanley Steamer, and Nelson Dingley, Jr., who had been governor of Maine and also served eight terms in the US House of Representatives. Women were granted the right to own property and they could vote on an equal footing with men within the governing association, which may have contributed to Florence's later interest in woman suffrage.

Florence evidently enjoyed her freedom and was not in a hurry to settle down. In 1892, at the age of 23, she took an extended trip abroad to Spain, Italy, Switzerland, Greece, Turkey, Africa, and the Holy Land, as well as to the art centers of Syria and Egypt.[6] She spent one entire winter in Egypt, traveling down the Nile in a *dahabeah* and lingering for several weeks in both Cairo and Luxor. The detailed journal she kept during this trip, and the many sketches she made, became the basis for some of her later writing.

Florence finally returned to Maine in 1894 to marry Robert Treat Whitehouse, a local boy and former schoolmate.[7] Robert's uncle, Seth Whitehouse, had partnered with Samuel Brooks in buying into Squirrel Island back in 1871, so it is likely that Robert also spent summers there. The Whitehouse family was highly regarded in Augusta, where Robert's father, William Penn, had served as the Kennebec County attorney, on the Kennebec Superior Court, and eventually as chief justice of Maine's Supreme Court. Robert's mother, Evelyn Treat, was the daughter of an affluent businessman from Frankfort, Maine. Robert was the eldest and only surviving child of the family. He had attended Harvard College as an undergraduate and had completed law school there as well.

The wedding was a simple ceremony held at her parents' house on Spruce Street, with only a few family and friends attending. She had made him wait to marry her—family lore has it that he actually sailed to Egypt to bring her back home—but Florence and Robert were well-matched and their marriage was a happy one. Young, educated women like Florence were looking for marriages in which they could enjoy equal status with their husbands, and Robert seems to have shared this view. They moved to Portland, where, with the help of Robert's mother, they bought an attractive wood frame house at 42 Deering Street, a respectable address for a couple just starting out. Robert was admitted to the bar in 1894 and joined the firm of Symonds, Cook, and Snow.

It was an exciting time to be young and living in Portland, then a city of about 40,000 people that boasted 50 women's clubs, a host of cultural amenities, and an active social schedule for families with means. Florence and Robert enjoyed the theater, literature, and music, and during the first two years of their marriage collaborated on writing and directing plays.[8] The one that received the most recognition was *The House Party*, which they performed with great success in Portland at Kotzschmar Hall, in Brunswick and Augusta, and on Squirrel Island *(see Figure 2)*. One reviewer enthused that it was "one of great variety, running the whole gamut from serious drama to light comedy and musical specialty. The situations are clear, the dialogue brilliant in parts, and the action rapid and well sustained to the end."[9] Florence and Robert directed the plays and acted in the lead roles.

The second play, *A Modern Sir Launfal*, was a short comedy with a "Gallic vivacity and grace and perfection in plot that recall Eugene Scribe himself."[10] *The Effendi*, the third work, they performed twice, and Florence later reworked it into her second novel. As Robert's professional and volunteer responsibilities increased, he had less leisure time and gradually left more of the writing to Florence.

They each pursued separate interests as well. Robert joined the Fraternity Club, an organization open by invitation only to men, in which they pursued scientific and literary interests. He was elected to Portland's school board and was active in the Republican Party. In 1900 he left private practice to become the Cumberland County district attorney. Florence joined Portland's Rossini Club, established in 1871 as the country's first musical organization for amateur and professional women musicians. The Rossini Club prepared an annual series of classical music concerts that helped raise scholarship funds for young musicians to further their studies. Florence sang in some of the concerts, and researched and presented papers on music history.

Florence also started the Author's Club to meet others who shared her passion for writing. Meetings were held during the winter months only, and for two years Portland's aspiring writers met twice a week to share their work. She was successful in publishing short stories in the *Youth's Companion* and other magazines. She gave several talks on Egypt, illustrated with her own sketches and photographs she had taken during her travels.[11] At Robert's urging, she gradually narrowed her focus to writing and illustrating a novel based on her experiences traveling in Egypt and the Sudan. She offered it to Little Brown and Company and they signed her immediately. *The God of Things* was published in 1902 to favorable reviews *(see illustration in Figure 3)*.[12]

The God of Things: A Novel of Modern Egypt is a rather moralistic romance set against the backdrop of ancient pyramids and ruins. The heroine, Dorothy, is traveling in Egypt when she meets and falls in love with Phillip, a man she later discovers had been married previously but whose wife had deserted him

FIGURE 2   Cover of program from *The House Party*, a play written by
Florence Brooks Whitehouse and her husband Robert.
Maine Historical Society Collections

years before. Dorothy's religious beliefs will not tolerate divorce, however, and she and Phillip experience a painful separation before being reunited at the end of the story. One of the book's most distinguishing features is its descriptions of Egypt seen through the eyes of Western travelers. As an artist and a writer, Florence had an eye for colorful details, and the novel is full of references to the scent of orange blossoms, the haunting beauty of the desert, and the bustle of Cairo's streets.[13] Little, Brown promoted it from coast to coast and Florence subscribed to a clipping service, pasting the reviews into a scrapbook. The congratulatory letters she also saved suggest that she helped market her novel by sending it to notable people of her acquaintance, including the Honorable Clarence Hale, a US District Court judge and a family friend, and Senator William P. Frye, then president pro tempore of the United States Senate.[14]

Buoyed by her success with her first novel, Florence immediately set about adapting the play *The Effendi* into a second book. Household help, including a cook and a nanny, helped her find time to write despite the fact that she and Robert already had two young children; William Penn had been born in 1895 and Robert Treat, Jr., followed in 1897. A third child, Brooks, arrived in 1904. Due to complications with that pregnancy, Florence was on bed rest most of the winter, which gave her time to complete her second novel. This one was illustrated by Isaac Henry Caliga, a well-known artist who occasionally illustrated books for Little, Brown. Since he had a studio in Boston, it is possible that Florence had either met him or taken lessons from him during the winters she had spent there.

The Effendi: A Romance of the Soudan enjoyed an even better reception than *The God of Things*, establishing Florence as an author of some note and a local celebrity in Portland.[15] The story is again set in Egypt, this time in Luxor during the British colonial involvement that had been playing out during Florence's own travels there. The novel opens with a lengthy prologue describing the last days of General Charles Gordon, a British war hero who was killed in the 1885 siege of Khartoum by the forces of the rebel Mohammed Ahmed, the self-proclaimed Mahdi. The events of the novel take place in 1897 and are shaped by the history of Gordon's death. There is romance, espionage, and intrigue woven together in the complex plot. Florence displays some Western biases; Muslim Arabs are generally referred to as heathens, for example, and there is a presumption throughout of the superiority of American and British culture. Nevertheless, there are many appreciative descriptions of the antiquities, the beauty of the desert, and of Arabic music.

The heroine, Elinor, is from Maine, and is in love with Randolph, a soldier in the British army. Elinor is an intelligent young woman who actively engages in the adventures of the book and helps resolve its mysteries. At one point, she and Randolph are kidnapped, and she is dragged off to a *hareem*. Elinor's quick thinking prevents Randolph from being tortured, and helps to win their release.[16]

Although it is not the focal point of the book, Elinor is also a woman suffrage supporter, providing an early indication of Florence's own views on this topic. In the book, Elinor muses that she herself had "never felt any of the restraints which Lyndall fought. She had been absolutely free and unrestricted from childhood." She contrasts her experience with that of another character, Doris, who has been much more constrained and tells Elinor it is futile for women to resist established laws. "We shall always be like dogs on the end of a leash, at the mercy of the man who holds the string," Doris tells Elinor. "The happiest woman is the one who forgets the leash." The reference to Lyndall is almost certainly to a character in a best-selling novel by Olive Schreiner, *The Story of an African Farm*, first published in 1883. Now hailed as one of the early feminist novels, it caused controversy at the time because of its discussion of feminism and free thought, as well as of taboo subjects such as premarital sex and transvestites. The fact that she mentions it in her novel, however obliquely, suggests that Florence had read and was influenced by the work. While clearly obedient to many of the proprieties imposed on young women of her class, Elinor often moves about Luxor unchaperoned, sometimes alone and at other times in the company of her young unmarried male friends. She has several suitors but is free to choose the man she will marry. She attended Smith College and continues to have a life of the mind. Florence contrasts this to the experience of the local women, who are confined behind walls, forced into polygamous marriages with men they do not love, taught only how to please their husbands, and who spend their days guarded by slaves.

The two novels suggest some evolution in Florence's beliefs; Elinor in *The Effendi* is a more independent thinker. She makes little reference to being guided by the religious values that lead Dorothy in *The God of Things* to refuse marriage to Phillip. Indeed, one wonders if Elinor, presented with the same dilemma, might make a different decision. Still, Florence was clearly not prepared at that point in time to address head-on the ways in which women's sphere was limited in American society, as she would when she joined the suffrage movement years later.

FIGURE 3 Illustration from *The God of Things*, Florence's first novel.

Florence's career took a backseat once their third son, Brooks, was born. Managing a household and three active young boys kept her busy, and if she worked on a third novel, she was not able to complete it. Any hopes she may have had of returning to more active writing were put on hold when Brooks developed polio at the age of four. At first he was almost fully paralyzed and was placed in an iron lung, but gradually sensation returned to first one arm, then the other, and finally to his left leg. Florence remained by his side during the crisis and its aftermath, using hot baths and massage to stimulate nerve and muscle development in the lifeless limb. Doctors tried to prepare her to accept that Brooks might never walk again, but she stubbornly continued her therapy. One day, after three years of home treatment, she saw a muscle jump in his leg. Florence buried her face with her hands and wept in relief.[17] Brooks continued to improve and was eventually able to walk with the help of leg braces, though he required corrective surgery on his foot several years later.

Florence did manage to write and publish at least one short story during these years. Entitled *By Way of Compensation*, it seems likely she wrote it for Brooks to comfort him during his recovery. The story features a homeless newsboy, self-named Theodore Roosevelt William Travers Jerome, who has a cherubic face and is the leader of the younger newsboys on the east side of the city where he lives. Like Brooks, little Teddy contracts polio and spends many months in a hospital. There he is cared for by a handsome young doctor and a beautiful volunteer nurse, Miss Edith, who plan to marry and adopt him. In a surprising turn of events, Teddy emerges as the hero of the story when he is able to rescue the young doctor from drowning in the lake during a visit to Miss Edith's camp. Many details of this story seem patterned after Brooks's own experience: the months in a hospital; gradual recovery to the point where he could move about in leg braces; and the sadness of being left behind by the older boys because he was too weak to keep up.[18]

From 1905 to 1913, Florence apparently committed herself to caring for her family. Her scrapbook, into which she had faithfully pasted every book review and published interview following publication of her novels, simply leaves off in 1905 and resumes in early 1914 as though those nine years never existed. What happened? After the heady period of early marriage and motherhood, and of achieving recognition as a playwright and novelist, was it difficult to give herself over completely to mothering? There is no evidence that she ever regretted her decision to become a mother, or mourned what she might have been as a writer had domestic duties not intervened. The threat of losing Brooks had to have been sobering, and perhaps caused her to reevaluate her priorities. Maybe it was enough, for the time being, to raise three healthy young sons and launch them into the world. Raising a family was not a retirement but merely a pause in her public life while she took care of some private business. Since Florence's achievements were always a direct result of her ability to identify her priorities and use every spare minute toward realizing her goals, we can be sure that she brought to motherhood the same focus and energy that she had brought to her novels. Her sons were all devoted to her, and in later life supported her in any way they could, a sign that she was as successful at this as she was in her other ventures.

Robert's career progressed well, and in 1905 he became United States Attorney for the State of Maine, a post he held until 1914.[19] This put the Whitehouses squarely in the middle of the reform movement that was then sweeping across Maine and the nation as a whole. Reforms were driven by middle-class men and women who sought to harness the power of local, state, and federal governments to improve society. In Maine, reformers pressed for enforcement of prohibition laws already on the books. They tried to eliminate government waste and corruption, improve schools, protect food safety, and save women from prostitution. They established city parks like Deering Oaks and the Eastern Promenade in Portland, and pushed to beautify the urban environment. As the State's Attorney and a reform-minded person himself, Robert was actively involved in many of these efforts.

By 1912 the Whitehouses' family responsibilities were finally beginning to diminish. Their eldest son, Penn, was enrolled at Harvard and young Robert was at Exeter. Brooks had survived his bout with polio and his health had improved, so he no longer needed such constant attention. Then 43, Florence may have felt that it was time to reclaim the public life she had laid aside. She and Robert joined the Civic Club of Portland at least as early as 1912. Another outgrowth of the progressive movement, the Civic Club had been established in 1898 to "make Portland a better place in which to live," and its membership roster read like a "Who's Who" of Portland. John Calvin Stevens was a member, as were the Flaggs, the Chapmans, and the Baxters, along with many others who the Whitehouses knew from a variety of civic, cultural, and social organizations. There were many couples, and both men and women served as officers of the organization; Mrs. Charles (Edna Frances) Flagg, for example, was a past president of the Club. The Civic Club met monthly from September to May and was divided into a number of departments. Robert sat on the

Advisory Board for several years, and both Florence and Robert were members of the Club's Department of Public Safety. This rather vague title could encompass a wide range of interests, but it is likely that the group focused at least some of its attention on what many considered to be the primary social evil of Portland life: prostitution.[20] Robert, in his capacity as State's Attorney, began researching this issue through his involvement with the Citizen's Committee. Other demands of modern urban life included improved sanitation, building inspections, and street lighting.

Her Civic Club membership helped kindle in Florence some of the moral outrage she felt about societal conditions, human problems that only changes to laws could address. There was a sense not only that society ought to do something about these issues, but that positive changes could be made if right-minded people came together to force changes to law and policy. Florence's fellow members included both women and men who were leaders on the local, statewide, and national levels in advocating for reforms, and who had the capacity to make positive change occur.

So it was that when Florence sat in the audience at Mrs. Hamlin's anti-suffrage lecture in 1913, her almost visceral response to Hamlin's arguments was a resounding *no*, even if she did not yet know enough about suffrage to argue with her. She was a wife and a mother, a published author, a person of stature in her community when it came to any issue other than voting. She was not prepared to accept that her sex alone made her unfit to vote.

Suffrage presented Florence with a unique opportunity. It provided a ready outlet for the reform-minded zeal her involvement in the Civic Club had nurtured. It drew on all the skills she had developed earlier in her life as a novelist and a playwright, and effectively gave her a stage on which to perform. Finally, the Maine suffrage movement was desperate for new leaders, and that may have clinched the deal for her.

II   MWSA's Rising Star

S everal years after she joined the movement, a reporter asked Florence why she gave herself so completely to suffrage. Florence replied, "Because I believe that the work I do for suffrage is fifty times more valuable to the community than ten times the work on charities or any social work would be." She noted that the charitable work did not get at the root causes of social ills. Low wages forced families to go hungry and to send their children to work instead of to school, and lack of other employment sent young women into prostitution. Easy availability of liquor meant that many men drank their wages instead of caring for their families. Poor sanitation in the homes and city streets made children sick. It was impossible to effect meaningful change without changing laws, and women needed the vote to do that. "When [women] do vote they won't be satisfied to skim the top of the pool of social corruption any longer, but they will pave it with clean cobble stones, and put a drain through it, and connect the source with the bubbling spring…Women are the conservers of the race, and men are the consumers…"[21]

Florence's conviction that women would prove to be an overwhelmingly positive moral force in governing society was echoed throughout suffrage literature, and was consistent with society's view that women were made of better moral fiber than men. The more radical portion of this statement is Florence's determination to examine the root causes of poverty and other ills, and to challenge the status quo. No other spokesperson for woman suffrage in Maine argued quite so forcefully or in such depth for the need for suffrage. Ironically, while Florence meant her words to galvanize support among forward-thinking people, her outspoken intention of wielding the vote to make fundamental social changes may have made Maine men more fearful of extending the franchise.

When Florence joined the movement in 1913, it was 65 years since the first women's rights convention, and winning suffrage had been the movement's primary focus for more than 40 years. Her research revealed that while they agreed on the vote as their primary goal, suffragists had suffered deep divisions around strategy, primarily over whether suffrage should be pursued state by state or through an amendment to the federal constitution. After the Civil War, the federal amendment enfranchising blacks established a precedent for national action, but many politicians argued that the Constitution specifically gave states the right to determine who was an eligible voter. As a practical matter, for decades this debate proved to be a useful way for suffrage opponents to delay its approval. At the state level, suffragists were told to get Congress to enact a federal amendment, while opponents in Congress told them to get approval from their state legislatures. For these reasons, most suffrage leaders believed it was important to operate on both levels simultaneously. Every state that approved woman suffrage added more pressure on the Congress to pass a federal amendment, while progress at the national level encouraged states to enfranchise women before the federal government usurped this right.

In the early years of the 20th century, the state-by-state philosophy was in ascendance, and after a 12-year stretch in which no new states were added to the suffrage column, momentum was beginning to build once again. Yet the state-by-state approach required herculean effort and was agonizingly slow. In 1913, after 65 years of struggle, only nine states and one territory had granted women the right to vote, and these victories had come at a high price. Between 1870 and 1910, suffragists across the country had mounted 480 campaigns in 33 states to get the question in front of voters. Only 55 of these, about 11 percent, were successful in getting referendums approved by state legislatures, and only two states actually approved suffrage in this way.[22] Still, by the end of 1914, men in 11 western states had given women the vote. Roughly four million women of voting age lived in equal suffrage states, and the presidential candidates were beginning to take notice.[23]

The National American Woman Suffrage Association (NAWSA), the country's premier suffrage organization, hadn't entirely abandoned the federal approach. Beginning in 1878, NAWSA regularly petitioned Congress to adopt an amendment to the Constitution enfranchising women. This was formally known as the Susan B. Anthony Amendment, because she drafted it and was first successful in getting it introduced, but suffragists generally referred to it as either the Anthony or the Federal Amendment. This was largely a symbolic act, however, as neither House nor Senate had even debated the bill for decades. In 1912 NAWSA's entire budget for passing the Federal Amendment was less than $10.00, and the woman in charge returned change at the end of the year![24] While they kept the option open, NAWSA leaders never aggressively pursued passage of the Federal Amendment until 1916.

Maine was slow to answer the suffrage call, and then it was decades before supporters achieved any noticeable results from their activities. Florence's father-in-law had been among those calling for suffrage in 1874. Along with 17 other people, William Penn Whitehouse issued a call in a Portland newspaper for a Woman Suffrage Convention to be held in Granite Hall in Augusta on January 29th and 30th.[25] The notice invited "...all who believe in the principles of equal justice, equal liberty and equal opportunity...and have faith in the triumph of intelligence and reason over custom and prejudice." Every seat in the hall was taken, and latecomers had to stand at the back and along the sides. Julia Ward Howe and Lucy Stone traveled up from Boston to be the featured speakers, though they were delayed by a day due to a snowstorm.

Judge Whitehouse served as chairman of the Convention's Committee on Resolutions. On day two, he introduced several resolutions that affirmed women's right to vote and called for changes to Maine's constitution to allow this to happen.[26] The conference concluded with a decision to form a women's rights organization in Maine.

Despite this enthusiastic start, suffrage organizing in Maine produced few results over the next 30 years. Organizers formed leagues in many areas of the state, including Portland, Augusta, Auburn, Saco, Skowhegan, Machias, and Hancock County. The leagues helped keep the suffrage issue visible at the local level and recruited new workers and resources for the cause. All were auxiliary to the statewide Maine Woman Suffrage Association (MWSA), which was itself affiliated with NAWSA. Maine suffragists settled into the slow, painstaking round of activities that were repeated in other states across the country. They sought endorsements for their cause from Granges, labor groups, churches, women's clubs, politicians, and individual community leaders. At the same time, they tried to pass state-level legislation related to women and their voting status. At various times from 1885 to 1907, MWSA tried to obtain municipal suffrage for all adult women, exemption from taxation for women because otherwise they would be paying taxes without representation, municipal suffrage for tax-paying women only, and statewide woman suffrage.[27] If full suffrage seemed too much to ask from the men running state government, they hoped that partial suffrage would prove more palatable and set a valuable precedent to help leverage broader voting privileges later on. All of these efforts were defeated, although the women gained experience through each campaign and succeeded in keeping the issue visible. In this ongoing legislative shell game, in some years the state Senate would pass the measure and the House would defeat it, only to vote the opposite way the next time it came to a vote.

From the start, Maine's huge size, dispersed population, and lack of affluence hampered organizing efforts. In 1900 its entire population was just under 700,000, a bit more than half what it is today, with most people living on farms or in remote towns that made them difficult to reach. With a small, rural, and relatively poor population, Maine was also a difficult place in which to raise money. Maine's industry was still heavily natural resource–based, with its chief products being lumber, ice, granite, and canned fruits and vegetables.[28] Suffragists sold candy and literature, charged membership dues, and took up collections after speeches, but they found money very scarce. This, of course, made it difficult to rent halls for speeches and debates, organize in remote towns, or purchase suffrage literature for widespread distribution. Lack of money also restricted travel outside the state. While it maintained membership in the national suffrage association, MWSA typically sent only one or two delegates to the national conventions, and Maine women had never been national leaders in the movement.

Then, in 1903, Hadassah Herrick of Harmony, Maine, bequeathed her estate of just over $2,000 to the Maine Woman Suffrage Association. This was an entirely unexpected but welcome event, for at the time the organization had just $52.36 in its bank account.[29] Her gift precipitated formal incorporation of the Maine Woman Suffrage Association; prior to that, so little money passed through it, they had not bothered with this step. Heddick's bequest supported more intensive lobbying and educational activities, and allowed suffrage leaders to broaden and strengthen membership from around the state. Vote by vote, the women built support in the state legislature until, in 1911, a majority in each house approved sending full woman suffrage to statewide referendum. This represented enormous progress, but it still fell short of the two-thirds majority required to pass the measure. Two years later, in 1913, they got the necessary two-thirds vote from the state Senate, and were just five votes shy of this in the House. Victory in 1915 seemed almost assured.

Their successes made it easier to recruit new members and in fact made it imperative that they do so. For years, MWSA had been led by just a handful of women, including Lucy Hobart Day, Fannie Fernald, and Helen Bates, along with a few others. These women rotated through the presidency and other key roles and together had close to 70 years of experience in suffrage work. They were getting older, though, and none of them was a particularly effective public speaker or writer. Their success in 1915 depended on their ability to recruit and train a fresh cadre of younger women who could draw and inspire audiences with fiery speeches. MWSA put the word out all over the state to bring in new volunteers; in November 1913, for example, Helen Bates (then MWSA's president) wrote to Ida Greenwood of Farmington to ask for help in recruiting "college girls" for a class in suffrage speaking. "We have very few speakers and I want to get the younger women into the work," Bates wrote. "We must get our bill through in 1915 and then we shall need speakers for the campaign."[30]

As a middle-aged mother of three, Florence was hardly in the same category as the "college girls," but Bates was delighted to have her. Florence launched herself into suffrage with the same focus she had applied to writing her novels. There were several organizations ready and willing to use her talents, as Maine suffragists sought new converts by creating separate suffrage leagues for women of like interests. Some of these were the Portland Equal Franchise League (for Portland women), the Junior Suffrage League (for the younger set), and the College Equal Franchise League (for college students and graduates). They were all affiliated with MWSA, Maine's premier statewide suffrage group. Florence joined them all except for the College Equal Franchise League. All four organizations cooperated in leasing office space on the third floor of the Press building in Portland's Monument Square.[31]

Florence's debut as a suffrage speaker came in the first week of January 1914, when she read a paper at a meeting sponsored by MWSA. Close to 100 women crowded into the Portland residence of Mrs. A. S. Hinds at 98 West Street to hear the speech. This was the product of Florence's lengthy research into both anti- and pro-suffrage literature, stimulated by Mrs. Hamlin's presentation at the Current Topics Club. Florence took the approach of listing "anti" arguments and then refuting them using facts drawn from a wide range of sources. The audience (largely suffrage supporters, to be sure) remained riveted throughout the hour-long speech. The reporter who covered the event wrote that Florence's speech gave new support to suffragists, forced those who were undecided to take a stand one way or the other, and left the antis speechless.[32]

Florence quickly became a fixture in the Maine suffrage scene. After a number of years of keeping a relatively low profile, she thoroughly enjoyed being in the public eye once again. She was a popular and effective public speaker, often featured in speeches and debates. Even allowing for the hyperbolic style of newspaper reporting at the time, her oratorical skill seemed to breathe new life into the suffrage campaign. Newspaper reports noted:

> "...[her paper] is a masterpiece of style and incontrovertible argument, while her enthusiasm and charming delivery added to the delight of all who listened."[33]

> "Mrs. Florence Brooks Whitehouse closed the debate for the affirmative by reading the cleverest and best prepared suffrage speech that has been given in this city in many years."[34]

> "Mrs. Whitehouse, in one of the most logical addresses ever heard in this city on the subject of equal suffrage..."[35]

In March 1914, Florence participated in a highly publicized suffrage debate at Portland's Riverton Park casino.[36] This was a competitive event organized by the Congregational Club, boasting three judges and a team of three speakers for each side. It drew the largest crowd the casino had ever seen, with close to 275 people sitting down to dinner before the debate in the casino's big dining room and two adjoining areas. There were so many people that some had to wait for a second seating for dinner, and an impromptu "singing school" was held to entertain the crowd while waiting for the later diners to finish. At 8:45 p.m., Dr. Jesse Hill, the club president, silenced the excited crowd and formally introduced the debate topic for the evening: "Resolved, that the privilege of suffrage should be granted to women on the same conditions that it is granted to men."

The women spoke by turn, alternating between those in favor and those opposed to suffrage, with Mrs. Barton Jenks of Concord, New Hampshire, opening for the proponents. She spoke of women's desire to improve social conditions, and noted that in the eleven countries where women already had the franchise, the death rate was the lowest in the world. She also held up a suffrage map that showed the suffrage and non-suffrage states, and noted that in the upcoming presidential election, enfranchised women would be influential in both the primaries and the race itself. In closing, Jenks appealed to the men of Maine to show themselves the equal of their western brothers in granting women the right to vote.

Ida Vose Woodbury led for the anti side. She began by stating, somewhat surprisingly for an anti, that women should either have full suffrage or none at all; asking for limited municipal suffrage as Maine suffragists had done several times was a "fallacy" that should not be permitted. Woodbury casually dismissed the argument that the vote could be used to increase working women's wages, declaring that the law of supply and demand alone governed this. In her view, there was no point in wasting votes on women, as a large percentage could not vote because of their youth or foreign birth. She closed with a favorite anti position—that the ballot was merely an expression of opinion that had little ability to change anything.

The proponents next sent up Mrs. Leslie. P. Rounds, who agreed that woman's proper sphere was the household, but then pointed out that the government was encroaching on her domain by mandating such things as children's school attendance, vaccinations, and work restrictions. Since everyone accepted that child-rearing was women's domain, it was only natural that they should take an interest in government. Women only wished to use their voting power to "straighten out the public housekeeping," she assured the audience, and to eradicate social ills such as diseases and the white slave traffic.

Mrs. Phillip W. McIntyre, the antis' second speaker, was the only one of the six women who had actually lived in an equal suffrage state, having moved to Maine from California. She reported that women who had the vote did not use it, even when voting on popular issues such as closing saloons in San Francisco. She pointed out that the division of labor between the male and female of the species was commonly practiced throughout the animal kingdom. Only female suffragists rebelled against this, and, she said dismissively, everyone knew that "there was no more restless and dissatisfied animal in the world than she." McIntyre painted an alarming picture of women, once enfranchised, attending political meetings and primaries and even seeking public office themselves! In her view, this would only waste much time and energy with no beneficial results whatever. In closing, she cited as fact the statistic that "ten per cent of the women want the ballot, ten per cent do not want it, and the other 80 per cent don't care whether they have it or not."[37]

Florence anchored the debate for the pro-suffrage forces, arguing for the vote on the grounds of both justice and expediency. Women had an inherent right to vote that was based in the Constitution, she said, and men had simply usurped this privilege over the years. Men had never had to demonstrate their worthiness for the vote as they expected women to do, and while women proved themselves worthy again and again, men still refused to grant them suffrage. She went on to supply a long list of the ways that women in equal suffrage states had succeeded in improving social conditions, which won her loud and frequent applause from the audience.

The final anti speaker, Mrs. W. B. Johnson, based her arguments in the Bible, quoting the prophet Isaiah as saying that the glory of Israel was lowest when women ruled. Women must focus on the home and on raising the next generation, she declared; they had no energy to spare for anything else. She also hinted that granting woman suffrage in the unenfranchised eastern states would open the door to the spread of Mormonism, with its dreaded practice of polygamy (alleging that Utah had granted voting rights to its women in part to help protect this practice).

When the evening was over, a slim majority of those attending thought that the pro-suffrage speakers had won, but the judges (all men) awarded the victory to the antis on the merits of their arguments. Yet this debate is interesting less for its outcome than for its illustration of the strategies employed by both sides to promote their cause. In general, the antis used emotional and often irrational arguments to paint a frightening picture of an equal franchise society. They played on people's fears of the loss of social and moral controls. Women would abandon their homes and children, become tarnished by involvement in dirty politics, and pursue immoral practices (even polygamy!). Men were threatened by the prospect of having to share power, and women by the idea of shouldering the "burden" of voting in addition to their other duties of running the home. Indeed, the antis often claimed that women, by their physical makeup, were simply unfit for the responsibility of voting (too emotional, not smart enough, lacking in physical strength). They made some effort to support their claims with statistics, but their most powerful arguments were emotional, not rational in nature.

The suffragists tended to follow a much more logical and rational line of argument. Furthermore, their statistics were much more likely to be grounded in research, such as tracking how women actually voted in the equal franchise states. They were certainly not above making emotional appeals, but they were more likely to base these in democratic ideals that were fundamental to the country's founding and near to the heart of every American. To refute antis' predictions of social chaos, they also painted a rosy picture of the future, in which women used their voting power to address every social ill. Far from abandoning their household duties, women would use the vote to create a more enlightened environment in which to raise their children. Effective speakers on both sides used a blend of rational arguments, humor, and outright sarcasm to entertain their audiences and win new converts.

Florence was capable of using a measured, reasonable style in her speeches, but she was just as likely to launch a verbal broadside against arguments or people she found foolish. She particularly disliked it when antis portrayed women as unequal to the "burden" of voting, or worried that men would find voting women less attractive. Two days after the debate at the Riverton Casino, she addressed the Woman's Council at the Columbia Parlor in Portland. Perhaps she was still smarting from the anti victory of two nights before or merely thought she had a more sympathetic audience, but the irritation and frustration in her tone were almost palpable. Her speech challenged the system that forced women to use indirect means to influence men's votes. "The indirect influence is demoralizing upon the user of it and it is an influence that is devoid of responsibility…because it need not bear any of the responsibilities of the decision…" she said flatly. The system was equally bad for men, she argued, because "…is not the influence about which we hear so much the playing of the influence of sex? The wheedling, the cajoling, the twisting around the little finger influence…" In such a system, Florence insisted, the actual issue women were trying to resolve was overshadowed by the means they had to employ to gain men's attention, to the detriment of society as a whole.[38]

She was similarly impatient with the antis' charge that voting would lessen women's attraction.

> The old idea of womanhood was founded on woman's incompetence, her weakness, and her insipidity. The nearer she could approach a beautiful backboneless imbecile, the nearer she approached the ideal woman. Man was her lord and master, she was his chattel and plaything, touching one side of his nature only…

Rational, spirited, and highly competent, Florence could scarcely have been more appalled by this vision of womanhood. There was no doubt that women had made some advances over the years; Florence's own upbringing and her marriage were based on a far more egalitarian view of sex roles. Yet these gains were precarious, and only through constant vigilance could women hope to sustain and strengthen their advancement. The suffrage movement offered insurance against slippage, and the promise that more progress would follow. Indeed, in Florence's view, the power to win continued improvements in women's lot was "a mighty surging force as impossible to stem as the flow of the Niagara."

This speech offers an early hint that Florence's views of feminism and the purpose of suffrage were broader than those of her more conventional Maine peers. While sharing their views that the ballot was the key to ending social ills that men were largely ignoring, Florence also viewed it as "the next step in the evolution of women."[39] Her larger goal was a more egalitarian society in which women were not constrained by artificial sex roles imposed by men. At first glance, these viewpoints do not seem mutually exclusive, and at this stage Florence may have had no inkling of how divisive they would prove to be. Nevertheless, they underscored the differences later on between the women who adhered to NAWSA's more conventional approach and those who embraced the tactics of Alice Paul and the National Woman's Party.

For the moment, though, Florence was content to work with MWSA. In addition to speaking frequently on suffrage, by March 1914 she had teamed up with Helen Bates to write a regular suffrage column for the *Portland Daily Press*, and the *Daily Eastern Argus* (another Portland paper) had expressed interest in this as well.[40] Florence and Bates also traveled to Augusta to organize a suffrage association there. They were hopeful that the legislature would approve a statewide suffrage referendum in early 1915, and having a strong league in the state capital would be critical for the intense lobbying required to win the last few votes and hold on to the faithful. Among those they recruited was the well-known author Laura E. Richards, who lived in Gardiner and was a friend of Florence's. [41] Richards was the daughter of Julia Ward Howe, best known as the author of the "Battle Hymn of the Republic," who had been an active suffragist and social reformer in her own right.[42]

By the end of 1914, Florence's immersion into suffrage was complete. She had been installed as chairman of the Junior Suffrage League and recruited to serve as a director of MWSA. [43,44] MWSA's officers at the time Florence first joined the board were as follows:

Miss Helen N. Bates, President: 65 Sherman Street, Portland.

Mrs. Hannah J. Bailey, Vice-President-at-Large: Winthrop Center.

Mrs. Emma E. Knight, Vice-President: 5 Knight Street, Portland.

Miss Anna Burgess, Recording Secretary: 8 Whitney Street, Portland.

Mrs. Lucy Hobart Day, Corresponding Secretary: 655 Congress Street, Portland.

Mrs. Sara P. Anthoine, Treasurer: 87 Emery Street, Portland (Chairman)

Miss Alice Blanchard, Auditor: Preble House, Portland.

Miss S. A. Clark, Supt. Literature: 21 E. Promenade, Portland.

Miss Margaret Laughlin, Supt. Enrollment: 118 Spring Street, Portland.

Miss Ella O. Woodman, Supt. Press Work: 492 Cumberland Avenue, Portland.

Helen Bates had been elected president of MWSA at its 1912 convention following many years of service to suffrage in other capacities. Corresponding Secretary Lucy Hobart Day had previously served as MWSA's president from 1897–1905. Vice-President-at-Large Hannah J. Bailey, Vice-President Emma Knight, and Recording Secretary Anna Burgess had also held various leadership positions dating back to 1907. Thus, by 1914 at least half of the officers had been steeped in the traditions of state suffrage work. Sara Anthoine was one of the younger "college girls" Bates was pleased to recruit, and she did seem to exemplify the new energy and enthusiasm they needed. During 1914, Anthoine doubled up on offices, serving both as Treasurer and as Chairman of MWSA's Organization Committee. At one point, she also assumed responsibility for its new Congressional Committee, which worked with NAWSA to influence Maine's congressional delegation to move the federal suffrage amendment through Congress.[45]

Bailey lived in Winthrop Center. She was another of the pioneers of the Maine suffrage movement, having served for six years as MWSA's president. She had also served as a board member of both the National and the World Women's Christian Temperance Union, was a former treasurer of the National Council of Women, and for three years served as Maine's representative to the National Board of Charities and Corrections. Born in 1839, she was now 75 and no longer actively participating in suffrage campaigning.

It is worth noting that, with the exception of Bailey, all of the board members lived in Portland. While travel time and expense made statewide board membership problematic, concentrating leadership in Portland must have hampered efforts to build a truly statewide organization, which in turn would have complicated planning and implementing campaigns to pass a suffrage referendum bill. MWSA leaders seemed aware of this; throughout 1913 and 1914, Bates and Day made repeated attempts to coax Ida Greenwood, in Farmington, to become an active member of MWSA's Executive Committee. They sent her invitations to meetings and then, when she again failed to appear, kept her informed of what had transpired, expressing their hope that she would make the next one.[46] This she was evidently unable to do, as she had several children and traveling to Portland for meetings was too time-consuming and expensive. Greenwood was active at the local level, however, serving for many years as chairman of the suffrage league in Farmington, where her activities included distributing suffrage literature at the Farmington Fair and speaking in Augusta.[47]

Despite her steadily increasing involvement in suffrage, Florence was still occupied with her own family during 1914. In late February, her son Penn, who was attending Harvard University, became very ill. Florence rushed down to nurse him and decided to bring him home to convalesce further.[48] This temporarily put on hold the suffrage organizing in Augusta. At the same time, Brooks, now 10 years old, was still enrolled in Portland schools and also needed her supervision. The polio had left his legs weak and the bones in one foot somewhat twisted, with the result that he found walking difficult, but Florence was determined that he would not lead the life of an invalid and encouraged him to stay active. While she was clearly one of the important new leaders of the Maine suffrage scene, her domestic responsibilities limited the time she could devote to the cause.

The Men's Equal Suffrage League

Florence's dedication to suffrage would have been far more difficult without the full support of her husband. Like his father, Robert believed in the justice and fairness of women's claim for suffrage and was willing to campaign publicly for it. The question was how best to do it. When William Penn Whitehouse had helped organize Maine's first suffrage organization back in 1873, more than half of the leadership positions (including the presidency) had been filled by men. Forty-one years later, women had progressed sufficiently that they were fully capable of running their own associations. Ousting women from leadership positions so men could run the show was clearly impossible. Still, excluding men from leadership positions was equally unthinkable.

The obvious solution was for men to have their own statewide suffrage organization, and on May 25, 1914, Robert and other supporters launched the Men's Equal Suffrage League during a public meeting at the Congress Square Hotel.[49] To address any lingering concerns about control, they staged a formal public "birthing" process in which MWSA president Helen Bates called the meeting to order and recognized a series of men to speak in favor of woman suffrage. Bates then formally handed over the meeting to Robert, who orchestrated the steps of forming the new organization. The symbolism was clear: the men would have their own league, but it was with the blessing of the women's suffrage association.

With a motto of "Equality is Equity," the new league's purpose was "to organize the sentiment for woman suffrage among the men of Maine and to diffuse information concerning the history and progress of woman suffrage."[50] Most significantly, the members would use their considerable political clout to lobby legislators to approve a statewide referendum on woman suffrage. The League's constitution was modeled on that of a similar organization in the state of New York. It divided the state into sections corresponding to the congressional districts and appointed a vice president in charge of each and also someone to serve on the League's Executive Committee. Robert was nominated to be the League's president, and though he tried to refuse this position, "the assemblage simply would not think of such a thing" so he was forced to accept it.[51]

This was a powerful and influential group of men, including some of the rising stars of Maine politics. Robert was still serving as State's Attorney and was active in the Republican Party. Ralph O. Brewster was another attorney, then serving as counsel for Chapman National Bank, who would be elected to the state House of Representatives in 1917 and go on to serve in the state Senate, as governor, and as a US Representative. Ira G. Hersey was at one time a prominent member of the Prohibitionist Party who later became a Republican and would serve as US Representative from 1917–1929. William R. Pattangall, a Democrat, served as Maine's Attorney General from 1911–12 and 1915–16, and was eventually appointed to the Maine Supreme Court. George Allan represented Cumberland County in the Maine House of Representatives, and Morrill N. Drew was prominent in the Republican Party.[52] C. S. Stetson was Master of the State Grange.[53] Together this group could influence legislators of all stripes.

Unlike MWSA, the League's membership was also drawn from all over the state, which substantially increased its power and reach. Few records of the group remain, so it is difficult to know exactly how it functioned, but it may not have required as many meetings as the women's suffrage organizations did. These men knew each other professionally as well as socially and worked with each other on a regular basis. Women were often tied to their homes because of family responsibilities, but the men were freer to travel and often had to do so in connection with their jobs. Finally, the men were all professionals who already knew how to draft and advance legislation, or to lobby and speak for whatever cause they were promoting. They did not need the same capacity-building that women, with less professional training and experience, would have required in order to be effective. Thus, the business of the League was probably transacted more informally, utilizing the existing "old boy network." Because of their business relationships, they could accomplish in one letter (or card game or hunting trip) what it might take women weeks to plan and achieve. With the men's help, the pro-suffrage forces concentrated on lobbying state legislators to approve a suffrage referendum in the 1915 legislative session.

The 1915 Suffrage Referendum Campaign

In mid-March 1915, Maine's state Senate voted overwhelmingly in favor of sending the question of woman suffrage to statewide referendum, with only four members opposed. Even as suffragists rejoiced they knew that the real test would come when the House voted on March 23rd. Both proponents and antis urged their members to attend, and the Maine Central Railroad provided reduced fares for people traveling to Augusta for the hearing.

On the day of the vote, Florence and other suffragists packed into the House gallery to witness the debate, as did the antis. Despite the late winter chill outside the State House, the room was bright with flowers. The antis pinned red roses to their chests, while each suffragist wore a yellow jonquil in her corsage. Many representatives sported jonquils in their lapels, and large yellow bouquets graced the desks of Representatives Lauren Sanborn of South Portland and Leonard Pierce of Houlton. Both were firm supporters of the referendum; Sanborn had introduced the measure in the House and would be the first to speak for it, while Pierce was the Democratic leader and would also issue an eloquent appeal.[54]

Suffrage proponents in the House displayed petition signatures demonstrating public demand for suffrage, and suggested that legislators should send the issue to referendum even if they did not support the measure personally. They repeated the claim that women's involvement in voting and lawmaking would elevate the level of discourse and cleanse politics of its unsavory elements, since everyone agreed that women occupied a higher moral plane. Women were increasingly well educated and had proven themselves in community and philanthropic work, so it was highly desirable that such women should vote (especially to offset the votes of less well educated or unsavory men). They employed the "no taxation without representation" argument, the rallying cry during the Revolutionary War, since many women paid taxes but had no direct ability to influence how those funds were spent. Finally, suffrage supporters quoted elected officials and leaders from equal franchise states who declared that women voters had produced no deleterious effects and many positive results in their communities.[55]

For their part, suffrage opponents argued that giving women the vote would necessarily enfranchise "undesirables" who were not of the pure moral character of their sisters, and whose votes might easily be purchased. Antis also claimed that voting was unfeminine, that it would wreak havoc on domestic harmony, and that most women believed they were well represented by the men. Some said that voting involved far too much effort, and that women were simply too busy managing domestic affairs. They also asserted that most women did not want the vote, though they never produced surveys or petition numbers to bolster that argument. They did not have to; if suffragists produced tens of thousands of signatures on a petition supporting enfranchisement, the antis simply pointed to the many thousands more women who had not (for whatever reasons) signed the petition and thus could not be said to want the vote. (Suffragists responded that such women represented a very small percentage of possible voters, and that in any case, since legislators did nothing to prevent undesirable *men* from voting, it was unfair to use this argument.)

Unfortunately for the "pro" forces that day, the antis had on their side Representative McCarty of Lewiston, who delivered the knockout blow. Alternating among irony, ridicule, and witty comments, he soon had the audience dissolved in laughter, and he was roundly applauded for his closing speech.[56] McCarty's humorous dismissal of suffrage claims won the day; the final tally had 59 House members opposing the referendum and 88 supporting it. This was a healthy majority, but still a full 10 votes short of the two-thirds needed to pass the measure. Despite the added clout of the Men's Equal Suffrage League, the suffragists had actually lost ground in the House since 1913, when they had lacked only five votes to achieve the necessary majority. In 1915, Maine was progressive enough to permit a vigorous discussion of the merits of woman suffrage, but not liberal enough to actually approve it. It was the twelfth defeat of suffrage in the Maine legislature.[57]

While the vote was not entirely along party lines, in general most Republicans favored suffrage and most Democrats did not. Suffrage was widely supported in the rural areas but not in the cities. For example, all of the members of the Portland delegation voted against it, while 100% of the Somerset and 80% of the Aroostook and Waldo County delegations voted for it.[58]

Observers were evidently struck by each side's use of flowers as symbols, because soon after the vote local newspapers saw a brief exchange of poetry that became known as "The War of the Flowers." The following poem, signed only "B," was sent by an anti to local newspapers, and started off the exchange:

The Jonquil and the Rose

The Jonquil and the Rose
They tell a tale of suffrage
In the good old state of Maine
That is full of lively interest
And proves the men still sane.
They tell that at the "Hearing,"
And sometimes since the close,
They have worn the lady's jonquil,
But—they've voted for the Rose.
Some say that men are foolish,
"The Creator made them so
To match up with the women";
But we doubt if it is true!
You see, while smiling blandly
And politely keeping pose,
They've been buttonholed with jonquils
But—they've voted for the Rose.
Most men are fond of flowers

But in preference draw no line,
To them the jonquil's "beautiful,"
And the red, red rose is fine.
And so it can't be prejudice
But conviction—made them choose.
They've worn the lady's jonquil,
But—they've voted for the Rose.

Those ladies who have spent much time
Around the statehouse dome,
Must now feel somewhat weary,
And may rest awhile at home.
Poor statesmen, nagged and badgered!
You have earned a long repose.
You have worn the lady's jonquil,
But—you've voted for the Rose.

The antis were gloating that legislators who had pledged to vote for suffrage failed to do so when put to the test. Providing a rebuttal in verse appealed to the writer in Florence, and she responded with her own poem correcting the antis' version of events in Augusta.

The Jonquil and the Rose (A Reply)

We have noticed in your columns
A most elucidating rhyme
Which must have kept the perpetrator
Working overtime.
It tells how at the Hearing
Which has just come to a close,
The "voters wore the Jonquil
While they voted for the Rose."

This is pretty propaganda
And though it isn't true to facts,
It shows the Anti-spirit
Embodied in their "tracts."

To score a point against us
For applause of fickle hands,
They stoop to write their arguments
On running, shifting sands.

The truth about the question
Is really quite immense
For only nine and fifty
Voters proved their lack of sense
By voting down the suffrage.
And 88 men chose
To wear the Suffrage Jonquil
While voting DOWN the Rose.

In all we had a surplus
Of fifty votes to spare
If we count the House and Senate
And our friends who stood firm there.
And while the Antis seem so joyous
That we hadn't two to one
They can't escape the knowledge
That we won at fifty-one.

We are proud to cede the Antis
The nine disloyal "reps"
Who renounced their party pledges
To aid the Suffragettes
And the Democrats, from the cities,
Which stand for rum and booze,
We also state, quite frankly,
We are honored, them to lose.

With the Senate six and twenty
And the House four score and eight,
We had a big majority
From those who legislate.
And in 1916 surely,
We will bring the war to close,
With the whole House wearing Jonquils
While Voting DOWN the Rose.

Florence's poem served as a tart reminder that even if they did not have the full two thirds required to pass the referendum measure, the suffragists had managed to get a healthy majority of both the House and the Senate, an impressive show of support.

Two other points Florence made in her poem are worth noting. In the fifth verse, she pointed out that nine "reps" had opposed the measure although their own party had pro-suffrage language in its platform. This was a problem experienced by suffragists across the country; for years elected officials had been pledging to pass equal franchise measures and then reneging on their promises when the time came to vote.

The fifth verse also admonished the Democrats for standing for "rum and booze." This was not an idle accusation, for the "liquor lobby" was well known by suffragists across the country for its role in defeating suffrage campaigns. They purchased the votes of elected officials when a suffrage measure was in front of a legislature, and in referendum campaigns they enlisted the support of every bar owner, saloon keeper, and distributor to get male patrons to oppose woman suffrage. The commercial distillery and brewery interests had enormous sums of money to pump into local and national campaigns, and since they were fearful that women, if enfranchised, would enact national prohibition, they were highly motivated to use this influence. The cities were more associated with "wet" interests, and in Maine these areas were represented by Democrats. The liquor lobby worried that if women won the right to vote they would make sure liquor laws were strictly enforced and strenuously oppose any efforts to overturn Maine's prohibition law. For these reasons, the liquor lobby routinely underwrote anti-suffrage activities, and the results of the 1915 vote suggested that they had been successful in influencing the Democratic vote.[59]

Despite their disappointing loss, Maine suffragists still believed they were building positive momentum. Nevertheless, it is possible that this experience predisposed Florence toward working with the Congressional Union when its organizers came looking for someone to establish and lead a new branch in Maine to work for the Federal Amendment.

III   The Congressional Union Comes to Maine

Following the legislative defeat of their referendum in March 1915, MWSA supporters started laying the groundwork for a new initiative two years later. It was disheartening to come so close to victory only to have it snatched away once again by the illogical arguments of the antis and the backroom deals arranged by the liquor lobby. Nevertheless, they had high hopes that in 1917 they would at last secure the legislative support needed to bring suffrage to a statewide referendum.

Florence wrote a new pamphlet to support the campaign, entitled *An Argument in Favor of "Votes for Women."* The 16-page pamphlet thoroughly analyzed reasons for supporting suffrage. While MWSA published it for distribution, it also served as the basis of Florence's stump speech as she traveled around Maine speaking to women's clubs and other gatherings. In the pamphlet, Florence posed the anti arguments and then responded to them with statistics supporting women's claim for suffrage. As with most of her suffrage writing, she was forthright and candid; she rarely minced words and at times seemed almost indifferent to the possibility of offending her audience.[60]

The pamphlet provides a useful glimpse into Maine laws during this period. Florence noted that in 1915 Maine had no minimum wage law, a ten-hour working day (in contrast to the eight-hour day adopted in five of the full-suffrage states), no "Mother's Pension Law" (akin to social security, which was still twenty years in the future), no reformatory for women, an age-of-consent law that effectively allowed girls to marry at age 15, lax child labor laws that allowed children to work in factories with little penalty to the owners, and "open non-enforcement" of the state's prohibition law. She also noted that there was a need for women's influence in the areas of public health, education, and community policing, which included providing better supervision of dance halls.

References to the plight of working women were woven throughout the pamphlet. In the excerpt that follows, Florence sarcastically reminds readers that many women knew nothing of genteel lives of leisure, yet even those who were more fortunate exposed themselves to harsh realities through their charitable work:

> Then the men, pushed to the wall, say: Politics are dirty; you will lose your charm if you enter them. We say: We may go into settlement work, frequent the houses of disease and filth in our rescue work; we may wander unguarded through the worst streets of your city on our errands of mercy; we may work in your shops and factories ten hours a day; we may stand in your laundries, our hands in hot starch, from 12 to 16 hours a day; we may work in your canning factories from daylight till 10 or 11 at night; we may scour floors in your offices and city buildings on our hands and knees, at 20 cents an hour; with no protest from you that we will lose our charm; *will you tell us what there is in politics so much more fatal to charm than these things?*

She pointed out that Portland men were more focused on public works projects like road-building, water supplies, public buildings, and the police. While acknowledging the importance of these things, Florence held that women were more likely to be concerned about libraries, art, overseeing the poor, and prison conditions. Men were interested in city-building, she argued, while women were concerned with conserving human life. The notion that men and women were different would have been commonly accepted at the time, but Florence brought the argument to the next level by insisting that women's interests ought to occupy an equal public policy sphere with those of men: "We assert that the 'feminine attitude toward life is of equal value with the masculine, and we demand the right to see that that attitude becomes imbedded in the institutional and social life of society.'"[61]

Florence ended the pamphlet with a discussion of feminism. She clearly considered herself a feminist, which she defined as "the moral, spiritual, and ethical awakening of woman to the realization that she is a human being as well as a biological fact." She decried the practice of educating women solely for "sex interest" and making "potential motherhood her only reason for existence." Women who had revolted against these stereotypes, she proclaimed, "…are physically stronger,…are mentally peers of the men,…have cast off the shackles of ignorance for the armor of self-knowledge, [and]...*are better companions, better wives, and better mothers.*"[62]

She was careful, however, to distinguish feminism from what she called "ultra-feminism," the latter being a term the antis applied to all manner of moral evils, from free love to the dissolution of family life, as well as to political movements such as socialism. Suffragists and feminists want the same things, Florence argued in her pamphlet, "economic independence for women; better and wiser marriage and divorce laws; one standard of morality for men and women; 'equality of opportunity, not identity of function, for women with men.'"[63]

Equality of opportunity for women, injecting women's values into the public debate, and labor laws that protect women and children as well as men—these seem a familiar agenda for feminists and labor activists of the 21st century. But in the early 20th century, suffragists were just beginning to forge strong ties between their cause and leaders of the labor movement. In 1910 over 8 million women were in the workforce nationally (up from one million just 30 years earlier).[64] By 1915 about 25,000 Maine women worked in manufacturing, with an additional 25,000 in nonindustrial employment.[65] Working conditions for women in factories were wretched; they were seldom protected from extremes of heat and cold, endured poor air quality, and had insufficient light. Sixty-hour work weeks (six 10-hour days) were the norm, yet women were often expected to bring home piecework they could complete after the evening meal. In some industries, women worked even harder, from 12 to 14 hours a day. Women were also paid less than men for the same work, which remains a concern for activists today. Finally, the few laws that existed to prevent exploitation of child labor were generally not enforced, so many children ended their schooling early to spend long days in factories.

Men were generally unwilling to enact labor laws that protected women workers, so the only other recourse women had was to join unions and strike for better pay and working conditions. Union membership grew steadily after the turn of the century, with approximately 2.1 million (just over 10% of the national workforce) enrolled by 1910.[66] But the major unions were all dominated by men who had little interest in representing women.[67] It was widely believed that women worked only for a brief period of their lives, from their teens to their mid-twenties at most, to earn a little extra spending money or to help their families before beginning married life. Since women had no long-term commitment to the workforce, union leaders reasoned that there was no point in trying to organize them. Then, too, most working women performed unskilled or semiskilled work that made them easily replaceable in the event of a strike. When this work was done by immigrants from Quebec, Eastern Europe, or Italy, language barriers were an additional obstacle for labor organizers.

While it was true that many women worked only until they married, those whose husbands died, deserted them, or simply failed to earn enough to support the family continued to work throughout their lives. They worked in low-skilled jobs because men systematically excluded them from training and management positions that would have been the route to better careers. Women were fully aware that the choice between a low-paid, dead-end job and an unhappy marriage was no choice at all; some joked that men deliberately created inhospitable working conditions for women in order to make themselves the more attractive alternative![68]

By 1910 labor activists understood that the most effective way to protect women and children from exploitive labor practices was through winning the suffrage fight. At the same time, suffrage leaders realized that labor activists provided a ready pool of trained, effective organizers and speakers who could be put to work immediately. Additionally, the need to protect children and improve working conditions for women provided a practical and compelling rationale for suffrage that could be used along with the arguments for fairness or justice.

As a member of the more affluent middle class, Florence was spared the necessity of working to support her family, yet she understood the connection between suffrage and protecting the rights of working women. In May 1915 she was MWSA's lone representative at a meeting in Boston sponsored by the Woman's Trade Union League (WTUL). The purpose of the meeting was to organize support in the New England states for an eight-hour workday for women; this, along with a minimum wage law, abolition of child labor, and ending night work for women was among the WTUL's chief concerns. The Massachusetts legislature had recently rejected a bill for an eight-hour workday, evidently swayed by manufacturers' testimony that such a law would make them noncompetitive with other nearby states. By organizing all the New England states to push for the legislation simultaneously, the WTUL hoped to eliminate that obstacle.

Florence was very moved by the testimony she heard at this meeting.[69] In the morning, the representatives heard from women who had worked in mills, laundries, and as telephone operators, and in the afternoon, they heard speeches from doctors and from WTUL workers testifying to the benefits of the eight-hour day. One of the first speakers was a woman named Mary Thompson, who had been born in Scotland (Florence noted she "had a delicious accent"). Although young in appearance (Florence guessed her age at 28), Thompson had worked as a weaver for 20 years. Textile workers, she said, were more like slaves than employees. Even moderately productive women commonly lifted 3,600 pounds of cloth and other materials every day. Pregnant women often worked right up until they delivered, returning to work after only a ten-day rest and, Florence noted indignantly, "leaving their puny baby to be cared for by some old relative too feeble to work." Thompson explained that while factory owners offered bonuses for greater production and efficiency, they managed to recoup these costs by charging higher rents for mill-owned housing or for mill-sponsored entertainment. Charging employees for the materials they used to make the product was another common strategy companies used to reduce expenses and increase profits.

Next, Maud Foley spoke for the shirtwaist workers, describing how women worked on machines that required them to watch from two to six needles at a time. A skilled worker might make from 3,000–5,000 buttonholes a day, or sew on 3,000–4,000 buttons! If the needle missed a hole, the risks of which seem high given the sheer numbers involved, the button would break and pieces fly up into the worker's face, sometimes injuring her badly.

Florence was most impressed with the testimony of a telephone operator, Miss Sullivan, who she described as "the prettiest Irish girl imaginable." The young woman, shy at first, soon warmed to her theme and described a harrowing job that is difficult to imagine with today's workplace protections. Telephone work demanded that operators stay alert every moment of their shifts, their hands constantly flying around the board in front of them. Each girl sat in front of a board that was about three feet tall and nearly the same width. The board was filled with rows of wire connections that had to be manually inserted into different sockets, depending on the status of the call. While tracking many calls at once, operators had to watch what was happening and negotiate with each caller: "This line is busy" or "This line does not answer." There were strict rules about the phrases operators had to use. On average, calls came in at the rate of three per second, which meant that operators had to have instant recall and coordination between what they said and what their hands were doing. Shifts were long, usually nine or ten hours a day, with little time for breaks. Most girls worked one out of every three Sundays, and many did extra work at night as well. It was small wonder, Florence thought, "that many girls became hysterical and had to be carried from the room." When this happened, though, an unfortunate coworker would have two boards to watch![70]

There was more testimony throughout the day, and by the end of it, Florence had agreed to continue representing Maine in the regional campaign for the eight-hour workday. She attended a follow-up meeting in Boston at the end of June, and subsequently began corresponding with Roscoe Eddy, Maine Commissioner of Labor and Industry, to discuss Maine labor laws and tactics for amending them. She also planned a meeting in Portland, on September 2, to which she invited Jane Addams as a speaker. This experience sparked Florence's interest in women's labor issues that continued after suffrage was won, and more than any other Maine suffragist, Florence incorporated labor issues into her suffrage speeches. Suffrage remained her first priority, however, and she stopped attending meetings on the eight-hour workday when the pressures of the suffrage campaign in Maine became too intense.

One of the most important byproducts of this labor research was her introduction to Florence Kelley, a well-known socialist, labor activist, and social reformer ten years her senior. Florence had a high regard for Kelley, speaking favorably of her in the suffrage pamphlet she wrote for MWSA. Kelley had attended Cornell University and the University of Zurich. Following her divorce from her husband, Kelley had moved with her three children to Hull House in Chicago, where she worked closely with Jane Addams. Kelley was widely known for her work with the National Consumers' League, where she fought to ban child labor and enact legislation protecting women workers, but she had also served on the NAWSA board for several years. Alice Paul later recruited her to organize for the Congressional Union, and sent her to Maine in the summer of 1915 to establish a branch there.

What was the Congressional Union, and what difference would it make to Maine to have a branch established there?

The Congressional Union

In the fall of 1912, two young women petitioned NAWSA to form a committee that would focus exclusively on passing the Federal Amendment through Congress. Alice Paul *(see Figure 4)* and Lucy Burns had recently returned from England, where they had participated in militant actions organized by Emmeline Pankhurst and her daughter, Christabel, through the Woman's Social and Political Union (WSPU). Both Paul and Burns had been arrested and jailed for picketing, had gone on hunger strikes, and been forcibly fed.[71] NAWSA leaders hoped such tactics would not be embraced in the United States, but they desperately needed the energy and ideas of the next generation of women. The current NAWSA president, Dr. Anna Howard Shaw, was 65. Jane Addams was in her mid-50s. Both women had worked on suffrage issues for decades, and they supported other causes as well. In contrast, both Paul and Burns were in their late twenties, single, and ready to commit themselves full-time to suffrage. Alice Paul clinched the deal when she offered to move to Washington, DC, at her own expense and be solely responsible for raising the funds she needed to pursue the work. Since it seemed to require no additional effort or cost, NAWSA voted at its national convention in December 1912 to create the five-member Congressional Committee under its organizational umbrella.[72]

Paul and Burns established the new Congressional Committee's office in DC in early January 1913. They set right to work raising money, organizing suffrage parades, and sending deputations to President Woodrow Wilson to make the case for woman suffrage and to request his support, as the leader of the Democratic Party, in ushering the Federal Amendment through Congress. While they had been joined by three helpers, by the spring of that year it was clear that a committee of five women could not bring effective pressure on Congress. They needed a body of women behind them who could work within their individual states to put pressure on their congressional representatives. As a result, Paul and Burns created the Congressional Union (CU), a membership organization of women who supported passage of the Federal Amendment. For a 25-cent donation women could become members for life, and by December 1913, the CU claimed a membership of 1,000 women across the country. Paul organized the CU without seeking formal permission from the NAWSA Executive Committee (which undoubtedly would have turned her down). While she insisted that it neither duplicated nor conflicted with the work of NAWSA's state associations, the CU triggered immediate confusion and hostility in the ranks. How could NAWSA have two separate membership bodies under one umbrella? Did funds raised for the CU belong only to that body, or should they be routed through NAWSA? Could the CU organize in states without the permission or approval of the existing state association?[73]

Paul argued that there was no conflict. The NAWSA state associations could continue to work with their individual legislatures to obtain suffrage either through state legislation or through a referendum process, as they had always done. Since the CU's sole purpose was to pass the Federal Amendment, it would concentrate on bringing pressure to bear on the congressional delegations. The two associations were pursuing separate but complementary strategies. This was perhaps disingenuous on her part; inevitably, the men responded negatively to the CU's demands for suffrage and its threats to hold the party in power responsible for failing to approve the Federal Amendment. They took their complaints to NAWSA's leadership, insisting that Alice Paul and the CU were causing irrevocable damage to the cause, which of course threw NAWSA into an uproar.

Despite this controversy, by the time of the annual NAWSA convention in December 1913, Alice Paul was able to report a number of exciting successes. For the first time ever the US Senate had created a majority committee on suffrage, and in May this Suffrage Committee had voted unanimously in favor of the Federal Amendment. In June the Committee brought its favorable report to the floor of the Senate, where it was discussed for several hours. The last time a body of Congress had debated the suffrage measure at any length was in 1877, so this was an important advance. The House of Representatives had assigned the Federal Amendment to the Judiciary Committee. Although Paul and her colleagues had submitted a request to the House Rules Committee to establish a majority Suffrage Committee like the one in the Senate, so far the Rules Committee had refused to act.

In addition to its legislative work, the Congressional Committee had organized a number of events to increase the visibility of the suffrage cause, and had raised almost $25,000 to support its activities. Even Paul's detractors had to acknowledge that in the space of twelve months the Congressional Committee had accomplished a remarkable amount. Her report was accepted unanimously by NAWSA's Executive Board, and convention delegates gave her a standing ovation, but the questions of structure, process, and accountability within NAWSA remained.[74]

By the end of the convention, delegates had instructed the Executive Board to form a new Congressional Committee which would remain firmly under NAWSA's control. Alice Paul and Lucy Burns were invited to continue serving on the new Congressional Committee, but they would have to give up the Congressional Union and follow NAWSA policy.[75] This they refused to do, opting instead to establish the Congressional Union as a separate organization and to request that it be accepted as an auxiliary member to NAWSA.[76]

NAWSA charged its restructured Congressional Committee to work for the Federal Amendment, but in doing so to oppose only those individual congressmen who were anti-suffragists. The policy of holding the party in power responsible for passing suffrage was dropped. NAWSA appointed a new chairman, Mrs. Medill (Ruth) McCormick, who quickly found the Congressional Union a threat to NAWSA's national work. Within six short weeks of being appointed chairman, she was complaining to Dr. Shaw that serving as chairman was "one of the most disagreeable tasks I have ever performed."[77] She demanded that NAWSA deny the CU auxiliary membership, threatening to resign if the CU was accepted:

> The harm already done in Washington cannot be exaggerated in regard to the policy of the Congressional Union [of holding the party in power responsible for failing to secure suffrage]. It is political suicide at the present time…to adopt such a policy, and the only way that the harm can be undone is by the National [NAWSA] taking a stand of repudiation of this action…You know that I am accurate in the statement that two or three days after it becomes known that the Congressional Union has been accepted as an auxiliary member of the National Association they will be sending out appeals for money and support as an auxiliary of the National, and as they are doing the same sort of work that we are in Washington, the confusion will continue and we will be in a "Kilkenny cat fight" for another year.[78]

In January 1914 NAWSA submitted the question of the CU's auxiliary membership to its Executive Council, which was composed of state association presidents and other key individuals. One of those who supported Paul and Burns' approach was Katherine Houghton Hepburn (mother of the actress Katherine Hepburn), who was president of the Connecticut Woman Suffrage Association. In a letter to her fellow Executive Council members, she argued that "Mrs. McCormick's idea of simply opposing the men who are anti-suffragists and bad besides would make it practically impossible for us to use the votes of women in the voting states…" Yet that was precisely where

FIGURE 4 W Alice Paul, Chairman of the Congressional Union/National Woman's Party
Women of Protest: Photographs from the Records of the National Woman's Party,
Manuscript Division, Library of Congress, Washington, D.C.

suffragists' leverage was greatest, she insisted. She urged NAWSA to approve the CU's membership request.

In the end, the NAWSA Executive Council rejected their request for auxiliary membership, so Paul and Burns were free to pursue their separate course.[79] NAWSA leaders evidently believed that the CU posed no long-term risk to their plans; throughout 1914 they assured each other repeatedly that the CU had no support and would soon retire from the field in ignominious defeat.[80]

This "Kilkenny cat fight" was intensified due to Paul's decision to create and strengthen member organizations in each of the 48 states.[81] The CU had not yet established a foothold in Maine, but in the summer of 1915, she encouraged Florence Kelley to meet with Florence Whitehouse. Kelley summered at her cottage in Naskeag near Blue Hill. After some initial meetings in Portland, Kelley left and then returned with Doris Stevens, a young organizer from Nebraska, to stir up more interest.[82] They succeeded in forming a new CU branch, and Kelley became one of its six vice presidents, representing Naskeag.

Much to the chagrin of the MWSA stalwarts, Florence not only joined the Congressional Union, which was heresy enough, but compounded the error by agreeing to serve as its chairman.[83] Later that fall she also accepted appointment to the Congressional Union's national council, a smaller advisory group composed of about 22 women across the country.[83A] In a few short weeks, MWSA not only lost control of its most effective organizer, but saw the emergence of a rival entity that would compete for scarce donations and volunteers and challenge MWSA's authority as Maine's leading suffrage organization.

On September 2nd Kelley helped Florence organize a luncheon and conference grandly described as the "Maine State Convention of the Congressional Union," held in the State of Maine room at Portland City Hall. Attendees were greeted with a bright yellow banner draped over the mantel, inscribed with the words "We Demand an Amendment to the United States Constitution Enfranchising Women." The timing of the conference took advantage of the fact that several prominent suffragists were vacationing in Maine: Jane Addams sent greetings from Bar Harbor; a Mrs. John J. White from Washington, DC, was noted to be summering at York Harbor; and there were several other women who were from states with sweltering summers. Helen Bates was there, no doubt to keep an eye on things for MWSA. Sarah Anthoine, the only other MWSA board member to join the Union board, attended as well. Kelley presided, and she and Florence were the featured speakers of the evening program. In the brief newspaper coverage of the day's events, the reporter noted a certain bellicosity in Kelley's attitude toward Maine's congressional delegation. Of the delegation's six members, Kelley pointed out, only one had voted for the Federal Amendment and three opposed it. Some members had "paired" when the vote came up, but Kelley was not impressed; "Pairing doesn't get anything" she told the reporter flatly, "it is votes that count." Women would no longer be content to accept men's maneuverings on suffrage.[84]

****

In mid-December, Florence was Maine's lone representative to the CU's annual meeting in DC, which Paul had cleverly planned to upstage NAWSA's annual convention scheduled for December 14–19. Paul frequently piggybacked on political conventions or other events to obtain free publicity and improve access to people she wished to influence. Paul also must have known that suffragists who supported NAWSA and the CU would be more likely to attend both events if they were held close together so they would not have to travel twice.

The CU's annual meeting would be the setting for Paul's latest publicity stunt. Three thousand miles away, at the Panama-Pacific Exposition in San Francisco, CU organizers had spent several months distributing suffrage literature to fair attendees. They also asked people to sign a petition supporting the Federal Amendment, and by August 1915 had collected nearly 500,000 signatures. Paul decided that envoys from the West should drive across the country, stopping in towns and cities along the way to collect more signatures and participate in mass meetings in support of the Federal Amendment. The envoys left San Francisco on September 16, launched by the first-ever Woman Voters' Convention, and were scheduled to arrive in Washington, DC, in early December, where there would be further meetings and demonstrations in their honor *(see Figure 5)*. In DC the envoys would ceremoniously call on the president to hand over the petitions, providing evidence that the women of the West wished the president to do everything in his power to move the Federal Amendment through Congress.[85]

Just as Paul intended, the envoys' journey across the country had secured terrific publicity for the Federal Amendment, and the stunt worked symbolically

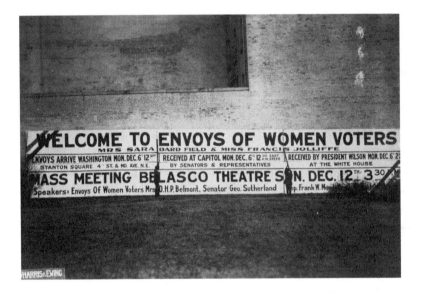

FIGURE 5 Welcome banner for the arrival of the suffrage envoys in 1915
Library of Congress, National Woman's Party Collection.

on many levels. In the early days of the automobile, few people had driven coast to coast, and In the early days of the automobile not many people drove from coast to coast, and it was rare for women to make the trip unaccompanied by men. Congressional Union organizers leapfrogged across the country, helping cities organize mass celebrations to welcome the envoys, collect more signatures on the petition, and send them on their way. Before every major city, the envoys stopped to decorate the car with the purple, gold, and white colors of the Union, and to string across it what became known as the "Great Demand" banner: "We Demand an Amendment to the Constitution of the United States, Enfranchising Women." Between bad roads and poor maps they had their share of adventures; getting lost, stuck in the mud, and pummeled by storms, but they emerged triumphantly in DC at the appointed time. Thousands of women greeted the envoys when they arrived in DC, and escorted them to the White House, where they presented the petitions to President Wilson.[86]

****

The week following the CU convention, Florence joined Helen Bates, Leslie Rounds, and Susan Clark at NAWSA's annual convention.[87] Usually only one or two MWSA members attended conventions, but in 1915 their presence was particularly critical because NAWSA had been thrown into an organizational crisis by the upstart CU. NAWSA was also being torn apart by its own support of the controversial Shafroth–Palmer Amendment that competed with the Federal Amendment originally submitted by Susan B. Anthony (which the CU was promoting).

The Shafroth Amendment was conceived by Ruth Hanna McCormick, head of NAWSA's Congressional Committee. It responded to complaints that the issue of woman suffrage should be decided by the states.[88] The amendment would require that a statewide suffrage referendum be held whenever more than eight percent of a state's voters, based on the most recent election, petitioned for it. This would remove from state legislatures the decision to have a suffrage referendum, sinc they were often more conservative and difficult to influence. Passing the referendum would require a majority of the state's voters.

Because they proposed to amend the federal Constitution, the Anthony and Shafroth amendments would each require a two-thirds majority of both the US House and the Senate to pass them, and then be ratified by three-quarters of the states. At that point, the Susan B. Anthony amendment would be the law of the land. The Shafroth Amendment, on the other hand, would then require extensive work at the state level—first to get eight percent of the state's voters to sign the referendum petition, and then another campaign to persuade a majority of voters to support suffrage when the referendum was held. If a state referendum failed, which many likely would, the process would need to be repeated. This represented a far greater amount of work.[89] While many suffragists who were loyal to NAWSA unquestioningly supported its position on the Shafroth amendment, others vigorously opposed it and dissension reigned.

Anna Howard Shaw's weak leadership on this issue further eroded NAWSA's ability to unite behind any course of action, and the organization was at a standstill. Earlier in the fall, Shaw had announced that she would step down as president when her term was up; a new leader would be chosen at the convention. Close to 1,000 women from all over the country, NAWSA's largest convention attendance ever, came to DC to show support for NAWSA and help choose their new president.[90]

It would take several days to sort out the leadership question, so convention delegates occupied themselves with business meetings and reports on state work. A small group of delegates still hoped NAWSA and the CU could resolve their differences and work together to pass the Federal Amendment. Early in the week a well-known writer, Zona Gale, successfully moved that the convention should immediately appoint a committee of five women to meet with five CU representatives to explore (1) the affiliation of the Union with NAWSA, and (2) whether or not formal affiliation occurred, how the two bodies could coordinate legislative strategies going forward.[91] The NAWSA convention appointed Carrie Chapman Catt, Ruth Hanna McCormick, Mrs. Stanley McCormick, Mrs. Antoinette Funk, and Miss Hannah J. Patterson as its representatives. Given that the two McCormicks and Funk had recently penned some of the most venomous screeds against the CU, it could hardly be expected they were in much of a mood to compromise. The CU representatives, who included Alice Paul, Lucy Burns, Mrs. Lawrence (Dora) Lewis, Anne Martin, and Mrs. Gilson Gardner, were equally entrenched, and the meeting was not a success. Despite its crippled state and the new muscle demonstrated by the CU, NAWSA negotiated as if it had the upper hand. The price of affiliation once again was for the CU to drop its policy of holding the party in power accountable and to agree to never again enter political campaigns. In addition, the CU had to promise to stay out of all states where existing

NAWSA affiliates were already operating, which would effectively bar them from any state work whatsoever. Not surprisingly, Paul refused to accept those terms, and the meeting ended in anger. Although they would see each other in legislative hearings, this marked the last time Catt and Paul met to discuss suffrage.[92]

It is surprising, perhaps, that NAWSA took such an uncompromising position, but Catt may have been reacting to an incident that had occurred the day before. Catt, Paul, and others had gone to testify before the House Judiciary Committee on the question of the Federal Amendment. The Democrats were still furious with the CU for campaigning against them in the 1914 elections, and this was the first opportunity they had to confront Paul and her coworkers about their strategy.

With only occasional protests from the Republican members, the Democrats fired questions at Alice Paul. Representative Taggart asked, "Why did you oppose the Democrats in the last election?" Although they had been through this several times already, Paul patiently explained how the Democratic caucus had blocked the Rules Committee from scheduling time for a House vote on forming the Suffrage Committee. As evidence, and much to the Republicans' amusement, she proceeded to read a letter from Representative Henry (D), chairman of the Rules Committee, in which he said that "…the Democratic caucus, by its direct action, has tied my hands and placed me in a position where I will not be authorized to do so unless the caucus is reconvened and changes its decision." The only recourse left to the suffragists, Paul reasoned, was to tell the women voters of the West how the Democrats were blocking progress on the Federal Amendment and urge a vote against them. This approach must have been effective, she pointed out, because after the election was over and Congress reconvened, the House leadership quickly reversed its opposition to scheduling a vote on establishing a Suffrage Committee.[93]

Next, the Democrats demanded to know what the Congressional Union was planning for the 1916 elections. Paul's response was "[w]e have come to ask for your help in this Congress. But in asking it we have ventured to remind you that in the next election one-fifth of the vote for president comes from suffrage states. What we shall do in that election depends on what you do." Representative Gard asked, "You are using this method because you think you have power to enforce it?" and Paul replied simply, "Because we know we have power."

The hearing ended a short time later, but not before Representative Taggart sneered, "Have your services been bespoken by the Republican committee of Kansas for the next campaign?" and Paul shot back, "We are greatly gratified by this tribute to our value."[94]

NAWSA representatives were appalled by this uppity performance, but if Paul and her supporters had entertained any doubts about the effectiveness of their strategy, this hearing laid them to rest. Angry and resentful the men might be, but for the first time, they understood there would be a consequence for dismissing the women and delaying passage of the Federal Amendment. The CU had demonstrated a growing strength and political presence in the western states; if they campaigned against the Democrats in 1916, it could mean the end of their majority in one or both houses of Congress, and the defeat of President Wilson, as well. The women had given them much to think about.

The summit between NAWSA and the CU, and the hearing before the House Judiciary Committee, served as the backdrop to the 1915 NAWSA Convention. Florence was not directly involved in either of them, but she and everyone else knew they were happening, and the tensions between the two suffrage organizations must have been a frequent topic of conversation over the tea table, at meals, and within the conference sessions themselves.

While there were certainly women present who supported both NAWSA and the Union, it is likely the majority bitterly opposed Paul's confrontational tactics. Among the latter group were the other members of the MWSA delegation, especially Helen Bates, who remained committed to NAWSA and its approach to winning suffrage. The failure of national suffrage leaders to find common ground could only have heightened Bates' unease at Florence's continued support for the CU. At the same time, Florence was a valuable addition to Maine's suffrage forces and had yet to do anything controversial herself, so for the moment Bates let the matter rest. Still, the prospect of dealing with this situation, which had all the signs of becoming very disagreeable, may have contributed to Bates' decision to step down from the MWSA presidency a few months later.

On the positive side, NAWSA gained much-needed new leadership at its 1915 convention. With great reluctance, Carrie Chapman Catt agreed to leave the New York suffrage group she had led so ably and assume the presidency of the national organization *(see Figure 6)*. The strict conditions she set were all accepted by the search committee; New York agreed to

FIGURE 6 Carrie Chapman Catt
Women of Protest: Photographs from the Records of the National Woman's Party,
Manuscript Division, Library of Congress, Washington, D.C.

support her appointment, she was able to handpick a new executive board, and NAWSA would drop its support of the controversial Shafroth Amendment.[95] Catt spent the next six months reorganizing NAWSA, replacing members of the executive Board with women who were skilled organizers, had few family responsibilities, and had independent income that would allow them to work full-time for the cause. By mid-1916, she would be ready to launch the "Winning Strategy" that would guide NAWSA's work until suffrage was won.

IV Let the Referendum Come!

In January 1916 Helen Bates wrote to new NAWSA President Carrie Chapman Catt to appeal for help with a "situation that is causing me much anxiety." At issue was Florence's insistence that there was no conflict between organizing for the Congressional Union and retaining an active role with MWSA. This might mean, for example, that Florence would organize a meeting for MWSA and then afterwards recruit women to join the Union ranks. Bates viewed this as "…an impossible arrangement. The State Association has always been loyal to the National and in sympathy with its non-partisan policy…" Yet Florence refused to resign from either organization and planned to outline, at the MWSA board meeting the following week, just how she would juggle working with both. Bates was secretly trying to organize MWSA board sentiment against Florence, although she acknowledged this was challenging because several other MWSA members also belonged to the CU. Bates thought a letter from Catt might help persuade a majority of MWSA board members to oppose Florence's plan. Bates ended by saying that she was sorry to see Florence join the CU because she "has been one of our best workers, but she came into the work only two years ago and I think that is one reason why she got into this—she did not know suffrage history." Florence's inexperience and naiveté led her down this wrong path, was the clear implication; more seasoned veterans like Bates were not so easily led astray.[96]

Despite Bates's opposition (and any action Catt may have taken), the MWSA board agreed to let Florence continue working with both organizations, and an uneasy truce prevailed. Later in January, Bates wrote Catt again to work out logistics of her visit to Maine planned for the following month. She warned Catt that "[i]t is very important that nothing be said to antagonize the

CU, as many of our suffragists have become connected with that organization." Bates fervently hoped that Catt's visit would help unite Maine suffragists and get them working in harmony once again. [97]

Following her appointment as president of NAWSA, Catt traveled extensively to assess states' strengths, rally the troops, and gather input on how NAWSA should move forward. She came to Maine with Maud Wood Park, whom she had chosen to replace Ruth Hanna McCormick as the head of NAWSA's Congressional Committee. Park, a Radcliffe graduate, had founded the first College Equal Suffrage League in Boston and went on to help organize chapters in 30 other states. Also traveling with them was Mrs. (Elizabeth) Glendower Evans, also from Boston, who was a prominent social reformer.[98]

The meeting was held at the Pine Street Methodist Episcopal Church in Portland, coinciding with MWSA's annual convention. Catt and her team spoke the evening before the convention and stayed to participate in the next day's activities. During the day, Catt and her colleagues wanted to gauge the strength of Maine's interest and enthusiasm for suffrage, the organizers' grasp of the work required, and their commitment to carrying it forward. One of Catt's key reforms was that NAWSA would be much more strategic in choosing "campaign states." This would avoid squandering scarce human and financial resources on states that lacked the capacity to carry off a successful referendum campaign. In order to win NAWSA backing of their campaign, MWSA members needed to impress Catt that they could field the volunteers and raise the funds needed to execute a statewide lobbying effort. For Bates this presented a bit of a dilemma; she needed Florence, one of her "most effective organizers," to help impress her visitors, but on the other hand she could not afford to antagonize Catt by allowing the state chairman of the rival CU to assume too prominent a role. Electing caution, Bates arranged for Florence to have a low profile. She sat in the audience until the last hour of the day, when the format took the form of a grammar school recitation. Along with Mrs. George French and Ralph Brewster, Florence was then permitted to speak for five minutes on the topic of "How to Secure State Endorsement of a Federal Amendment." She was not allowed to speak, however, to "Why We Need Both Federal and State Work"; Mrs. Leslie Rounds, Mrs. Ralph (Grace) Jones, and Robert Whitehouse were each assigned that topic.[99]

Despite Bates' efforts to smooth over the tensions among her members and present a united front, Catt and her team were evidently not impressed with

Maine's lead suffrage organization. When it appeared later in the year that there were sufficient votes in the state legislature to send the suffrage question to referendum, Catt would advise against Maine undertaking such a campaign.

Following the NAWSA visit, Florence shifted her focus to organizing for the CU. In March she was joined by Mrs. Frederick H. (Louise) Sykes of Connecticut, who served as Second District Chairman for the Congressional Union in her own state. The two women toured the state, stopping in Augusta, Bangor, Waterville, Rockland, Brunswick, and Biddeford. In each town, they spoke at meetings hosted by local suffragists, and were successful in organizing CU leagues in Rockland and Waterville. In Bangor they joined with MWSA supporters in lobbying delegates to the state Democratic convention.[100]

Until this point, Maine suffragists had been able to keep their differences out of the papers, but from this tour of the state emerged the first faint signs of discord. To begin with, the Portland Sunday paper led its description of the tour with the statement that "[t]here is probably no woman in the State more enthusiastically alive to the needs of the women of the State than Mrs. Robert Treat Whitehouse…," which may have irritated MWSA stalwarts who had joined the movement long before Florence and had received less recognition. The article further noted that Florence, "always progressive," was one of the first Maine women to join the "modern movement" among suffragists, the CU. Despite devoting long hours to organizing support for the Union, the newspaper noted innocently, Florence maintained her involvement in the "parent organization," the National Woman Suffrage Association [*sic*], "feeling that there is nothing conflicting in working with both organizations."[100]

Florence remained adamant that there was no conflict between the two because the CU concentrated on passing the Federal Amendment through Congress while NAWSA worked to obtain suffrage at the state level. The CU's effort to unilaterally impose this division of labor galled NAWSA loyalists. After all, NAWSA had for years claimed to work at both levels, even if the national work had been minimal. Alice Paul and her supporters were proposing that they would take charge of getting suffrage through Congress, leaving NAWSA to manage the ratification campaign in the states. While this separation of duties may have looked promising on paper, in fact both groups would need to be active in the states to bring pressure to bear on legislators, and their tactics differed so dramatically that conflicts were inevitable. The NAWSA faithful also bridled at the hint of condescension in the tones of

CU organizers when they spoke of the expense, the labor, and the difficulty involved in winning enough state campaigns to enact suffrage nationally. After all, it was those very state campaigns that had enfranchised enough women voters in the West to make the CU's national strategy possible. While she was certainly aware of the tension she was causing, Florence evidently hoped that her personal integrity and long-term relationships with MWSA members would bridge the divide that existed between the two suffrage organizations in Maine.

Alice Paul encouraged state branches to organize by congressional district rather than by county in order to improve the effectiveness of lobbying efforts, as it was harder for US Representatives to ignore their own constituents. Florence served as chairman for the 1st District, since there was no one else as qualified to handle it; Mrs. Guy (Anne) Gannett of Augusta chaired the 3rd District; and Miss Gladys Niles of Bangor headed up the 4th. Florence had found no one to fill this role in the 2nd District (her note in the margin of the list sent to Union headquarters read "Nobody in thought even. Dead").[101]

Florence's comment illustrates a fact that plagued Maine women throughout their battle to win the franchise: the state was extraordinarily difficult to organize. Perched on the very northeast corner of the country, it was a somewhat insular state whose residents were not easily swayed by national movements. Maine had never been in the forefront of the suffrage struggle; curiously, it had enacted statewide prohibition in 1851, far in advance of the national movement, but that level of activism never extended to votes for women. Fundraising was a constant headache for Maine suffragists. Perhaps because it was so difficult to wrest a living from the rocky soil, people were unwilling to part freely with their money. A fundraising event that in other states yielded many donations in the $10, $25, or even $50 range generated far less money in Maine.[102] People attended suffrage speeches and listened politely, sometimes even enthusiastically, but they kept their money in their wallets and did not volunteer. Even the founding meeting of the CU's Maine branch resulted in only 36 women members, hardly the massive show of support the organizers would have liked to have seen. Florence addressed this bluntly in a letter she wrote in early April 1916, responding to an appeal from CU headquarters for Maine delegates to help rouse the women voters in the western states. "I am very much afraid that you will do no good in circularizing Maine for delegates for the trip through the West," Florence wrote. "There is very little interest and littler money." She noted that she and

Sykes had just done a tour of the state and had met no one who would be willing to travel west for this purpose. "We must be content if we wake them out of their indifference to suffrage in Maine, for some time to come I am afraid. I am sorry, and would help if I could."[103]

New suffrage leaders in Maine, even as late as 1916, showed more determination to avoid controversy than to make any progress toward winning suffrage. In early 1916, Florence was successful in organizing a new MWSA league in her old hometown, Augusta. Mrs. William R. Pattangall, who was elected the Augusta League's treasurer, was a strong states' rights advocate, and although she was the only one quoted in the news release, we can presume that many of her fellow members in the Augusta league felt the same. While she was very much in favor of Maine granting full suffrage to women, Pattangall said she had "...not as yet become convinced that federal suffrage is desirable," her chief concern being that men might take exception to any effort to impose woman suffrage through national action. "I have no particular plan of my own as to the best way to bring about full suffrage in Maine," Pattangall admitted, but then suggested that the legislature might be more easily persuaded to extend municipal suffrage to women, which it could do without amending Maine's constitution. Once women proved their ability to participate in town elections, she was sure that full suffrage would follow quickly. Pattangall's views were likely influenced by those of her husband, who was then the state's attorney general. While a staunch supporter of woman suffrage (he was a founding member of the Men's Suffrage Referendum League), he was also a firm believer in states' rights and opposed the Federal Amendment.[104]

No wonder Florence was frustrated! Shortly after her note to headquarters about the apathy of Maine suffragists, she wrote a similar letter to Alice Paul describing her organizing tour with Mrs. Sykes. "The great cry seems to be poverty and the people who joined the C.U. were very much afraid they would have to work and earn money," she observed wryly. She also dutifully reported on all the things the CU headquarters had requested of her, such as lobbying legislators at the state Democratic convention,[105] passing resolutions to send with the envoys touring the West,[106] and sending telegrams to urge the US House Judiciary Committee to report the Federal Amendment out favorably to the floor of the House so that the full membership could vote on it. In closing, Florence said wistfully about the western tour, "I hope it will be most successful, and I wish very much I could go with you." Florence was

torn between her responsibility to her family and her desire to be in the thick
of things at CU headquarters. She never expressed those sentiments about
NAWSA; it was the CU's daring that captured her spirit and imagination. In
the short term, however, she decided it was best for her to stay home and focus
on fundraising.

During this period, Florence seemed eager to build her relationship
with Alice Paul and the other organizers at headquarters. She sent them
some suffrage verses, hoping for their inclusion in *The Suffragist*, the CU's
newspaper, but though they were pronounced "entertaining," they were
returned for lack of space. She also sent Paul an article her father-in-law, Judge
William Penn Whitehouse, had written on suffrage and that the *Lewiston
Journal* had printed, for which Paul later wrote to thank her. [107,108]

****

Despite her new focus on the CU, Florence remained committed to her
state work with MWSA. Due to ill health, Helen Bates resigned the presidency
of MWSA at the end of March 1916, and the members chose Mrs. George S.
Hunt to replace her. She was to be an interim president only, however; MWSA
would elect new officers at its annual meeting in October. Then 70 years
old, Hunt was a close friend of Florence's and someone she much admired.
Florence described her as "a fine specimen of womanhood, a woman who has
been at the back of every movement for the uplift of women and children in
the state for 50 years." For over three decades, Hunt had led the WCTU's effort
to win legislative approval of a women's reformatory in Maine. Yet Florence
knew that Hunt was not capable of leading MWSA through a state campaign;
she lacked the energy and organizational skills to pull it off. In fact, MWSA
was facing a grave leadership crisis. The organization had not been successful
in recruiting and preparing younger women for leadership positions, which
was why they were forced to bring back a member of the old guard when Helen
Bates resigned.

Florence was clearly the right choice for the MWSA presidency, and she
had been offered it more than once, but only on the condition that she resign
from the CU. (She had been offered the presidency of the Portland Equal
Franchise League under the same conditions.) This she flatly refused to do.
Instead, she resigned as chairman of MWSA's Organization Committee and
took over the Legislative Committee. Bates had been serving as the Legislative

chairman in addition to the presidency, but owing to her health issues and other responsibilities as state president, she had not accomplished much, and no one believed Hunt could handle both roles. With a state campaign on the horizon, it was crucial to have a Legislative chairman with the organizing skills, time, and energy to manage relationships with legislators.[109,110]

In her new capacity, Florence wrote to 660 Maine men who were either current state legislators or candidates for office, asking them to declare their position on submitting a suffrage referendum to the people. She enclosed a stamped, self-addressed envelope to expedite their replies, and by the following month had received overwhelmingly positive responses. Even more promising, Carl E. Milliken, the Republican gubernatorial candidate who was favored to win the next election, had publicly declared that the "time was ripe" to put the suffrage question out to referendum. With substantial support from both the executive and the legislative branches, the measure was sure to pass in 1917. [111,112,113]

Over the 4th of July, Florence and Robert headed out to their rustic retreat on the north shore of Panther Pond in East Raymond, Maine. In front of the great brick fireplace in the main room of the cabin, surrounded by the peace and stillness of the woods, Florence sat down to write a long and thoughtful letter to Alice Paul. The prospect of a state campaign was exciting, but it posed a dilemma for Florence, as she explained. She was receiving considerable pressure from NAWSA and from the state association to take over the presidency of MWSA in October, and she knew there was no one better equipped for that role than she was. "[U]p to two years ago, suffrage was a dead issue in the state and there is no one who has given the time or taken the interest in it that I have," she wrote. She was torn between the CU and her loyalty to the state of Maine. "I love the C.U. but I can't help feeling if the state goes into a campaign it is my duty to work for that with all my strength." She would only accept the chairmanship of MWSA if she could "openly and frankly" avow her support for the CU, she assured Paul; still, this move would force her to step down as the president of the CU's Maine branch. Her quandary was that there was no one waiting in the wings to run the CU, and it would certainly languish without her direction. It had a paper membership of 150 and a few people who, though very enthusiastic, needed to be told what to do, but no one who could serve as leader. Which should she choose? Without her assistance, the referendum campaign would surely fail, but for the better part of a year she would be able to do nothing else.[114]

Maine had never managed to place a referendum on suffrage before the people, and there was no way to predict how the voters felt about the question. History showed that most state campaigns were unsuccessful and virtually all failed the first time, so realistically a Maine referendum had little likelihood of passing. Then, too, as NAWSA organizers had noted, MWSA suffered from a lack of skilled, committed, and well-organized volunteers, and this would make the campaign that much harder. Yet how could Florence sit out a campaign that, if it were successful, would tip the national scales in favor of woman suffrage? Maine would be the first state east of the Mississippi to grant full suffrage to its women, surely the sort of significant contribution to the cause that she longed to make. Not for the first time, Florence regretted the commitments that prevented her from being closer to the real action on suffrage. "I wish I were in the thick of the fight. I should love it," she wrote impulsively to Paul. Then, returning to the business at hand, she ended the letter with a plea for advice. "I shall hope to have a letter from you which will help me a little in settling this problem which seems to be forcing itself into my horizon."

Alice Paul responded swiftly to this threat of losing her only effective worker in Maine to yet another doomed state campaign, though, as she always did, she approached the matter on very rational grounds. At this stage of the work, she noted, state campaigns not only diverted much-needed volunteer time and financial resources away from work for the Federal Amendment, they were extremely problematic when they failed. "Do you feel that there is any possibility of Maine succeeding in a referendum campaign?" she asked Florence. A losing campaign "...not only means a loss of money and energy, but it erects an actual barrier against our progress in Congress, for the congressmen from states where suffrage referendums have failed are prejudiced against us. They consider that they have had a mandate from their people to vote against suffrage at Washington."[115]

Paul reminded Florence that the work she did for the referendum was no different from the work that was required to build support for the Federal Amendment; the difference was that the latter would be focused on changing the views of a few congressmen, not the general voting public. Given the choice, why wouldn't she choose to influence the votes of just a few key men, rather than tens of thousands?

To revive her interest in the CU, Paul encouraged Florence to attend a conference in Colorado Springs the following month, at which the policy and strategies to be used in the fall campaign would be determined. She also suggested that Florence connect with Mrs. Lawrence (Dora) Lewis, a highly skilled CU organizer who was going to be summering in Northeast Harbor, to see if she might help drum up more interest in the work for the Federal Amendment. Leaving nothing to chance, Paul wrote Lewis the same day and asked her to meet with Florence while she was on vacation. "None of us has seen her since last December when Miss Stevens was in Maine," she wrote, and they were in danger of losing her to a state campaign.[116] It is likely Mrs. Lewis responded to this appeal; the two women already knew each other, because Lewis had been present at the launching of the Maine branch the year before. Between Alice Paul, Dora Lewis, and her own inclinations, Florence was persuaded to continue as Maine's CU chairman, at least for the present.

Through the first half of 1916, the Democratic leadership of the US House of Representatives stubbornly refused to take action on the Federal Amendment. In response, Alice Paul called a convention of CU advisers, organizers, and state presidents to launch the National Woman's Party (NWP). The NWP, to be composed of the women voters of the 12 equal-franchise states, would be a political party dedicated to winning woman suffrage through federal action. Paul hoped that the NWP would "have the same significance as a factor in the coming election as had the Progressive Party when it was launched four years ago." Amid much ceremony, the CU sent 23 envoys out from DC to whip up enthusiasm for the new party among women in the enfranchised states, and to encourage them to attend its first convention, planned for early June in Chicago's Blackstone Hotel. Alice Paul cleverly scheduled her event to occur in the few days prior to the Republican and the Progressive Conventions, when reporters were arriving in town and were hungry for news. The CU supplied plenty to cover when 1,500 women met to form the country's newest political party. Convention delegates quickly elected Anne Martin of Nevada as chairman (Alice Paul was appointed vice chairman) and set about making their political presence known.[117,118]

In the upcoming fall elections, the country would choose a president as well as the entire House of Representatives and one-third of the Senate.[119] The four million women with voting rights represented one-fourth of the electoral college, and one-third of the votes a presidential candidate would need to win office. The freshly minted NWP invited representatives from the other political parties to address the convention one Tuesday evening and, in a sign that the men took its voting power seriously, all accepted. Posters advertised this as "Representatives of All National Parties Address Convention on Claims of Their Party to the Support of Women Voters"[120]; clearly this was a skeptical audience, and not one that was likely to part with its votes lightly. "We do not ask you here to tell us what we can do for your Parties, but what your Parties can do for us," Anne Martin told the assembled men, and a resounding cheer went up from the audience.[121] The only question the women were concerned with was how the various parties stood on enfranchising women through the Federal Amendment.

Within weeks of the NWP's founding convention each of the five national parties adopted a pro-suffrage plank in their platforms, an unprecedented achievement. The Democrats fiercely debated including such language, but they had been put on notice at their own political convention that if they failed to support the Federal Amendment the NWP would campaign against them in the enfranchised states in the fall elections.[122] Yet while they endorsed suffrage, both the Republican and the Democratic Parties affirmed their belief that it should occur only through state action, not through a federal amendment. This was unacceptable to Alice Paul and her supporters, for whom nothing less than amending the federal constitution would do. The impasse held for several weeks until the Republican presidential candidate, Charles Evans Hughes, broke with his own party platform and came out in support of the Federal Amendment, marking the first time a major national candidate had taken this position. This gave voting women a clear choice between reelecting President Wilson and the Democratic Party's state-by-state plank, and the Republican Hughes.

The stage was set for a showdown in the fall elections in the 12 equal-suffrage states. The August meeting Alice Paul urged Florence to attend was where the National Woman's Party would plan its campaign against the Democrats for failing to support the Federal Amendment. Florence did not make the trip to Colorado Springs, but she did agree to spend some time organizing in the West before the elections. Alice Paul very likely hoped that participating in the campaign against the Democrats would rekindle Florence's passion for Federal Amendment work and encourage her to abandon Maine's state referendum. If she had been free to go, Florence might very well have picked up and headed west immediately, but Brooks, now 12, was still at home so she must have felt that she could only be gone for a short period. She also chose to delay her trip until after MWSA's annual meeting, scheduled for October 12–13. The critical decisions of who would lead MWSA in 1917,

and whether Maine would pursue a statewide suffrage referendum, would
be settled at that meeting. Florence was caught in the middle of a tug-of-war
between MWSA and the CU.

While the CU was busy launching a new political party, NAWSA had spent
the first half of 1916 taking care of some long overdue internal business. After
reorganizing the national office and completing her state-by-state assessment
of suffrage strength, Carrie Chapman Catt produced what came to be known
as her "Winning Plan." For the first time, NAWSA's membership would be
united behind a single national strategy, the passage of the Susan B. Anthony
Federal Amendment. In order to lobby Congress full-time, NAWSA would
move its national headquarters from New York to Washington, DC. NAWSA
would not abandon efforts to win statewide suffrage referendum campaigns,
but instead would concentrate each year on a handful of key states, preferably
those with substantial electoral votes, and only those in which the likelihood
of success was high. It would no longer squander its resources by supplying
organizers or financial assistance to state campaigns where a referendum was
unlikely to pass. Once enough states were won, Catt reasoned, Congress would
bow to the inevitable and enfranchise women through national action.

In many respects, Catt's Winning Plan borrowed heavily from the CU, but
with one important distinction: NAWSA refused to hold the political party
in power responsible for its action on the Federal Amendment, choosing
merely to hold individuals accountable for their votes. Catt remained bitterly
(and publicly) opposed to what she regarded as the more militant strategies
of the Union, which eliminated any chance of their working in harmony.
NAWSA seldom lost an opportunity to denounce publicly the CU's tactics,
and generally blamed the CU for any reversal of suffrage's fortunes at the
state level or in Congress. For her part, Alice Paul rarely leveled the same
criticism toward NAWSA, hardly even acknowledging its existence, but from
the trenches her organizers complained frequently about the behavior of local
NAWSA organizations. In their letters to Paul, they spoke of banners ripped
down, contracts to rent halls mysteriously revoked, and newspapers refusing to
run CU articles. NAWSA's deep animosity toward the CU forced suffragists to
choose between the two organizations; it was simply too difficult to continue
working with both. While this caused problems in all states, in Maine the issue
was particularly acute because there were so few effective suffrage workers.
Florence was key to suffrage success in Maine; without her speaking, writing,
organizing, and fundraising abilities, a state referendum campaign was less

likely to succeed. These skills also made her essential as the leader of Maine's branch of the CU. The time was fast approaching when she would have to choose between the two.

****

Entering into the 1916 elections, then, suffragists found themselves engaged on two fronts. On the one hand, they faced entrenched opposition in Congress to the Federal Amendment, and a country that remained at best indifferent—and perhaps even hostile—to the idea of woman suffrage. On the other was the suffrage civil war that pitted NAWSA and the CU against each other. There were signs, however, of a third front developing, as the war that had engulfed Europe since 1914 was inexorably involving the United States as well. While still officially neutral, America was supplying England and France with ships and munitions critical to their success, and the war's progress was front-page news on a daily basis. American volunteers were already overseas, fighting alongside British troops. Pro-war sentiment was further aroused when the Germans sank American ships, often without warning, resulting in civilian casualties. Public sentiment was gradually shifting toward more active US involvement, but President Wilson understood that many people embraced his efforts to keep the country neutral. He could not afford to risk this support in his upcoming reelection bid, and deliberately campaigned under the slogan "He Kept Us Out of War."[123]

The administration's policies complicated the NWP's campaign in the West among women voters because women were more likely to oppose the war and thus would naturally prefer to reelect Wilson. To keep the focus where they thought it properly belonged, Alice Paul and her organizers adopted the anti-Wilson slogan "He Kept Us Out of Suffrage," and this banner decorated NWP speaking platforms throughout the western states.

In 1916 Maine was one of two states that held all its elections (except for president) annually in September; Mainers voted for president in November along with everyone else. This was the origin of the old adage "as Maine goes, so goes the nation," because for years the outcome of Maine's votes in September accurately predicted how the rest of the country would vote two months later. Although this predictive pattern had already begun to fade by 1916, when the Republicans won elections in Maine that September, it may have made the Hughes campaign complacent about the outcome of the

FIGURE 7 Demonstration against President Wilson in Chicago in 1916.
Library of Congress, National Woman's Party Collection.

presidential vote in November. Campaigning hard against Wilson in the equal-franchise states, the NWP organizers could tell Hughes was in trouble, and they fired off letters to Alice Paul imploring her to get the Republicans mobilized. Paul was in a quandary; the NWP's policy was to campaign *against* the party in power if it refused to work actively for the Federal Amendment, but it could not be seen working *for* any political candidate. Still, Hughes had endorsed the Federal Amendment and his presidency could help bring the suffrage battle to a speedier conclusion. Paul did quietly convey to Hughes's national headquarters her organizers' doubts about the strength of his support among western voters, but her warnings were brushed aside. Hughes would win in November, his campaign staff assured her.[124]

After briefly considering deploying Florence to Kansas, Paul sent her instead to Wyoming to join up with young Margery Gibson Ross, who had served as the CU's organizer there since the 1914 elections. In mid-October, Florence took the train to Chicago, stopping at the NWP's office there to help out for a couple of days before continuing west. She found the office to be a veritable beehive of activity where women wasted no time in idle chit-chat. She was impressed that every woman there knew what her job was and stayed busy at it until it was done. The Chicago branch had a brightly painted automobile in which organizers roamed the city, stopping at street corners to address the crowds that were drawn to its distinctive appearance. [125,126]

During her stopover in Chicago, Florence was thrilled to join an NWP demonstration against President Wilson, who was scheduled to speak at a nearby auditorium. The demonstration was to be a peaceful one; the 100 women participating had received strict instructions to stay silent and let the banners they were carrying tell the story of the Democratic Party's role in preventing passage of the Federal Amendment. They marched quietly from the NWP office to the corner of Michigan and Congress Streets, near where Wilson would deliver his speech, and lined up on either side of the road. Their banners read: "Mr. President, How Long Must You Advise Us To Wait?" and "Vote Against Wilson, He Opposes National Woman Suffrage" and "Wilson is Against Women"[127] *(see Figure 7).*

Aside from some minor heckling, all was quiet until Wilson entered the hall. At that point, a crowd of unruly onlookers charged the demonstrators and attempted to wrest the banners from their hands. In a report she sent home for her suffrage column in the *Lewiston Journal*, Florence vividly described the pandemonium that followed, as both men and women among the attackers tried to destroy the banners and wrestled with the picketers, who held on grimly:

> Two men seized the banner I held with Mrs. Bertram Sippy, Illinois Chairman of the Congressional Union, dragged it from us fighting their way out the street. Other men seized the other banners. If the women resisted they were slatted about till their hands were shaken off, or pounded on their knuckles till they gave up. Some of the women had their clothes torn. One elderly woman was dragged halfway across the street. The police did not attempt to quell the riot. I appealed to a mounted policeman and he laughed.[128]

Florence went on to describe how the picketers retreated to the NWP headquarters, pursued by the angry mob that "stood outside the building and continued their demonstrations of malediction." The next day, she exulted, the Chicago NWP headquarters was deluged with congratulatory phone calls. The "dignified and fearless" behavior of the women, contrasted with the rudeness and violence of the people who attacked them, generated positive publicity for the suffragists and sympathy for their cause. This marked a turning point for Florence, as she could see that even while actions like peaceful picketing enraged onlookers, the events also generated enormous publicity and support for the CU.

Florence left Chicago for Wyoming a couple of days later and remained there until the election took place. Margery Ross had arranged for Florence to speak first in Douglas, where she addressed a large crowd gathered to hear Rep. Frank Mondell, a Republican who represented Wyoming in the US House of Representatives. Mondell had introduced the Federal Amendment in the House and was a long-time suffrage supporter. The theater was packed, and the largely Republican audience was, not surprisingly, very receptive to her plea to vote against the Democratic Wilson, so she had a triumphal beginning to her speaking tour. This was just as well, because she spoke next at a movie theater between showings of a film, to an audience composed primarily of Wilson supporters. Some refused to listen to Florence at all, and others left as soon as she mentioned defeating the Democratic Party, but, as she wrote Paul, "I said my say." After the initial uproar and rush to the exit, those who remained behaved decently enough, though she doubted she had won any converts.

Florence much admired Margery Ross, whom she found "very efficient, fearless and splendidly informed." It amused Florence to observe the NWP organizers' effect on local politics: the Republicans actively courted their support while the Democrats feared and attacked them. They would sneer, for example, that the NWP organizers were "the silk stockinged aristocracy from the East who come to the West to tell the western women how to vote." The Republicans begged the suffragists to endorse Hughes publicly, but this they refused to do. "Privately I say I hope Hughes will win, publicly that Wilson will lose," Florence wrote home.[129] But Hughes's campaign in Wyoming was as lackluster as it was everywhere else, so the prospect of a Republican victory seemed increasingly remote. Whether this stemmed from Republicans' lack of interest in their candidate or from utter complacency was unclear, though Florence suspected both were true.[130]

Florence was surprised at the extent to which Wyoming women took their voting power for granted; it simply did not occur to them that women in other states were deprived of the same right, and she discovered that much of her role was to wake people up to this basic fact. When they learned this, they were eager to supply examples of how well equal suffrage worked in Wyoming, and Florence returned home with a stack of names and addresses, "enough to fill a large address book," of people who would testify for suffrage. Although both men and women promised to vote against the Democrats, the threat of war troubled many people, and it was clear that the NWP would not win the support of those who placed preserving peace ahead of woman suffrage. Many Republicans she spoke to planned to vote for Wilson over Hughes because they believed the president's claims that he would keep the US out of the war. "Even intelligent women accept that on its face value," observed Florence in some exasperation; she had her own doubts about Wilson's intention to make good on his promise.

The trip west was a lark for Florence from start to finish. Despite a busy schedule that included travel to five or six different cities and two speeches a day, she found time to take a quick side trip into Yellowstone National Park and to take note of the scenery she passed through. Her reports to the *Lewiston Journal* included almost as many descriptions of the scenery as of the work she was there to do, a happy jumble of travelogue and NWP reportage. In marked contrast to her usual columns, which generally followed a logical progression, it appears that she simply jotted down her thoughts as they occurred to her and mailed them off to the *Journal* without bothering to edit them into any particular order. "We had a wonderful ride in an automobile over impossible roads but thru a beautiful country where snow-capped mountain peaks rose 10,000 feet in the air, and nearer hills showed peaks capped by red rocks, looking as if a giant's paw had clawed them, leaving the wounds angry and bleeding" she enthused in one paragraph. This was followed immediately with "[a]t Buffalo we had a wonderful meeting. Nearly 500 people, two-thirds men, made up our audience, and they were unwilling that we should stop talking at all." Tagged on to the end of a section entitled "Stirred Up Wyoming Women," in which she analyzes women's feelings about the vote, was the complete non sequitur "[m]ore than 5000 tourists went to the [Yellowstone] park via Cody last summer, many coming from the East in automobiles." She was thrilled to be in the thick of things, ecstatic to be traveling in new territory, and just bursting to share her experiences with everyone back in Maine.

She was quite as taken with Wyoming's people as with its grand scenery, especially the men, whom she described as "splendid, in most cases much finer than the women. They are courteous, kind, and chivalrous." The typical Wyoming woman was "big-souled, big-hearted" but a little too focused on her daily concerns for Florence's taste. Still, she admired the way they managed their households and children singlehandedly, for there were no servants to be had in Wyoming. Lacking any domestic help, women simply brought their children to all sorts of political meetings "as the squaws do here in the West," and Florence was amazed at how well behaved they were. No proper matron in Maine would have dared disrupt a political meeting by dragging her children to it; she kept them home with the nanny where they belonged.

Wilson won the 1916 election, of course, beating Hughes even in the twelve equal-suffrage states where the NWP had campaigned hard against the Democrats. As the suffragists had feared, the desire for peace had trumped the issue of woman suffrage. They were long experienced in finding hope amid the ruins of failed campaigns, however, and their reactions to the 1916 election results were predictably optimistic. They had succeeded in waking western women to the plight of their eastern sisters, and in four years the West would be far better organized in support of woman suffrage. Although he had won the election, Wilson's margin of victory had narrowed considerably in many of the states, and it was clear that future candidates would have to be mindful of the women's vote in their campaign strategies. On her way back to Maine, Florence stopped at the NWP office in Chicago for an hour between trains, and found the women untroubled by the election results, as full of energy and purpose as ever. This was particularly true of her fellow campaign organizers in the equal-franchise states. "There is a splendid loyalty for the W.P. shown by all the women who have been to the West," wrote Florence defiantly as a closing note to her *Lewiston Journal* column. "We all feel it is the way to win, and that we will win if we keep up the fight for the S.B.A. federal amendment."

Ironically, Maine's Republican leaders tried to blame women voters in the West for Hughes's defeat. Florence bluntly and unequivocally challenged this assertion, pointing out in a letter to the editor that in all the suffrage states men outnumbered women. "[I]t is, therefore, untrue to lump the women en bloc as voting for Wilson, and it is stupid to attempt to do so, as even if they had so voted they could not have carried any one of the states without the help of a large number of the men. In Nevada, there are 221 men to every 100 women; in Wyoming, 219 to 100…." In Illinois, the only state where men's and women's votes were tallied separately, 70,000 more women voted against Wilson than for him, evidence that the NWP campaign had been highly successful. The actual reasons for the defeat of the Republican candidate, Florence concluded, were "the lack of organization, lack of speakers, lack of interest, and lack of leadership in the Republican party. They were not equal to the demands of the campaign and they deserve what they got."[131]

The glow of Florence's trip west soon faded in the face of the chilly reception she received back in Maine. Her fellow suffragists were less than thrilled with her newspaper reports of getting swept up in the Chicago riot, and of organizing Wyoming voters against Wilson. This behavior was simply too outrageous to tolerate, and the MWSA faithful closed ranks against her. She returned to find that she had been stripped of her position as chairman of the Legislative Committee. From then on, she could "address envelopes and stick on stamps," but she could not have any official (or public) role within MWSA.[132]

This was problematic because there was every reason to expect that Maine would have a referendum campaign in 1917, and it was unthinkable to Florence that she would not play a prominent role. Just before she left for Wyoming, MWSA had held its annual meeting in Portland at the spacious State Street home of Augusta Hunt, who was still its acting president. Nearly 100 women from across the state came to the event, making it one of the best-attended annual meetings MWSA had ever held. Mrs. Hunt took the unusual step of serving coffee as a beverage, rather than the traditional tea, and perhaps it was the extra dose of caffeine that emboldened the women present to consider a campaign in the face of strong opposition from NAWSA. Florence, as Chairman of the Legislative Committee, had conducted the research over the spring and summer that proved they would have the necessary legislative support for the referendum, as well as the approval of Governor Milliken and other influential leaders, and she laid this evidence out for the assembly. Yet under Carrie Chapman Catt's new Winning Plan, this was no longer a sufficient test of whether a state should proceed with such an effort. Catt adamantly opposed a Maine campaign because she did not believe MWSA would succeed. Before Maine could even think of a campaign, it should have amassed a war chest of at least $6,000, she warned them (MWSA had a balance of just over $160 in its account at the time). Finally, she reminded MWSA that her new plan prioritized allocation of NAWSA's resources to those states with the most electoral votes and the greatest likelihood of success. Maine, compared to New York and other states with referendums planned in 1917, had few electoral votes to offer and was entirely unproven, and as a result could expect little help from NAWSA.[133]

As much as she wanted Maine to be in the forefront of the suffrage battle, Florence joined Catt in advocating strongly against a 1917 referendum campaign. This may have been in part an effort to appease Alice Paul, who still believed a Maine referendum campaign would be a losing proposition. Florence argued that Congress would pass the Federal Amendment within a year, and then it would just be a matter of persuading three-quarters of the states to ratify it. She also warned that, once the campaign began, Maine would find itself up against not just the antis, whom no one considered a serious threat, but against the well-financed liquor lobby that had mobilized successfully against suffrage referendums in New York, Nebraska, and other states. With no prior experience of a state campaign, Maine had not yet encountered the full force of this opposition, but Florence had read and heard enough from other state organizers to know that the liquor interests would do whatever they could to defeat the referendum. "It would seem foolish," she told those assembled, "for the Maine suffragists to ignore the actual experience of other states who had fought, bled--and lost-- in recent attempts to obtain successful referendums on this question."[134]

Her fellow suffragists were heedless of these warnings, however; they had simply worked too long to secure a state campaign to let one slip through their fingers when it was so tantalizingly within reach. One after another, they rose to refute Florence's arguments and demand in dramatic fashion that Maine enter the fray. Mrs. French led the charge for the campaign, rising to declare, "I do not want to cease from forging ahead and working for a mighty principle relating to human liberty, even if the liquor interests do come in for the fight! I can yet trust the voters of Maine!" She reminded the listeners that the suffragists would not shoulder the burden of the campaign alone; the WCTU claimed 6,000 members in Maine, almost all of whom could be counted on to work for the referendum, and she believed both the churches and the Grange would support it as well. She also disputed Florence's claim that suffragists could get the Federal Amendment through Congress in the next year, as they lacked the necessary votes. "I say, therefore, let us ask the coming Maine Legislature for the referendum; let us work to win and do the very utmost that we can! Tho' we lose this trial, we would have wrought an incalculable miracle of education..."

Mrs. Ralph K. Jones, with "Titian hair...radiant face, and golden voice," next bounded to her feet to assert that, since Maine already had prohibition laws on the books, the liquor interests lacked the organization that they had in other states, and might be expected to put up less of a fight. This observation met with enthusiastic applause from those assembled, and as the meeting wore on, the women worked themselves up to such a fever pitch that Jones spontaneously shouted out, "Let the referendum come! It is a glorious fight anyway! And there is no such thing as an unsuccessful campaign!"

This expressed exactly the sentiment of the women present, including Florence, who, it appeared, had merely been playing devil's advocate. Significantly, she elected not to mention the one argument Alice Paul had made to her that would have refuted Mrs. Jones's claim that "there was no such thing as an unsuccessful campaign." The fact was, as Paul had written Florence several months earlier, failed referendums sometimes solidified legislative opposition to the Federal Amendment, because the congressional delegation could claim with some justification that their states opposed granting women the franchise. With the exception of US Senator Frederick Hale, who was still undecided, Maine's delegation at that time supported the Amendment, so perhaps Florence felt the risk was minimal. As a final test, she asked women to stand if they were willing to commit all of their spare time to working for suffrage if Maine's state legislature approved a referendum. By this she meant that "for two years you will respond when called upon to work; that you will sacrifice the other outside interests, if suffrage needs you; that suffrage will be first!" Twelve women instantly rose to their feet, and another dozen or so committed to working half-time. Still others agreed to work one or two hours a day, and Florence, evidently believing they had sufficient strength to justify going ahead with the campaign, pronounced herself satisfied. MWSA would push for a referendum campaign in the upcoming legislature.

Why did Maine, which had long been content to bring up the rear of the pack, choose this moment to try to run with the leaders, especially when Catt warned them against it? The most likely explanation is that, after literally decades of work, they finally had a state legislature that was favorable to woman suffrage. To let this opportunity get past them was unthinkable. It would have sent mixed messages to the very men they had lobbied so hard if MWSA did an abrupt about-face and withdrew the request for a referendum when it was quite clear they had the votes in the legislature to pass it. Furthermore, very few had experience lobbying for the Federal Amendment, and many MWSA members remained opposed to the national approach to winning suffrage, even though this was now NAWSA's principal strategy. Perhaps they thought that the best way to support the national campaign was for Maine to conduct a successful statewide referendum.

Finally, they were naïve and believed they would win. Maine had never had a suffrage referendum, and there were no polls to indicate popular sentiment one way or another. This left them free to imagine that the "good old state of Maine" would prove generous to its women, even as all evidence from other states suggested a first campaign would end in failure. A successful referendum would make Maine the first state east of the Mississippi to grant full suffrage to its women, which would surely breach the defenses the conservative East had erected against the franchise. "As Maine goes, so goes the country," they repeated optimistically throughout the campaign, and they truly imagined a sort of domino effect taking place as Maine led the way to national enactment of woman suffrage. They would bask in the rosy glow of approval from their fellow suffragists across the country, and Maine would come out of the shadows to claim her rightful place in the history books as a leader in the fight for women's rights. The call to battle was simply, in the end, irresistible.

Yet Catt's concerns that Maine was not up to the ordeal of a state campaign were well-founded. MWSA had virtually no funds in its treasury, and historically had struggled to raise even small amounts of money to finance the work. The organization lacked the sort of united and effective leadership that would be critical to a successful campaign; in fact, its members remained sharply divided over the issue of the CU and whether to work exclusively for the Federal Amendment. While it had more members than ever, most were concentrated in Portland, Augusta, Farmington, and Bangor, which hampered canvassing in the vast rural areas of the state.

There was also the issue of class differences. Virtually all of MWSA's members were educated, affluent, middle-class women. MWSA allied itself with the Women's Christian Temperance Union, the state Grange, and a number of women's clubs, but their memberships were also solidly middle class. Thus, while it may have appeared that everyone they knew supported woman suffrage, this was in part because they stayed within narrowly prescribed circles. Indeed, as the antis liked to point out, women who joined the WCTU frequently belonged to the Grange and other clubs as well. This suggested that the combined membership of these organizations was far less than the suffragists claimed because the same women were getting counted more than once. Finally, MWSA was never particularly successful in reaching out to working women, whether on rural farms or in the factories and mills. Until Florence began focusing on labor issues in 1915, there is no record of MWSA having anything to do with organized labor. There is also little evidence of effective organizing in the French Canadian communities, by far the largest immigrant population in the state and key to winning cities such as Lewiston, Auburn, and Biddeford. Compared to other states, Maine had some significant gaps in its support for suffrage.

MWSA would also lack the services of the one person everyone agreed had been their most effective organizer and was responsible for all the recent canvassing that showed they might count on a campaign in 1917. Perhaps the MWSA leaders believed that victory was so assured they no longer needed Florence's assistance, or maybe they gambled that Florence would never pass up the opportunity to help lead a state campaign and would thus recover her senses and reject the CU. In any event, Florence was not among the slate of officers elected at the close of the annual meeting in October. Instead, MSWA chose Katherine Reed Balentine to be their new president.

Balentine was the daughter of Thomas Brackett "Czar" Reed, who had represented Maine in the US House of Representatives from 1876 to 1899.[135] She had just returned to Maine from California, where she had lived for five years, and had the added distinction of being the only Maine suffragist to have lived and voted in an equal-suffrage state (California enfranchised its women in 1911). Her move back to Portland could not have been better timed; here was a woman, the daughter of one of Maine's most distinguished politicians, who could speak of suffrage from personal experience. She had the stature to lead the organization, though it remained to be seen whether she had the necessary skills. Gertrude Pattangall of Augusta, whose husband had just been elected to the Maine legislature, would serve as vice president at large, and Stella Yates (Mrs. Benjamin) Brewster of Portland would be second vice president. Helen Bates, who appeared to have regained her health (although not enough to resume the presidency) agreed to serve as correspondence secretary.[136]

MWSA members were also delighted to welcome into their ranks Deborah Knox Livingston, a young woman who had moved to Bangor four years earlier with her husband, a minister. Since 1912 Livingston had served as the national superintendent of the Women's Christian Temperance Union's department of franchise, and she had recently done some organizing work for NAWSA.[137] She was described by one Maine newspaper as being "among the half dozen great orators of America," and her presence may very well have tipped the scales in favor of NAWSA supporting a campaign in Maine. Catt insisted that MWSA appoint Livingston to spearhead the 1917 referendum campaign, and NAWSA paid her salary.[138] With a woman of Livingston's skill and talents they must have thought they could afford to lose Florence.

Florence had stubbornly refused to accept the MWSA presidency, despite pressure from Catt and others to do so, because she would not abandon the CU. Committee appointments had not been settled before she left for Wyoming, but she hoped to retain her role as chairman of MWSA's Legislative Committee. The reports of her exploits in the West, however, convinced her more staid MWSA colleagues that Florence was too radical and uncontrollable, that she could not be trusted to march in step with everyone else. Although she was permitted to remain a MWSA member, she was offered no official role to play in the upcoming referendum campaign that she had done so much to bring about. And while she remained president of the CU in Maine, Alice Paul would certainly have frowned on her using the mantle of that organization to support the sort of intensive state campaign work Florence had in mind. It looked as though she would have to sit this campaign out.

Florence's friends in the Maine branch of the CU unexpectedly came to her rescue. Fed up with the narrow-mindedness of MWSA's members, and equally affected by the pressure to choose between membership in the CU or MWSA, they met secretly to form a completely new organization, the Suffrage Referendum League of Maine. One night, as Florence sat at home

"thinking hard about [her] future attitude toward the state association," there
was a knock on her front door. A small group of men and women filed into her
parlor and explained to her that they had formed a new league, and at their first
meeting had chosen Florence to be their president! The Suffrage Referendum
League of Maine would allow its members to work for the referendum while
remaining active with the CU "without feeling themselves outcasts." Clearly
delighted with this proposition, and very touched by their faith in her, Florence
accepted immediately. The news hit Maine's small suffrage community
like a bombshell. As Florence chuckled in a letter to Alice Paul, her former
colleagues at MWSA were apoplectic: "'Antagonistic.' 'Trying to make a split.'
'Got to have everything her own way,' & etc., were some of the nice things one
who listened heard." The new Referendum League planned to cooperate with
MWSA if they received cooperation in turn, but Florence and its members
stubbornly insisted that they intended "to work for the referendum as they saw
fit, without dictation from the National [NAWSA] or the State [MWSA]."[139]

Alice Paul must have read this letter with dismay. While Florence assured
her she would work for the CU whenever possible, they both knew that the
state campaign would absorb most of her energy in the coming months. Paul
wasted no time in recriminations, however, and did not even mention the state
campaign in her reply to Florence. Instead, she tried to keep Florence focused
on CU work. "I wonder if you could not arrange to come to Washington
sometime this winter. I wish so much you could arrange to come, if you feel
that you will be able to come at all, in time for the memorial service, and be
here for the opening of Congress after the holiday recess. We are planning
another demonstration...and will be glad to have you take part."[140]

Things were heating up in Washington. Throughout 1916, despite every
sort of pressure the suffragists could bring to bear, the Democrat-led House
of Representatives kept the Federal Amendment buried in the Judiciary
Committee. Frustrated, the CU decided to increase the pressure, and in early
December they shocked the nation with a stunt reminiscent of the more
militant suffragists in England. As President Wilson delivered an address
to the 64th Congress, five CU members sat in the front row of the visitors'
balcony. They knew that one of Wilson's themes would be Puerto Rican men's
need for the vote, though of course he would remain silent on the justice of
American women's demand for suffrage. On cue, as Wilson mentioned Puerto
Rico, the five women unfurled a banner they had smuggled in under a cape
and dangled it off the balcony for everyone to see. The words on the banner

read: "Mr. President, What Will You Do For Woman Suffrage?" The President glanced at the banner, hesitated briefly, and then resumed his speech, but the entire hall buzzed and whispered as a Senate page quickly tore the offending banner from the women's hands and escorted them from the chambers.[141] Newspapers throughout the country carried the story the next day, and even CU supporters, Florence among them, were divided as to whether it was an effective strategy. "The affair in the House met with a great deal of criticism in the East," Florence wrote Alice Paul a few days later. "I am more or less uncertain myself about the wisdom of that kind of demonstration. It seems likely to hurt the cause more than it helps. But I do have great faith in your judgment and you are there to see if it pays."[142]

Even as she wrote this, plans were well under way for the Union's next public demonstration, the memorial service for Inez Milholland Boissevain that Alice Paul had urged Florence to attend. Milholland was a writer who had gained national fame in 1913 by leading a suffrage parade in DC all dressed in white and riding a white horse. Her flowing robes and beautiful face captured the public imagination, and she became an emblem of pure womanhood's quest for liberty. Milholland was also a passionate and articulate speaker, and in 1916 Paul had scheduled her into grueling cross-country speaking tours, despite the fact that she was suffering from pernicious anemia and tonsillitis. In the fall of 1916, as she was addressing a mass meeting in Los Angeles, she fainted on the platform as she uttered the words, "Mr. President, how long must women wait for liberty...?"[143] Milholland died in a hospital two months later. She was mourned everywhere as a martyr to the suffrage cause, and the CU planned a huge memorial service for her in the Capitol on Christmas Day, the first time the Capitol had ever been used for this purpose for someone other than a member of Congress.[144]

Florence did not attend Milholland's memorial service. Brooks was still young and it would have been hard to leave him at Christmastime. She must also have been troubled by the knowledge that her two eldest sons, Penn and "Bobbo," were of military age. If the United States entered the war in Europe, as seemed increasingly likely, they were planning to enlist. In that case, December 1916 might be their last Christmas together as a family, and there was simply no way Florence would be absent during the holidays.

She also missed the opening of Congress the following month, and the "other demonstration" Alice Paul had referred to obliquely in her letter. At 10 a.m. on January 10, 1917, twelve women filed out from Cameron House, the

Congressional Union headquarters across Lafayette Park from the White House. They were dressed in the suffrage colors of purple, white, and gold, and carried two banners on which were printed the questions, "Mr. President What Will You Do For Woman Suffrage?" and "How Long Must Women Wait For Liberty?" They walked across the park and took up positions on either side of the iron gates of the White House, standing silently throughout the day. From time to time they were relieved by other picketers, who stood as resolutely—and as mutely—letting their banners speak for them. They ended their vigil after dark but returned to stand all the next day, and the next.

Picketing was by then a fairly common tactic in labor disputes, and certainly Florence had participated in the NWP's banner-carrying procession against Wilson in Chicago the previous fall, but no one had ever picketed the president outside his own front gates. National reaction ran the gamut from fierce support to outright condemnation, but many viewed these fresh antics of the CU with a sort of amused condescension, at least initially. Newspapers reported gleefully that President Wilson, returning from his morning golf game, had driven through the gates shortly after the women had taken up their position and, unrecognized by them at first, had smiled and tipped his hat. The editors of Portland's *Daily Eastern Argus* accorded the silent sentinels just one wry comment: "[I]t had been thought President Wilson had as much trouble as one man ought to face, but now he must take on the added annoyance of having the irrepressible woman suffrage warriors camping on his trail."[145] The *Washington Herald* editors spoke for many when they wrote dismissively that "[i]t is to be expected that the suffrage sentinels in front of the White House will become such a fixture within a week that they will not be noticed at all. And without being noticed women will not 'carry the banner' in public." Ignore them and they will go away was the unmistakable message, but it missed the irony that in the very act of writing this, they provided the publicity suffragists were seeking.[146]

Katherine Reed Balentine, MWSA's new president, wasted no time in distancing her organization from this latest controversy. "In view of the fact that many letters have come to me criticizing the activities of the Congressional Union in Washington, I take this opportunity to say that the Union is a separate and distinct organization from the National American Woman Suffrage Association, and the policies of the two are totally different."[147] MWSA, as NAWSA's Maine affiliate, heartily embraced the national organization's dignified and nonpartisan approach to winning suffrage, and Balentine stated flatly that under no circumstances should it be "held responsible for the actions of an organization with which it is neither connected nor in sympathy."[148]

Members of Maine's congressional delegation joined in the general chorus of disapproval. In early January, Florence had written to the six men to ask their positions on the Federal Amendment and received replies that must have caused her some anxiety.[149] Senator Bert Fernald was among the first to respond. He had been favorably inclined toward suffrage, he wrote, but due to the actions of certain suffrage leaders, he had lately become less enthusiastic. "A most disgusting event took place at the convening of Congress, when the President was reading his message, and had not the participants in this affair been women they would doubtless have been arrested and summarily punished. I presume you are familiar with the incident mentioned," he wrote indignantly.[150] Fernald was referring here to the banner incident, not the picketers, so although the letter was dated January 10, he must have been unaware, as he dictated the letter, of the women standing outside the White House gates. He told Florence he was still likely to support the amendment, but he was displeased by the CU stunt and there was a hint that additional actions of that nature might change his mind.

Wallace H. White, a Republican who had just been elected to serve as the 2nd District representative to Congress, was even more direct. He had previously been firmly in support of the amendment but was now "... thoroughly out of patience with some of the methods of campaigning adopted by the women." He condemned both the banner incident and the picketing, and warned that his support for suffrage was waning. [151]

These letters Florence dutifully forwarded to Anne Martin at CU headquarters. The CU leadership appeared unconcerned about the veiled threats they contained, and even welcomed them as evidence that suffrage agitation was working, but they were considerably more troubling for Florence. In the first place, they appeared to substantiate MWSA members' contention that the CU's actions eroded rather than increased support for the Federal Amendment. Secondly, the women in Washington were somewhat sheltered from the sort of personal attacks experienced by organizers working in their home communities. While CU headquarters certainly received plenty of mail (and press) opposing its actions, the women there had the benefit of each other's company on a daily basis and were in a position to witness the positive results in Congress. Women like Florence, who worked in their home cities and towns, had to trust in the assurances from headquarters that the fight was going well as they faced unrelenting criticism at home. They were also much more likely to come face to face with their critics—in the shops, in church, at their children's schools, or simply while walking down the street. Their critics were people with whom they had worked, played, and associated for years, individuals whose high opinions in other times, perhaps, they had cared about and courted.

Woman suffrage was no longer a radical or terribly controversial concept; even when they rejected it, people often did so in a fairly tolerant way, without heat. Many of its opponents acknowledged that it would come eventually, at some vague point in the future, but simply felt that society was not ready for it at the present time. Society was accustomed to women *asking* for the vote; it was women *demanding* the vote that generated anger and condemnation, because it violated social norms governing women's proper behavior. It required considerable backbone and nerve to persevere in activities that a good portion of one's local community considered to be not just a political mistake but evidence of moral failure. The events of the coming year would test the resolve of Florence and her fellow Suffrage Referendum League members as they campaigned for the suffrage referendum in Maine and supported the increasing militancy of their colleagues in Washington.

V The War, the Pickets, and Maine's 1917 Suffrage Referendum

In January 1917, Florence joined 100 other women from around Maine at a NAWSA "Suffrage School" held to prepare MWSA for the upcoming referendum campaign. The majority came from Portland, but Rockland sent six, and there were representatives from Brunswick, Bangor, and several other towns, as well. At least two other members of the new Suffrage Referendum League attended along with Florence: Mrs. Frederic W. (Louise) Freeman and Mrs. Phillip Keith, although it is unclear whether they were representing the League, MWSA, or perhaps even the Portland Equal Franchise League.[152]

Despite her legitimate concerns regarding Maine's capacity, and her desire to focus on states with the greatest prospects of success, Catt had grudgingly approved Maine's campaign and agreed to hold the school there. She could see that MWSA members were determined to pursue a suffrage referendum campaign even without her blessing, and must have decided that they should be as prepared as possible.

NAWSA's Suffrage Schools were two-week courses offered in all campaign states to train women in effective organizing, public speaking, and lobbying techniques. Catt sent three women to teach the course: Mrs. Halsey W. Wilson and Mrs. Frank J. (Nettie) Shuler, both from New York State, and Mrs. T. T. Cotnam from Arkansas. Deborah Knox Livingston, in her new capacity as MWSA's referendum campaign chairman, served as a fourth instructor. Wilson, Shuler, and Cotnam were veterans of campaigns in their own states, and they used the course curriculum and materials developed for New York, which also expected to pursue a suffrage referendum in 1917.

The Suffrage School provided participants with a thorough grounding in suffrage history, and offered facts and figures with which they could lace their speeches and newspaper articles. Instructors sought to place suffrage

in the context of recent trends such as women's growing involvement in
the workforce, increasing numbers graduating from college, and leadership
development resulting from membership in a wide array of women's clubs.
The school's primary purpose, however, was to help women transition from a
"woman's club" mentality to a political action model. Club meetings and teas
were fine for providing general education over time, but a state campaign by
necessity operated within a very tight time frame. With limited financial and
volunteer resources, suffragists had to create an efficient and effective political
organization that could deliver the votes on the day of the referendum. Thus, a
good deal of the course was devoted to teaching the women how to build and
operate within the framework of this new organizational structure, using the
pyramid design shown in the diagram in *Figure 8*.[153]

Within each of these levels, the instructors offered different strategies
for reaching out to and mobilizing public opinion, with the ultimate goal
of persuading men to support the referendum. Each election district, for
example, should have a leader who was responsible for local education efforts
and recruiting people to work for suffrage. She would also be a member of
the committee, just higher in rank. So, for example, the women in charge of
the election district would be members of the State Representative District
committee. There was no room for ineptness or sloth in this formula; if
an election district leader proved herself unequal to the organizing tasks
associated with her position, "…it should be clearly understood…she will be
asked to resign."

Organizers at every level were encouraged to identify different groups they
might work with in their communities and to approach them in different ways.
This included members of professions, such as teachers and doctors (and their
wives); church workers; society groups; temperance; the Grange; or Mother's
clubs. Each might require different strategies. Immigrant groups, for instance,
might need suffrage literature printed in their own language. The instructors
emphasized the need to be sensitive to cultural differences, especially when
doing house-to-house canvassing, and to consider even such details as the
appropriate style of dress, which time of day it was acceptable to canvass, the
type of literature to distribute, and how to pitch the appeal. "ADAPT your
APPEAL to the different groups of women," the instructors advised. "Let the
pleasure lovers FINANCE suffrage with cards, balls, and social affairs. Let
those with consciences see their DUTY to the community. Let the tax-payer
and wage-earner see the INJUSTICE of their condition. Show the generous-

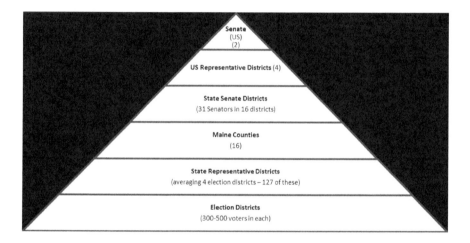

FIGURE 8 Illustration of pyramid structure used to organize support for woman suffrage. Figure reproduced from the original in the Maine Historical Society Collection.

hearted their opportunity of HELPING."[154]

Whatever the method, the instructors emphasized the message that it was time for women to concentrate on suffrage. Organizers could acknowledge that there might be other goals worth working for, but they should stress that, whatever they might be, suffrage was the key to achieving them. The mantra was: "Not suffrage only, but first." Failure to unite behind suffrage would delay its enactment for years, requiring a steady investment of funds and human resources to achieve it. After suffrage was obtained, those resources could be deployed elsewhere, and women would have the added strength of the ballot when they sought to correct societal wrongs.

Maine suffragists generally thought the school was a great success. It provided a thorough education in suffrage organizing, generated a great deal of positive publicity, and, at an evening meeting open to the general public, raised $1,200 to support the referendum effort. This was by far the largest amount MWSA had ever succeeded in raising on a single day, and while still far short of the $6,000 Catt had recommended, it was a big improvement over what they started with. It would remain to be seen, though, whether they could apply the lessons learned to Maine, and whether the competing suffrage organizations could set aside their differences and work together to achieve a victory.[155]

First they had to usher the referendum measure through the Maine legislature so the campaign could officially begin. Representative Willis Swift from Kennebec County introduced the suffrage resolve in the House on January 25, 1917. It was referred to the Judiciary Committee, which set its hearing date for the following Thursday at 1:00 p.m. in the hall of the House of Representatives.[156] When the day arrived, spectators looking for good seats poured into the hall as soon as the House concluded its morning session. To the right of the Speaker's desk, suffragists arranged a map of the country showing the states where women already had voting rights. The bright-yellow MWSA banner was placed there, too, along with a large basket of yellow jonquils. Suffrage supporters, all sporting jonquils on their chests, sat on the right side of the room, and the antis, wearing roses, claimed the left. Despite their private conviction that they would prevail in the legislature, the suffragists pulled out all the stops preparing for the hearing. The lessons of Suffrage School were still fresh in their minds, and this would be the first opportunity they would have to demonstrate their strength and unity. Then, too, the antis were coming out in force to oppose the resolve, expecting to assemble 100 suffrage opponents at the hearing. The suffragists would have to match that if they wanted to make a good showing. By the time the meeting began, the great hall was so crowded that latecomers had to stand outside the doorways, peering over the shoulders of those in front.[157]

The terms of the session were established in advance, and it resembled a debate rather than an open hearing. Each side would have 90 minutes to present its case to the Judiciary Committee. The pro-suffragists won the right to make the opening remarks; they would reserve 15 minutes of their time for a rebuttal after the antis had finished. Deborah Knox Livingston, as MWSA's referendum chairman, made the opening remarks and introduced each speaker in turn, and Mrs. John A. (Elizabeth Payson) Merrill of Portland did the same for the antis. Each side had taken care to select its best speakers to present its case. In addition to Mrs. Merrill, the anti speakers included Mrs. Morrill Hamlin, whose clever barbs kept the audience laughing, and Mrs. Sidney W. (Julia St. Felix) Thaxter. All socially prominent women from privileged backgrounds, the anti speakers argued against suffrage on the grounds that it placed too heavy a burden on women who were already stretched to their limits rearing children and managing their households.

The pro-suffrage speakers represented a more diverse support base. Katherine Reed Balentine followed Livingston's opening remarks with a discussion of her experience as a woman voter in California. Mrs. George F. (Lizzie Norton) French spoke as a representative of the State Federation of Women's Clubs, Charles S. Stetson represented the Maine State Grange, and Judge Edward Reynolds lent an air of legal authority. The last speaker was Henry M. Donnelly, then deputy state Labor Commissioner, who made organized labor's case for woman suffrage.[158]

Florence spoke in her capacity of President of the new Suffrage Referendum League. They may have wished to, but MWSA leaders could not exclude her from the proceedings. It appeared that by mutual agreement Florence and her fellow speakers avoided the topic of suffrage militancy in general and the White House picketing in particular, then entering its fourth week. (The antis, of course, had no such scruples; Mrs. Merrill, for example, spoke disparagingly of "suffragists…[who] have shown they believe in intimidation and coercion.")[159] Florence did open her remarks with a description of Wyoming's entrance into the Union as the nation's first equal-suffrage state. Since virtually everyone present would have known of her recent involvement in the NWP's campaign there against the Democrats, this may have been an oblique reference to suffrage activism of the type not favored in Maine. She quickly moved on to other arguments, however, making the case for suffrage on the basis of justice and political expediency. She estimated that women contributed almost 25% of Maine's taxes, and echoed others' assertions that denying women full participation in government amounted to taxation without representation. Women had proven themselves worthy of the ballot over and over again, she pointed out; they were succeeding in colleges and universities, in factories and professional positions, and in improving their communities through their good works. They were fully worthy of the franchise, and the committee should recognize this by voting unanimously in favor of the resolve.

She closed her remarks with a poem she had written for the occasion, prefacing it with the simple statement, "We have no quarrel with you. We are simply grown up, and we want you to realize it."

> I have no quarrel with you; but I stand
> For the clear right to hold my life my own;
> The clean, clear right. To mould it as I will,
> Not as you will, with or apart from you;
> To make of it a thing of brain and blood,
> Of tangible substance and of turbulent thought.
> No thin gray shadow of the life of man.
> Your love, perchance, may set a crown upon it;
> But I may crown myself in other ways.
> As you have done who are one flesh with me.
> I have no quarrel with you—but henceforth,
> This you must know; the world is mine, as yours,
> The pulsing strength and passion and heart of it;
> The work I set my hand to, women's work,
> Because I set my hand to it.[160]

Uniquely among the pro-suffrage speakers that day, Florence's remarks combined general arguments for woman suffrage with a very personal and moving statement of her own autonomy as a human being. It was her manifesto, a challenge issued not just to the men on the Judiciary Committee, but to everyone else in the room, suffragists and antis alike. In asserting her right to live her life independently and on an equal footing with men, she was reminding them that the issue was not just suffrage, but the larger issue of women's role in society. Florence was through with asking men for permission to think and feel and act the way she wished; from now on, she would be answerable only to her own conscience. This poem set the tone for her suffrage work over the next three years.

The Judiciary Committee accepted Florence's remarks and all the testimony with good humor, and the following week they forwarded the referendum measure to the full legislature with an "ought to pass" recommendation. The opponents tried to table and delay the final vote, hoping that other legislative work would swamp the legislature and make it impossible to act on it at all during that session.[161] Since the legislature met biennially, this would effectively delay it for two more years. The pro-suffrage legislators were alert to such tactics, however, and easily outmaneuvered their opponents.

Representative Edward P. Murray from Bangor, who was the Democratic floor leader, sought to defer the final vote on the grounds that he would be away from the House on business and the Democrats had not yet caucused on the issue. Representative Percival Baxter from Portland, a staunch suffrage supporter, led the effort to bring it to a vote as quickly as possible. The national Democratic Party was firmly in support of enacting suffrage through state referenda, he reminded his colleagues. The suffrage question had been around for years, and everyone present had had plenty of time to make up his mind on the matter; in fact, he pointed out, the suffrage question had been debated in the legislature long before any of them had started their terms. "For many years it was the joke of the Maine legislature…It was often passed by the House only to be defeated in the Senate. Sometimes it was passed in the Senate only to be defeated in the House," he told his colleagues.[162] The patience and hard work of suffrage supporters had forced Maine people to give the measure serious attention, and it was time for the legislature to do the same. Moreover, he argued that it met the three tests suggested for all referenda by former Attorney General William Pattangall: 1) That the question must not be "inherently vicious," meaning that it cannot propose harm to any group; 2) The voters have to understand what is being proposed; and 3) Those requesting the referendum must make a well-considered and reasonable appeal to the legislature.[163]

Representative Edgar E. Rounds, also from Portland, opposed "railroading" the measure through the House. He suggested that women, not men, really ought to vote on the question to get a true indication of whether women wanted the franchise; since he guessed that not more than 10% of Maine women really were interested, he obviously believed this would defeat the measure and lay it to rest. His contribution was pointedly ignored, however, and after some other parliamentary skirmishing, the vote was scheduled for February 21st.

When the day of the House vote arrived, each legislator found on his desk a pamphlet entitled "This Little Book Contains Every Reason Why Women Should Not Vote."[164] Upon opening it to inspect its contents, he found that every page was blank. This little gambit amused suffrage supporters and irritated its opponents, but fortunately there were many fewer of the latter. More serious food for thought was provided by Florence in a letter to House members the day before the vote. She reminded them that since the Maine legislature had convened in January, both North Dakota and Ohio had extended the vote to women, increasing to 94 the number of electoral votes controlled by suffrage states. Signs were very good that Indiana would soon follow suit, adding its 15 votes to the electoral column. In 1920, even if no other advances were made, suffrage states would contribute 25% of all votes for president, more than enough to swing an election victory to one side or the other. Woman suffrage was gaining momentum, and neither political party should be foolish enough to face women voters in 1920 with a record of having blocked its advancement. Whether it was this argument or the simple desire to pass on to voters the burden of deciding, the final vote found 113 legislators in the "yea" column, and only 35 voting "nay," a larger margin of victory than the suffragists had hoped for.[165] The referendum date was fixed for the following September 10th, a Monday.

The suffragists counted this a great victory and looked ahead eagerly to the vote in September. But there were warning signs that the campaign would not be as easy as they expected. To begin with, during the debate many legislators stated their belief that only 10 to 15% of women wanted the vote. Legislators are generally attuned to public opinion, and although they had no formal polls, they must have had some way to gauge their constituents' views on this issue. Even those who supported suffrage conceded that it was backed by a vocal minority of women. Yet they also knew there was little political risk to them in voting for the measure, because while a small percentage of the voters desperately wanted women to vote, and another small percentage vigorously opposed it, the vast majority appeared completely indifferent to the idea. Their interest in moving it through the legislature was purely practical. If the voters decided the question, it would be removed from the legislative agenda and they could focus on other issues. While several legislators paid lip service to the justice of women's claim for suffrage, they agreed that the outcome of the referendum was in doubt.

Of equal concern was the complaint voiced by Representative Edward W. Larrabee of Bath that the suffragists were no more than "a handful of wealthy women that you can count on your fingertips, traveling up and down our State of Maine in their wild frenzy, foist[ing] legislation upon our statute books..."[166] The image of middle-aged society matrons in a wild frenzy is amusing and absurd, but the sober truth was that Maine's suffrage leadership did not represent the diversity of women in the state as a whole. There were no farm wives, factory workers, or fishermen among them, few French-Canadians or Irish or other immigrant groups. This would cost them dearly in the months to come.

****

The Suffrage Referendum League of Maine established its headquarters in Portland in a storefront at 662 Congress Street. The red brick building sat at the end of the row and had large bay windows on either side of the entrance in which League members could post suffrage propaganda. Frederic Freeman, who was a close friend of the Whitehouses and a gifted artist, furnished the logo for the stationery *(see Figure 9)*. The figure had a martial air, but with a humorous twist that surely appealed to Florence, even as it must have irritated her former colleagues in MWSA. In the center of the circular seal, Freeman drew the head and shoulders of a young woman sporting a tricornered hat and military-looking epaulets; next to this were the words, "The Spirit of '76." The woman's gaze was steady and resolute and her firm chin raised, giving her a slightly defiant air. The League's name was inscribed in white letters in a black border surrounding the seal. Its colors, noted beneath the seal, were green, white, and gold. Suffragists used symbolism to great effect, and the colors were intended to convey strong emotional messages: white stood for women's purity in both private and public life; gold for the sunrise that signaled the dawn of a new day; and green signaled the hope and renewal found in spring. The League was openly laying claim to the revolutionary spirit that sparked and won America's battle for independence, and, in effect, declaring war on suffrage opponents.[167,168]

Was it also declaring war on social conventions that constricted free thinking and set artificial boundaries for behavior, for men as well as for

FIGURE 9   Detail from the letterhead of the Suffrage Referendum League.
Maine Historical Society Collection.

women? This is highly likely, since the League by its very existence defied the status quo. It owed allegiance to neither of the two national suffrage organizations. In stark contrast to modern suffrage practice, its executive and advisory boards included both men and women. NAWSA's bylaws, by contrast, prohibited men from serving on its own board or on those of its affiliates. Florence and her friends likely modeled the board structure after the progressive Civic Club, in which both women and men served as officers in full equality.

The League's board was also similar to the Civic Club in that it included several couples. Frederic Freeman was the League's treasurer, and his wife, Louise, served on the executive board. Anne Gannett was vice president, while her husband, Guy, was on the advisory council, as was Florence's husband, Robert. Most members were close friends and business associates of the Whitehouses who had rallied to support Florence and to create an organization that would embrace a more diverse set of suffrage views and methods than MWSA permitted. Actually working to obtain suffrage may have been a third and lower priority for them, judging from Florence's correspondence during the campaign, although it is also true that other events in 1917 shifted their priorities in ways they could not have predicted when they formed the League.

While there was certainly a concentration of Cumberland County members, through its advisory council the League was able to achieve a much broader statewide membership than any other suffrage organization. Some of the members were quite prominent, such as Guy Gannett, a well-known businessman and a state representative from Augusta; Charles S. Stetson, a leader in the Maine State Grange; and Albert Burleigh, from Houlton, who was President of the Bangor & Aroostook Railroad Co. Ralph Brewster would be elected to the Maine House of Representatives later in 1917, and was a leader in local Republican politics. Surely such a well-connected board would help sway public opinion in favor of the referendum measure the following September.

In early 1917, Maine's suffrage campaign was poised to achieve a success that would lead the country to full national suffrage and earn the state an exalted place in suffrage history. If Maine's referendum passed in September, then New York's voters would surely follow suit in their own referendum in November. Together the two states would break through the logjam of eastern states that had refused for so long to enfranchise their women, and passage of the Federal Amendment would inevitably follow. There was much optimism that Maine would approve suffrage; after all, Mainers had led the country by enacting prohibition long before any other state, demonstrating their willingness to be out in front on controversial measures, and many prohibitionists also supported suffrage. Suffrage was also enjoying more support in Maine than it ever had. One hundred women had attended the week-long Suffrage School, and there were three active suffrage organizations in the state (MWSA, the Men's Equal Suffrage League, and the new Suffrage Referendum League) that united men and women in working for the campaign. A single event during the Suffrage School had raised $1,200 in pledges for MWSA, very likely more than an entire year of fundraising had yielded in earlier times. With this unprecedented show of support, how could they lose?

****

The United States declared war on Germany on April 6, 1917, officially entering the conflict it had been supporting financially for months. War fever had been building steadily in the wake of repeated German submarine attacks on American ships, attacks that caused the deaths of innocent Americans and substantial financial losses for businesses, not to mention severe blows to American pride. Although Wilson had won reelection in 1916 on the strength of having kept the country out of the war, by the time he took his second oath of office the following March, sentiment had shifted in favor of involvement. In Maine, progress of the war had been front-page news on a daily basis almost from its inception, and editorials sneered at Wilson's cowardice before the bullying Germans. When he finally addressed Congress and asked for the declaration of war, the country was ready to support it.[169]

The United States' entry into the war posed a serious dilemma for the suffrage movement. Suddenly, the country was seized with a patriotic fervor that measured all activity against whether it contributed to winning the war. The Democratic caucus decided that Congress would only consider what President Wilson decreed were "emergency war measures" from April 1917 until six months after the war ended. Suffrage, of course, was not on the list of war measures requiring action, yet women all over the country were expected to turn their hands to war relief. In this environment, continuing to agitate for woman suffrage made women risk appearing selfish at best, and at worst, dangerously unpatriotic.[170]

Recognizing that American involvement in the war was inevitable, in late February Carrie Chapman Catt called together her executive council to consider how NAWSA should respond. Many suffragists, including Catt herself, were long-time peace activists. In any other situation, they would have quickly denounced the war mongering and urged leaders to remain neutral. However, these were not ordinary times; the suffrage measure was stalled in Congress and could remain there indefinitely if women organized to oppose the war. Supporting the war effort wholeheartedly, on the other hand, would prove women's value and make it much more difficult for men to withhold the franchise once the war was won.

After two days of secret sessions, Catt and her associates emerged to deliver their verdict at a mass meeting held at Poli's Theatre in Washington, DC. "We are opposed to war, but if it comes you will find us prepared and ready to serve," they announced. NAWSA would not pass up this opportunity to gain a political advantage for suffrage, despite the strenuous objections of peace activists. Catt estimated NAWSA's membership at 2 million women who were accustomed to hard work, were well-organized, and were highly skilled leaders at the local level. These skills could be transferred swiftly to the innumerable tasks of war relief—selling war bonds to help finance the war, raising money for the Red Cross, rolling bandages, and knitting socks and mittens for soldiers. All war-related activity would be accomplished under the umbrella of the Central Committee of the Woman's Council on National Defense, which was chaired by former NAWSA president Reverend Anna Howard Shaw.[171]

The war work would be layered on top of existing suffrage activity. Catt refused to abandon suffrage entirely; the country could not be allowed to forget that the price of women's support for the war was passage of woman suffrage. She sent word to local affiliates that women would simply have to find the time and money to continue suffrage organizing while at the same time handling their new wartime obligations. This was asking for superhuman effort, especially for those suffragists working in suffrage referendum campaign states, since money and resources were already stretched very thin in reaching out to voters. For the time being, though, they could stop lobbying on the Federal Amendment. Respecting Congress's decision to consider only emergency war measures, the NAWSA board voted in April to concentrate solely on suffrage work at the state level. This was a decision Catt would soon come to regret. In early August, she complained to Ethel Smith, who was handling publicity work for NAWSA, that she was fed up with seeing news clippings about NAWSA members carrying their own packages, or working in fire departments. It was nice to hear that Mrs. Roessing, then in charge of NAWSA's congressional lobby, was spending her time putting up fruit preserves, but "nothing goes out to indicate that we are even aware that there is a Federal Amendment," wrote Catt in some exasperation. But "[a]s a matter of fact, we do not care a 'ginger snap' about anything but that Federal Amendment at present."[172]

Smith tartly reminded Catt that she could *not* write about NAWSA's Federal Amendment work because there was no such work being carried out. "It takes activity to make news—and our policy was to lie low," she wrote. "I can't see how to write an amendment story without implying congressional activity on our part—and as I understand it, it was to avoid that appearance of activity that our lobby work was called off, and news of the state congressional work suppressed."[173]

In contrast, Alice Paul refused to be distracted from her single-minded pursuit of the Federal Amendment, putting her at odds once again with NAWSA as well as with Congress. Too often in the history of women's quest for suffrage they had been asked to sacrifice their interests to a higher cause: to the Civil War and ending slavery; to securing the vote for Negro men; to enfranchising Native American men and then immigrant men. Each time, women were promised that, in return for supporting voting rights for different groups of men, their own appeals would be heard more favorably, and each time men reneged on their promises and failed to enact woman suffrage. Paul would not repeat the mistakes of the past. Then, too, Paul and a number of her advisors were Quakers whose religious beliefs would not permit them to support war. Any individual member was free to pursue war work or advocate for peace as her conscience dictated, but the organizational power of the National Woman's Party would not be harnessed for war relief as NAWSA had chosen to do. The one concession to the scarcity of resources brought on by the impending war was the merger of the Congressional Union into the National Woman's Party, which occurred in early March. From that point forward, Paul would carry out her suffrage organizing under the banner of the NWP.[174]

Paul's decision to continue the White House picketing despite the war caused a great deal of controversy. For several months after it first began the picketing was conducted peacefully; every morning a group of women would take their places at the gates, carrying the white, purple, and gold banners of the NWP and holding aloft their signs asking how long women would have to wait for liberty. Passersby noted their presence, but in many respects they became part of the scenery of the capital city. Once the United States entered the war, however, the women's presence became more irritating, particularly once the banners began quoting President Wilson's lofty statements about freedom and justice. A frequent quote used on NWP banners was one from Wilson's April 2, 1917, speech: "We shall fight for the things which we have always held nearest our hearts—for democracy, for the right of those who submit to authority to have a voice in their own government." Foreign diplomats, now visiting the White House with great frequency on war business, had to cross the picket line and were thus treated to whatever the banners that day were saying, causing added embarrassment to the administration. Hostile crowds began gathering in front of the pickets, hurling jeers and insults at the silent women.[175]

In May, Carrie Chapman Catt published an open letter to Alice Paul calling on her to remove the pickets, describing them as discourteous to the president and a "futile annoyance" to Congress.[176] She also quoted US Representative Harrison, who had vowed never to vote for establishing a suffrage committee in the House as long as the picketing continued. Here was clear evidence that Paul's strategy was producing negative effects, Catt said, and it was time to halt the demonstrations. Paul told reporters that she would not bother to reply to Catt's letter, and hostility continued between the two suffrage leaders and their organizations.

The picketing moved to an uglier phase on June 22nd, when Lucy Burns and Katherine Morey (from Boston) were arrested for demonstrating by the White House gates. Major Raymond Pullman, Chief of the District Police, warned Alice Paul that further incidents would lead to arrests, but since Congress had legalized peaceful picketing in 1914 under the Clayton Anti-Trust Act, no one really believed the threats would be carried out; the authorities simply had no basis on which to make the arrests. Burns and Morey were charged with obstructing traffic on the sidewalk but were quickly released with no penalties or fines. In the next several days, the police made 27 more arrests in which the women were charged and released immediately, but when some of them made a beeline from police headquarters back to the picket line, it was clear the arrests were not a sufficient deterrent. On June 27th, six picketers were arrested, fined $25 each, and sentenced to three days in jail when they refused to pay.[177]

****

The controversy in the nation's capital over the pickets caused tensions back in Maine, where the suffrage referendum campaign was finally kicking into high gear after floundering for several months. The decisive win in the state legislature in February had brought an initial rush of jubilation followed by a severe slump. A number of factors were at play here, including a long winter that stretched into an unusually wet spring that made rural roads impassable and hampered organizing efforts outside the cities. This was troubling because rural votes were critical to offsetting the anti-suffrage "whiskey" vote in the cities, where bars and saloons were concentrated. The country's entry into the war was, of course, a huge distraction, as money and volunteers that had been pledged to suffrage were almost overnight diverted to war relief instead. It was May before suffragists sorted themselves out and got the campaign back on track, with only four months remaining until the referendum vote.

Like everyone else, in the months after the US entered the war Florence found her suffrage organizing taking second place to war relief work. Public pressure to support the war was enormous, but she had her own reasons to change her stance: Penn and Bob had both enlisted in the Aviation Corps soon after Wilson issued his declaration. Penn, newly graduated from Harvard University, planned to get a pilot's license and fly dirigibles.[178] Bob was training to become a fighter pilot. Florence was torn between her pacifist beliefs, the desire to do everything possible to bring the war to a speedy conclusion so her boys could come home quickly, pressure to exemplify patriotism to avoid criticism of her personally and the suffrage movement generally, and her commitment to the suffrage referendum campaign. During this time of crisis for her family, her state, and for the country as a whole, what should be her role? Since the Suffrage Referendum League was not affiliated with NAWSA, she was not obliged to undertake war work, nor was she bound by the NWP's insistence that its chapters continue their sole focus on passing the Federal Amendment. It was up to her and to the League's board to decide how to proceed. In the meantime, MWSA, following instructions from NAWSA headquarters in Washington, moved quickly to encourage its members to undertake war relief, so it may have been local political pressures as much as anything else that encouraged the Suffrage Referendum League to do the same.

Florence arranged for the League office on Congress Street to serve as a "matchmaking" service between employers with jobs to fill and civilians looking for employment. She also began handling public relations for the Portland chapter of the American Red Cross, which opened in February, and organized fundraising events for relief work *(see Figure 10)*.

Until WW I, the American Red Cross was a relatively small organization. Established by Clara Barton in 1881, the Red Cross offered disaster relief services, both domestically and abroad, for the next 23 years. In 1905 Congress gave it the charter under which it still operates today, authorizing it to serve as a means of communication between members of the American armed forces and their families, and to provide disaster relief within the United States and abroad. The congressional charter did not cause any immediate changes. The Red Cross continued to grow slowly over the next several years, offering assistance to disaster victims such as the families of the young women who were caught in the Triangle Shirtwaist factory fire in New York City, and to the survivors of the *Titanic* sinking. It was WW I that led to the extraordinary growth of the Red Cross; in 1914 it had just 107 branches, but this number mushroomed to 3,864 in 1918. During this same period, membership grew from 17,000 adults to more than 20 million, and 11 million young people joined the new Junior Red Cross.[179]

The Portland Red Cross chapter had a full-time staff of seven women but relied extensively on volunteer help, which was how Florence came to serve as its public relations coordinator. This was a strategic move on Florence's part, for both personal and political reasons. If anything happened to Penn or Bob in the Aviation Corps, her involvement with the Red Cross might improve her access to information. It put her skills as a writer to good use. It was also a highly visible role with an organization that was much trusted, even venerated, by the general public, which might help offset negative press Florence or the Suffrage Referendum League might receive.

Florence ran the Red Cross's publicity department with the help of her close friend Louise Freeman. According to a history of the Portland chapter, the two of them were "almost constantly on duty," ensuring that something about the Red Cross was published in local newspapers on a daily basis. National news was received from Red Cross headquarters in DC, but they were responsible for reporting on local fundraisers and events.

Portland, gripped like the rest of the country by a patriotic frenzy, threw itself into support of the war. By mid-June, Portlanders' subscriptions to Liberty Loan bonds reached almost $5.7 million, about $143 per capita. On

FIGURE 10   Florence Brooks Whitehouse in Red Cross Uniform, Gass Family Collection.

June 18th, the American Red Cross launched a national effort to raise $100 million in donations for its Red Cross War Fund, and Portland's share of this was $150,000. A large clock placed in Monument Square showed the progress of the campaign. On the face of the clock were the words, "Red Cross War Fund Campaign: Portland Should Keep Time With Other Cities." The short hand indicated the day of the campaign (it lasted only a week) and the long hand showed the amount raised. The campaign got off to a tremendous start with $41,578 raised in the first day. By day three, pledges had more than doubled to $103,000, and Portland easily exceeded its quota by the end of the week. Within a few weeks, Portlanders had raised nearly $6 million to support the war effort, either through purchasing bonds or outright donations to the Red Cross.[180,181]

It is small wonder that there was little left over for the suffragists when they went looking for funds. It was hardest on the Suffrage Referendum League. Without a strong national organization to back it, the League was entirely reliant on local giving, and lack of funds several times brought Florence's activities to a standstill. She was desperate for paid organizers who could devote themselves exclusively to suffrage since the Red Cross work occupied so much of her time. To keep it going, she and Robert more than once had to put their own money into the campaign.

Despite these challenges, Florence dedicated substantial time to suffrage work. During May and June she got some organizing help from Laura Hughes, an activist known for her work on labor reforms (especially child labor laws), improving public education, and promoting good government. Originally from Toronto, Canada, Hughes had recently moved to Chicago and become friends with Jane Addams.[182] It is likely Florence was introduced to her through Florence Kelley, who also had ties to Chicago, Jane Addams, the labor reform movement, and to the Equal Suffrage Referendum League. Hughes stayed with the Whitehouses; since the League was struggling to raise funds, room and board may have been all they had to offer her. As a fundraiser, they planned a big open-air rally in Augusta in June. Outdoor meetings had the advantage of accommodating large numbers of people without having to pay a rental fee for a hall. Unfortunately, torrential rains forced the meeting to relocate to Library Hall, and only a handful of people braved the storm to hear the speech. Hughes's speech was titled "Are Women Patriotic?" and addressed the topic of women's wartime service. Most women want to serve their country, Hughes observed, and it was the antis who were unpatriotic by denying women the opportunity of doing this through the ballot box. While Hughes's message was received enthusiastically by the handful of people present, as a fundraiser it was a failure. The League was still out of money and would have to continue its campaign on a shoestring.[183]

Undeterred, Florence set her sights on her next goal: to publish a "suffrage edition" of Portland's *Daily Eastern Argus*, a Democratic-leaning Portland newspaper that supported suffrage. Under this arrangement, the Referendum League would serve as "editors for a day." Its members would be responsible for obtaining articles, photographs, and advertising for that edition of the newspaper and for promoting its circulation. This was an effective publicity strategy since they could use material from noted suffragists across the country as well as those within the state. It also had the potential of raising much-needed funds, as the League would retain a portion of the sale of every paper. Any copies left over could be sold later on or given outright to people whose opinion they wished to influence, because the suffrage information would still be timely.

Florence served as business manager of the special edition, the city editor was Augusta Hunt, and Louise Freeman (a former Broadway actress) served as "dramatic critic." The Woman's Page editors were Mrs. Laura E. Richards and Mrs. W. F. (Helen) Leonard. Together, the women proved quite adept at finding articles to interest everyone. Florence solicited material from Jane Addams out in Chicago and from Alice Stone Blackwell, who was editor-in-chief of *The Woman's Journal*, a weekly suffrage newspaper. The Honorable Jeanette Rankin, the first woman to be elected to the US House of Representatives, contributed an article about women's use of the ballot in her home state of Montana. There was also a letter to the editor from a Mr. A. A. Slade, superintendent of schools in Cody, Wyoming, whom Florence had met in her travels there the previous fall, enthusiastically recommending suffrage to the men of Maine. Laura E. Richards contributed an article on "How Women Helped in War Time One Hundred and Fifty Years Ago" during the American Revolution. Robert Whitehouse wrote a lengthy article on "The History of Man Suffrage" that disproved the notion that men always had universal suffrage, and traced efforts to win it back to thirteenth-century England. Other articles demonstrated the link between suffrage and women's clubs, suffrage and temperance, and suffrage and reform laws such as those providing equal guardianship of children.[184,185]

There were even cartoons: Frederic Freeman, who served as the League's treasurer, produced marvelous sketches under the pen name "Will Ourcadie" that poked fun at anti arguments *(see Figures 11-13)*. Every Wednesday, the *Argus* published a new Ourcadie cartoon, and on the same day, the League posted the original in the big storefront windows of its office on Congress Street. These were reprinted in newspapers around the state, and several made it into the suffrage edition of the *Argus*. A few of these are reproduced on the following pages.[186]

The League arranged to print 6,000 copies of the suffrage edition, and while admitting to "one or two mistakes," Florence felt they had brought it off quite well, especially since nothing like it had ever been attempted in Maine. The *Argus* editor, Mr. Richardson, was pleased enough with the effort that he suggested the League publish another edition in early September, right before the referendum date.[187]

Despite the success of the paper, there were signs that the campaign was not creating the converts the suffragists desperately needed. In Portland, when the League members were trying to sell the suffrage edition on the streets, they encountered a disturbing number of men and women opposed to suffrage. There were also banners and signs posted along Congress Street in Portland urging men to VOTE NO! News of this reached NAWSA headquarters in DC, and Nettie Rogers Schuler wrote Florence to ask her about it. Some of this was to be expected from a city where liquor interests were concentrated, and Florence was uneasy about it, but she could see no alternative to slogging ahead. In the same week the suffrage edition came out, she also delivered a suffrage speech at the movie theater in Westbrook, and debated a well-known anti, Marjorie Dorman, in front of a crowd of 300 people.[188]

Florence had heard that Dorman was known to have ties to the liquor lobby, but NAWSA was unable to confirm this so she could not use this information in the debate.[189] Florence admitted she found the sort of "airy persiflage and ridicule" that characterized Dorman's speech difficult to refute, but was pleased with her own performance and received much praise afterwards from her supporters.[190]

The antis, like the suffragists, maintained a cadre of women available to deliver speeches, to participate in debates, and to organize against suffrage. They apparently saw no irony in traveling around the country telling people that women should remain in the home; evidently the threat of having the vote foisted on women was great enough to override the requirement that they stay out of the public sphere. Dorman came to Maine under the auspices of the

Maine Association Opposed to Woman Suffrage, who proposed the debate. This may have been the last suffrage debate in which Florence participated, although she continued to deliver speeches. She enjoyed debates, but had to admit their effect was mostly to confirm the beliefs of the supporters who showed up for either side. Very few people went to a debate undecided and wanting to hear both sides of the argument in order to make up their minds. Suffrage had been a topic of discussion for so long that people had already staked out their positions.

****

Up to this point, the Suffrage Referendum League had managed to coexist relatively peacefully with MWSA. In the *Argus*'s suffrage edition, for example, Florence included a letter co-written by Carrie Chapman Catt and Katherine Reed Balentine, as well as a photo of Deborah Knox Livingston and a nice article describing her work. Florence liked and admired Livingston, and the two were able to collaborate on some organizing efforts. Livingston was an attractive woman of great personal charm. She was born in Glasgow, Scotland, but had moved with her family to Pawtucket, Rhode Island, when she was ten years old. She took an early interest in temperance and was elected president of Pawtucket's branch of the Women's Christian Temperance Union (WCTU) when she was only 19 years old. Within a short period, she became president of the Rhode Island WCTU, a position she held for nine years. In 1912, due to her interests in the suffrage movement, she was elected Superintendent of Suffrage for the WCTU nationally. Soon after that, her husband was called to serve as pastor of the Columbia Street Baptist Church in Bangor, and she moved with him to Maine in 1912. Her work for prohibition and suffrage had taken her to cities across the United States, to Canada, and to Great Britain, and she was known as a powerful and persuasive speaker and writer.[191]

Livingston's capacity for organized, focused work matched Florence's own, so it is not surprising that the two women worked well together. Livingston was the younger of the two by about ten years and seems to have been freer than Florence was to move about the state. She served as MWSA's primary spokesperson for the campaign; after it was over, she estimated that between February and September she traveled 20,000 miles and delivered 500 speeches.[192] Florence's primary criticism of her was that she did too much herself and did not delegate enough work to others,[193] an observation that could

FLORENCE BROOKS WHITEHOUSE
Chairman for Maine, National Woman's Party

Simple Simon met Mrs. Pieman, going to the fair;
Said Simple Simon to Mrs. Pieman, "Let me taste
   your ware."
Said Mrs. Pieman to Simple Simon, "Will you
   advance my measure?"
Said Simple Simon to Mrs. Pieman, "If that's the
   price — with pleasure."

FIGURE 11   Florence Brooks Whitehouse, Maine Historical Society Collection.

FIGURE 12   Cartoon created by Frederic Freeman for the Suffrage Referendum League in 1917. Maine Historical Society Collection.

have been made about Florence herself. They might have made a great team had they not fundamentally disagreed on suffrage tactics. Livingston did not approve of the NWP's pickets and denounced them publicly in early July, soon after the arrests began in DC.[194]

Tensions at the state and local level reflected the growing hostilities between the two national suffrage organizations. NAWSA leaders were furious with the NWP over the impact the continued picketing was having in Congress. Congressional allies had assured them that the measure to create a Suffrage Committee in the House of Representatives, which had been stuck in the Rules Committee for more than 18 months, would see action once the emergency war measures were out of the way, possibly as early as June. House members were confident of a unanimous, favorable vote from the Rules Committee if the women would only be patient and wait a little longer. NAWSA leaders were not happy with the delay, but they accepted these assurances and agreed not to press their case during the remainder of the session.

Alice Paul and her colleagues, on the other hand, refused to accept any rationale for postponing the formation of the Suffrage Committee. It seemed to them that the war was just one more excuse in a decades-long string of subterfuges men had adopted to avoid enfranchising women, and they continued to lobby and picket. They were angry that the Wilson administration cited lofty democratic ideals as a rationale for involvement in the war. If women were denied the vote, how could the United States claim to be a democracy? They were determined to expose Wilson's hypocrisy, and a new opportunity came when the president sent Elihu Root to Russia to appeal for its support of the war. Russia had recently granted its women the vote, a nice gesture even if the opportunities to use it seemed limited in American eyes. In a speech in Russia that was widely covered by American newspapers, Root made much of the fact that America was a democracy. When the Russian delegation arrived at the White House on June 20th to confer with the president, they found Lucy Burns and Dora Lewis standing outside the gates displaying a banner that read:

> President Wilson and Envoy Root are deceiving Russia.
> They say we are a democracy, help us win a world's war
> So that democracies may survive.
> The women of America tell you that America is not a democracy.
> 20 million women are denied the right to vote.

President Wilson is the chief opponent of their national enfranchisement.
Help us make this nation free.

Tell our government that it must liberate its people before it can claim free
Russia as an ally.

The media reported this with shock and outrage, and the following
morning, when the women began their vigil with the same banner, a group of
boys ripped it from their hands while the police watched and did nothing to
protect them.[195] The women returned to headquarters for new signs, including
one that read simply: "Democracy Should Begin at Home." Later that day,
police joined onlookers in cheering as a mob attacked the pickets, tearing the
banners from their hands and destroying them. The following morning, June
22nd, Lucy Burns and Katherine Morey were arrested for "obstructing traffic"
soon after appearing at their posts. The court dismissed the charge and they
were released the same day, but more arrests occurred the next day, and on
June 25th, twelve women made the trip to the police station in the back of the
Black Mariah. Each time pickets were arrested, more women appeared to take
their places on the picket line.

Within a week or two of the "Russian banner incident," Florence sat down
to write a note to Alice Paul. While assuring her that she still had the utmost
faith in Paul and her lieutenants, Florence told her bluntly that "...there is not
a shadow of a doubt that you are hurting the Maine cause in the picketing."
People had come to accept the silent pickets, but accusing President Wilson
of "deceiving Russia" insulted both the president and the country as a whole.
The fact that it was true had no bearing on the matter, Florence wrote, it was
still akin to "telling your children's faults to strangers," and resentment was
running high. The antis were holding street meetings to protest this most
recent insult, connecting Florence and the Suffrage Referendum League to the
NWP even though they were independent. Thus, until after September 10th,
she would have no choice but to keep the NWP quiet in the state of Maine.
Posters in the window of the Suffrage Referendum League's headquarters
would continue to plead the case for the Federal Amendment, but she would
not organize meetings for the NWP until after the referendum was over. She
was not criticizing Alice Paul's decisions about picketing, she stressed, except
as they affected the state campaign, and after September 10th she planned to
work exclusively for the NWP. [196]

In fact, the Russian banner incident marked a turning point in the picketing.

FIGURE 13 Cartoon created by Frederic Freeman for the Suffrage Referendum League. Maine Historical Society Collection.

In a week's time, the NWP pickets crossed the line from being mildly irritating and faintly ridiculous figures to being treasonous militants deserving of imprisonment. The entire country was in an uproar over it. The events in DC were front-page news across the nation, and the subject of editorials and letters from readers. Congressmen complained publicly that the scandalous behavior made them question whether women deserved the vote at all, and threatened to withdraw their support for the Federal Amendment unless the picketing ended.[197] NAWSA blasted the NWP in news releases, and secretly sent its chief lobbyist, Maude Wood Park, to the major newspapers and wire services to request that they minimize coverage of the pickets.[198] Park reasoned simply that since the pickets wanted publicity, if the country ignored them they would have to give up and go home. The Wilson administration joined this effort at censorship, and subsequently, the editors of both the *Washington Times* and the *Washington Star* agreed to minimize coverage of the NWP demonstrators.[199] Most of the other editors Park spoke with said that they could hardly avoid covering what was, after all, a major news event, although many did agree to minimize coverage as much as possible. NAWSA also requested that they stop referring to any NWP members as "suffragists." In a bizarre twist, they pointed out that the word "suffrage" did not even appear in the NWP's name (as it did in NAWSA's), clear evidence that its members could not be considered legitimate advocates! The real suffragists were members of NAWSA, and the proper way to describe NWP activists was with the words "militants" and "pickets."[200] Although newspaper editors initially seemed agreeable to this request, they eventually ignored it and the activists were generally referred to as the "suffrage pickets."

More arrests followed, the Wilson administration still laboring under the delusion that by cracking down on the pickets it could convince them to stop. The actual effect was quite the opposite. The NWP pickets chose July 4th, the nation's Independence Day, for their next major action, this time carrying a banner quoting Wilson saying, "Governments Derive Their Just Power From the Consent of the Governed." This tactic made it more difficult to charge them with making treasonous remarks. How could quoting the president's own words be treasonous? On this occasion, the police and a mob met the women a few blocks from headquarters, before they had even taken up their positions at the White House gates, and within minutes the signs were destroyed and the would-be picketers placed under arrest. They were again fined $25 each and, when they refused to pay, sent to jail for three days. The irony of being arrested and jailed on the day the country celebrated its independence, solely for asking for their own political freedom, was not lost on the NWP suffragists, and they made the most of this publicity.[201]

Among the women arrested were Joy Young, a young suffragist from New Hampshire, and Helena Hill Weed, both of whom Florence had met in her suffrage travels. Young had worked for the leftist publication *The Masses* as well as for *The Suffragist* (the NWP's official newspaper), and had been one of the other organizers in the West during the 1916 elections. Young had invited Florence to speak on suffrage at an event in New Hampshire later in the summer, which, though she was sorely tempted, Florence declined to do until after the referendum vote was over. Too many people were watching her, waiting for signs of militancy, and she thought it best to lie low for the time being. After September 10th, Florence assured Young, she could make herself available at just about any time. Florence had met Helena Hill Weed on several occasions, and in fact Weed had written Florence earlier in the spring asking if she would hire her to work on the Maine referendum campaign. Due to the Suffrage Referendum League's meager finances, however, Florence could only offer her room and board, but since Weed could not afford to work without pay, they were unable to reach an agreement.[202]

On Bastille Day, July 14th, the NWP pickets carried banners reading "Liberty, Equality, Fraternity" toward the White House, but again they were intercepted and arrested a short distance from headquarters. On this day, the watching crowd was relatively quiet, and the arrests seemed routine until the 16 women were sentenced to a shocking 60 days in Occoquan Workhouse, located outside DC in Lorton, Virginia. Protests erupted all over the country in response to this very heavy-handed sentence, and the women only served three days before President Wilson pardoned them. While they were there, however, they were treated as any other prisoners; they had to don prison garb, eat wormy food, sleep in filthy cells, and work in the sewing room.[203]

By mid-July the stress of the summer heat, an unrelenting work schedule, the tension generated by the picketing, and her arrests had combined to make Alice Paul gravely ill. She was forced to leave DC to recuperate for several weeks in a sanitarium. Following initial alarm that she might not survive her illness, she recovered sufficiently to continue some direction of the NWP, albeit from her bed in Philadelphia. Lucy Burns took over day-to-day operations, and the picketing continued on a weekly basis.

In August, Lucy Burns wrote wording for a new banner that would provoke even more hostility and criticism than the "Russian" incident earlier in the summer. "Kaiser Wilson, Have You Forgotten Your Sympathy With the Poor Germans Because They Were Not Self-Governing? 20 Million American Women Are Not Self-Governing/Take The Beam Out Of Your Own Eye" read the banner the women carried out of headquarters on August 14th. The comparison of Wilson to the German kaiser infuriated the watching crowd, which immediately attacked the women and tore their banners to shreds. In short order, all the women lost their banners and headed back to Cameron House to regroup. The crowd followed and remained outside, so ugly and angry that the women were afraid to leave the building, electing instead to hang their "Kaiser" banners from the balcony. Some men in the crowd fetched a ladder and climbed up to pull the banners down; in the ensuing struggle, a gun went off and the bullet pierced a window on the second floor. Although no one was hurt, the incident rattled the women's nerves, and the siege continued for hours. Well into the evening, the mob continued to try to climb over the back garden fence to break into Cameron House. It was a long sleepless night as everyone stood watch and prepared for the worst. The police observed but did nothing, claiming they had no orders to intervene. While there were no further incidents that night, tensions mounted still more in the next several days as the NWP pickets continued to try to display their Kaiser banners, and were met each time by mobs. Frighteningly, the police themselves began joining in the attacks on the women, knocking them down and kicking them.[204] The situation appeared to be getting completely out of control.

****

The picketing sounded a steady, ominous drumbeat throughout the summer of 1917, perhaps an echo of the war in Europe but one that many heard to be out of step. In Maine, news of the picketing was met with heated condemnation. No one protested the fact that the suffragists' civil rights had been violated repeatedly, that they were denied police protection, arrested on spurious grounds, and illegally jailed for asking for political freedom. The general sentiment was that they deserved whatever they got. In the face of this sentiment, and given the high stakes of the referendum campaign, Florence continued to lie low. There was no way she could agitate for the Woman's Party, either the pickets or anything else, until after the referendum was over, she told Paul. Her inaction earned her a spot on NWP's list of state chairmen who refused do as they were asked in promoting the cause.[205]

By July the suffrage referendum campaign in Maine was running as close to full throttle as it ever would, given the competing claims the war effort imposed on volunteers and donations. NAWSA was fully backing the Maine campaign and in July sent at least five different national organizers to help with organizing work. Of these, the most colorful was Lola Trax, from Maryland's Eastern Shore. She had organized several publicity stunts in Maryland to raise awareness of suffrage, one of which was to recruit five other women (the "suffrage army") to hike 125 miles through mountainous areas of Maryland, stopping to give speeches in small rural towns. The women wore Panama hats and dark-blue linen uniforms with violet and white shoulder sashes, which were Maryland's suffrage colors. Trax also traveled nearly 1,000 miles around Maryland in a prairie schooner drawn by two draft horses named Susan B. and Margaret B., to call attention to women's demand for suffrage. She pulled no similar publicity stunts in Maine, merely delivering some speeches during her tour of the state, but she did attract more interesting and extensive news coverage than some of her colleagues. MWSA paid some of the expenses of national organizers, but NAWSA helped schedule them, advised on organizing strategies, and supplied publicity materials at low cost.[206]

The out-of-state organizers had broader experience and were in a better position to assess whether or not the Maine campaign was in trouble and needed reinforcements. They must have thought it needed a boost, for in late July both Carrie Chapman Catt and Nettie Schuler arrived for an extended visit to rally the faithful and breathe some excitement into the campaign. Schuler was a veteran of New York's suffrage campaign in 1915 and was assisting in its 1917 campaign as well. She had also been one of the instructors at the Suffrage School back in January, so she was already acquainted with a number of the women in Maine.

Catt and Schuler stayed for almost a week, enduring a typically strenuous schedule. They arrived on July 24th on the night train from New York, pulling into the station in Winthrop at 8 a.m. From there they made their way to Augusta and spent the day closeted with all of the out-of-state workers to hear their reports and map out strategy for the next six weeks. Mrs. Guy Gannett hosted a tea at her house from 4 to 6 p.m. that afternoon, attended by members of the Augusta suffrage contingent. Catt and Shuler stood in a receiving line so that they could meet every woman present. That evening, they spoke at a big rally presided over by Governor Milliken. The following day, they met with all the suffragists working in the central and western parts of the state, departing that evening for Bangor, where they stayed until Saturday. In Bangor, Catt and Schuler addressed another crowd and continued working with Deborah Knox Livingston and other suffragists on details of the campaign. On Saturday, they left Bangor for Bar Harbor, where they held a series of additional meetings.[207]

The Augusta mass meeting was held in City Hall, a large brick building perched on a hill overlooking the Kennebec River. MWSA opted for a patriotic theme for this event. The organizers arranged for the Second Regiment Band to play rousing music to entertain the waiting crowd and to accompany the meeting as well. A large American flag stretched across the back of the City Hall stage, reminding the crowd of women's patriotism during this time of war. Flowers decorated the front of the stage, the predominant color being, of course, suffrage yellow. Deborah Knox Livingston served as the master of ceremonies, and when she introduced Governor Milliken as a staunch supporter of woman suffrage, the audience rose to its feet in respect and gratitude. Milliken told the crowd that in his opinion the question was not *whether* women would vote, but *when*, and urged the men of Maine to lead New England in granting women the franchise. He then introduced Catt, who recited the progress woman suffrage had made nationally and internationally in the last year, largely, she believed, as a result of women's contribution to the war effort. Russian women had already voted several times since the revolution in that country. Three-quarters of the provinces of Canada had approved woman suffrage, and the prime minister was sure the rest of the country would follow shortly. In Great Britain, a suffrage bill had passed the House of Commons by a 7 to 1 vote, and there was great confidence that the House of Lords would follow suit before the end of the year. France had promised its women the vote once the war ended, and leading political parties in Italy, Hungary, Romania, and Prussia (Germany) had also come out in support of suffrage.

Catt pointed out that seven America states had given women at least presidential suffrage in the last year, five of them since Maine's legislature had voted in February to authorize the referendum. The momentum for woman suffrage was inexorable, and Maine men should simply get on the train or be left stranded on the tracks of history. She cautioned that the actions of the women pickets in DC should not influence men against the referendum. The women involved in the picketing were not members of NAWSA, and NAWSA heartily disapproved of their activities. It was foolish to hold all women accountable for the few that chose to picket, just as it would be to say that when men rioted and destroyed property, all men were bad and should have their voting rights revoked.

It is possible that when Catt mentioned the pickets all eyes turned to Florence, who was certainly their most prominent supporter in Maine. Even though she had deliberately deemphasized her involvement with the NWP during the campaign, she had steadily refused to denounce the pickets or question publicly the judgment of NWP leadership. She sat in the audience with her supporters, including the faithful Louise Freeman, Augusta Hunt, and her house guest Blanche W. Welzmiller. There was also another group, somewhat larger, that included Helen Bates and several other MWSA stalwarts. Indicative of the current level of tension, the two contingents from Portland signed in separately.[208]

While Florence's continued support of the NWP actions certainly irritated her former MWSA colleagues, there were other issues contributing to the division. To begin with, Catt and Schuler's visit to Maine completely bypassed Portland. It is unclear whether they simply believed that Portland was already better organized than the rest of the state and thus needed less attention, or if they wished to snub Florence. Since Florence complained with some frequency that she was doing most of the work, and she was most focused on the southern part of the state, there is reason to believe that the former was true. They may have trusted Florence to get the job done. On the other hand, Deborah Knox Livingston was based in Bangor and was crisscrossing the state to drum up support for the referendum, so MWSA certainly had some capacity in northern and central Maine. In any case, all the negotiations for Catt and Schuler's visit were handled by the MWSA leadership, and Portland never made it onto the itinerary. Florence tried to make her own arrangements, telegramming Schuler in early July to inquire if she and Catt could stop over in Portland to attend a garden party after they were finished in Bar Harbor. Blanche Welzmiller would be the featured speaker, and the event would raise money for the Red Cross Yarn Fund. Schuler politely declined the invitation, noting that their itinerary was already full.

During Catt and Schuler's visit, both Florence and Robert Whitehouse participated in a meeting in which representatives from local suffrage leagues and allied groups reported on their referendum organizing efforts. First to report were the MWSA state organization and the various city and county leagues. This group included the Men's Equal Suffrage League that Robert still chaired. These were followed by reports from the WCTU, the Federation of Women's Clubs, the Grange, and a stream of other organizations for which suffrage organizing was only an ancillary activity. Only after they had reported was Florence called upon to discuss the Suffrage Referendum League's activities, and even then, Catt deliberately interrupted her presentation partway through and said it was time to move on. This was a clear snub, and it infuriated the Whitehouses. Since Florence was in some ways the lightning rod in all this, Robert took the lead in writing to Deborah Knox Livingston to complain about MWSA's high-handedness and poor treatment of its sister league. He reminded her that they should all be focusing on the referendum, not on petty rivalries that deflected the public's attention away from the vote. He was able to clear the air somewhat, to the point where Florence was able to communicate directly with Livingston once again.

For Florence, the incident with Catt was simply the culmination of a long list of grievances. She had done her utmost to cooperate with MWSA, she told Livingston, responding to every request "…with enthusiasm," but in return had gotten "nothing from them but knocks." The blame for this she laid squarely on Katherine Reed Balentine and Helen Bates, acknowledging that they were extraordinarily difficult to work with and half-humorously suggesting that they were influenced by darker forces. "You are quite right—you are not responsible for them—I am sure the Lord would not like to be and whom else is there left—only the one who is prompting them I fear, Satan Himself." Still, Florence thought that she and Livingston could have formed a strong partnership, and wished that Livingston had stood up to Bates and Balentine from the outset.[209]

Following these incidents, Florence was much sharper in her criticism of the state association and less willing to bail out its volunteers when they failed to follow through on a course of action. A huge tension point was the petition drive MWSA undertook during the summer to collect signatures from women over the age of 21 who wanted the right to vote. In order for this to be a meaningful exercise they had to collect tens of thousands of signatures; after all, there would be little public relations value to claiming that only a few thousand women cared about voting. At a time when much of Maine's population lived outside of the cities this required an active outreach effort, traveling to small towns and going door to door to get signatures from women who stayed at home. It was an enormous undertaking since relatively few women could drive or had access to cars, and almost all were distracted by war relief efforts besides. It was also summertime, and many volunteers were unwilling to let the referendum campaign interfere with their vacation plans. Florence, who had her own car, agreed to help collect signatures in York and Cumberland counties, only to find that she was receiving virtually no assistance in this from MWSA volunteers. In early August, she lost her temper with Thirza Davis, who was supposed to be collecting signatures in Westbrook. "I was perfectly horrified to find when I called at your house in Westbrook that you had left the town and gone off for a vacation..." Florence scolded her. "[A]t this crucial time, when the whole success of the campaign in Maine depends on the loyalty of the few members who are working, it seems a pity that vacations could not wait until after the 10th. We should have 1176 petitions from Westbrook in order to carry. We have one name. Do you not feel this is a disgrace to Cumberland County?"[210]

Davis evidently took exception to this criticism and wrote Florence a haughty reply from her vacation home in Limerick. Florence recognized that she could not afford to completely alienate the few workers who remained and was more conciliatory in her response, but remained annoyed that Davis had packed up and left for vacation without a word to anyone. Except for one brief weekend on Squirrel Island, Florence and Robert took no time off that summer of 1917. Between the suffrage referendum and her Red Cross work, there was simply no time to spare. Instead, in early August Florence sent a suffrage flag to Captain Williams, who skippered the *Nellie*, the ferry based in Boothbay Harbor that serviced Squirrel and nearby islands. "I want you to fly this from the very highest point of your flagstaff just under the American flag where the Antis cannot get it," she wrote, "and when it is worn out I will give you another." Even if Florence could not make it to Squirrel, the flag would serve as a daily plea for suffrage to those who traveled back and forth to the islands.[211]

The final weeks of the campaign were filled with hectic activity, complicated by the fact that the Suffrage Referendum League still had no money. The hoped-for funds from the June edition of the *Argus* were slow to come in, and donations continued at a mere trickle. Florence wrote to anyone who had hinted at a willingness to support the campaign. On August 20th, she wrote to her friend Helen Maxey, who was vacationing on Squirrel Island, asking that she use her influence with her father to get a $100 donation from him. "We are very hard up for money and cannot have the help that we need on account of finances." Twenty days before the vote, Florence was still hopeful that they might win if they had money to hire speakers, rent halls, and print and distribute publicity materials. While it was true that the Red Cross had siphoned off a large share of donations, Florence was puzzled that it had been so difficult for her to raise money for the League's activities. She wrote Maxey, "Mr. Whitehouse and I are putting a thousand dollars in the campaign ourselves, and we do not feel we have a right to exceed that, although I am very much afraid we will before the thing is over." This was an impressive amount of money for the Whitehouses to donate, equivalent to over $18,000 in 2013 dollars.[212]

At this point, Florence had to admit the truth of what Alice Paul had warned her about: state campaigns swallowed an enormous amount of time and money that would be better utilized in lobbying Congress to pass the Federal Amendment. In the midst of her begging letters, she wrote to another friend she knew from Squirrel Island, urging her to attend an NWP conference in New Hampshire. It was clear that she was fed up with the state campaign. "To me," she wrote wearily, "after working as I have in this campaign morning, noon and night, I feel that I shall turn all my energies to working for the Woman's Party for the Federal Amendment when it is over."[213]

The pace of the campaign intensified as September 10th drew near. There were many meetings and speeches, and suffrage supporters sought to place daily appeals for the vote, or coverage of their activities, in every edition of Maine's larger newspapers. The antis, on their side, brought in speakers from out of state, held teas and rallies, and wrote letters to the editor. A big focus was to discredit the suffragists' petition drive, which now boasted 38,000 signatures. The antis charged that there was widespread fraud with those lists, including women who signed multiple times, those whose names somehow appeared on the list even though they opposed suffrage, and signatures of women who were not even residents of Maine. They further claimed that in some instances the names of infants, the feeble-minded, and even men were placed on the lists to swell their numbers.[214]

While admitting to a few errors, which they corrected, the suffragists heatedly denied these claims and countercharged that the antis were financed by the liquor interests. "Who is John B. Maling?" wondered one letter writer to the *Portland Evening Express* "And who is paying his salary?" Maling had been crisscrossing Maine throughout the summer, calling on political and community leaders and giving speeches in which he told of woman suffrage's disastrous effects in Colorado. He claimed to have had some position of authority in Colorado state government, but further investigation revealed that in fact he had been merely the handyman for one of the most notorious crime bosses in that state. The former managing editor of the *Denver Times* was quoted as saying that politically Maling was "a person of no consequence" in Colorado. After his "boss" left town, he was left without a livelihood, and he was simply peddling his anti-suffrage views for money. The suffragists were able to confirm that he had worked against suffrage in Iowa, and possibly in other states as well. There was strong suspicion that the liquor industry paid his salary each time.[215]

The suffragists had certainly anticipated the liquor lobby's involvement in the suffrage campaign, since it had been active in other states, but the "whiskey interests" were generally careful to avoid working openly as a lobby. Yet somehow the antis seemed to have plenty of money for hiring halls, recruiting speakers, or hiring organizers, and never had to undertake extraordinary fundraising efforts as the suffragists did. A large portion of the funding also came from Mrs. John F. (Laura) Hill of Bangor, the widow of the former governor of Maine and reputedly the richest woman in the state. She underwrote many of the activities of the Maine Association Opposed to Woman Suffrage, doing whatever she could to defeat the referendum.[216,217]

One of the people following the Maine campaign closely was Walter Clark, who was then Chief Justice of the Supreme Court of North Carolina. Clark took a keen interest in woman suffrage as well as other social reforms, and wrote to offer Florence (at his expense) copies of his own suffrage speeches that she could distribute to voters. "The whiskey interests will finance the fight against you," he jotted in the margin of his letter. "Tho [*sic*] you have Prohibition, the liquor men know that the vote of the women will make it more effective."[218]

Florence accepted his offer promptly. "We are perfectly sure that the Whiskey interests are working here in Maine," Florence replied in her letter to him. "In fact they have already begun to do their circularizing and last week a man representing the liquor interests [probably Maling] made two visits to the city in aid of the Anti cause." The Portland Mayor, Wilford G. Chapman, was firmly anti-suffragist and was also strongly suspected of having ties to the saloon keepers.[219]

In August MWSA replicated Florence's arrangement with the *Argus* and had a suffrage edition of the *Lewiston Journal* that came off quite well. Florence, who by this time had made peace with Deborah Knox Livingston, if not the rest of MWSA's leaders, sent her "heartiest congratulations" on the issue. "It was a 'crackerjack' edition, and cannot fail to do a tremendous amount of good," she added optimistically.[220] The two women collaborated on generating daily press coverage of suffrage activities, which meant having to organize events and speeches in multiple cities every day that would produce something new to write about. This required constant juggling of schedules and venues, and bringing in speakers from out of state who would be notable enough to draw crowds and generate news coverage. They had to produce announcements of the events as well as the news releases covering what the speakers had said. Florence and Livingston kept in constant touch, moving speakers and organizers around the state so they would not become stale in any one location. Significant advance planning was necessary because they had to do it all through the postal service, as telephone calls and telegrams were too expensive. In one letter to Livingston, Florence said, "I think it would be perfectly splendid to have Miss Engleman…and [will] confer with you later. Just now I am going off to a street meeting at one of the factories where a socialist labor man is going to speak…" Or later, "I am sorry about Mrs. Kelley, but I am negotiating for Helen Todd, who is considered one of the finest speakers in the suffrage cause. She has offered to come to me for her expenses, and if I can get the money I shall employ her." A week later, Florence wrote Livingston again. "Thank you for your two letters. Sorry about Mr. Weatherby, but we did not dare to advertise a meeting because we could not get in touch with him…I will see him tomorrow and give him your message about Cherryfield."[221,222]

At the invitation of the *Argus* editor, Florence planned a second suffrage edition with that newspaper, this one scheduled for September 6. It was to be a final appeal to the voters, trying to marshal the best arguments and at the same time showcasing the women who had worked so hard on the campaign.

To improve revenues from this second attempt, Florence (as advertising manager) sent letters to the *Argus*'s regular advertisers offering a direct business proposition. Place an extra advertisement in this edition, she said, and we will ensure that it gets to double the number of readers that it ordinarily would. Since they planned to print double the issues, advertisers could assume that 15,000 people would read the newspaper. Every effort would be made to deliver the paper into the hands of rural residents, and "[i]t is a known fact that once a farmer, far removed from the cities, receives a newspaper, that paper does not leave his hands until he has read all it contains, both news and advertising." That single issue of the *Argus* could generate 10% new customers, which would more than cover their advertising costs. Regardless of whether or not they supported suffrage, this was a deal they could not afford to miss. A full-page ad would cost $39, a half page $19.60, and a quarter page just $9.80.[223]

In an ominous sign of the campaign's prospects, the suffrage issue never happened. It is unclear whether Florence could not generate sufficient interest among potential advertisers to make the issue pay, had difficulty securing enough suffrage material to fill the paper, or some of both. At this stage, anyone working for suffrage was exhausted from the rigors of referendum organizing coupled with work for the Red Cross or other war-related activities. Florence herself had spent the summer shuttling between the Red Cross office, the suffrage headquarters on Congress Street, and towns throughout Cumberland County collecting signatures for the suffrage petition. It was up to her to make the suffrage edition happen, and layered on the frantic pace of the final days of the campaign, it may have been too much for her to do.

She might also have wondered if it would make any difference in the outcome of the campaign. On August 30th Florence received a letter from Charles E. Gurney that must have caused her some disquiet. Gurney, a Republican, had been state representative from Portland in 1916 and would go on to serve in the state senate for two terms beginning in 1919. In the interim, he was an attorney in private practice and a friend of Robert's. He wrote to say that he was surprised at the opposition to woman suffrage he was hearing from "intelligent and broadminded" men in his community, many of whom gave as their reason the actions of the NWP pickets. He suggested that the Suffrage Referendum League board ought to consider "...the official repudiation of such conduct as the friends of the measure in Washington have been resorting to. It is certainly prejudicing the cause here in Maine." It would be good idea to have the newspapers point out "with large headlines" that the Maine suffragists had fought the campaign in a "...clean, high-minded, straightforward, and honorable manner." Whether or not Florence brought this to the attention of her board, in the end the Suffrage Referendum League issued no such pronouncement. Its founding principle was that it would be accepting of all styles of advocacy for woman suffrage, and Florence refused to withdraw her support for the suffrage pickets, even if doing so would have won more referendum votes. The NWP actions made her local work more difficult, but she would defend the women in Washington.[224]

Although Florence had not yet joined the picket line, both Alice Paul and Lucy Burns had urged her to do so, and she was sorely tempted. The NWP was planning another mass picket on September 1st, similar to a demonstration back in March in which 1,000 women had participated. Attempting to reassure the more skittish NWP members, Lucy Burns pointed out in her invitation that "[t]here is no reason why this orderly demonstration should be interfered with." Since large numbers of women would be participating, it was unlikely anyone would be singled out for arrest, she assured them. Still, Florence believed she should not picket until after the referendum vote because the negative backlash, especially if she were to get arrested and jailed, would be substantial. She had worked too hard on the referendum campaign to risk losing it over joining the picket line. Given Congress's continued intransigence, there were certain to be other opportunities to join in after September 10th. And with the vote fast approaching, she could not afford the travel time to DC, so she reluctantly refused the invitation.[225]

Carrie Chapman Catt returned to Maine for mass meetings on the eve of the vote. This time she went first to Waterville to speak at the Opera House the Friday before the vote, traveling back down to Portland on Saturday for a large rally that evening at City Hall. Her Portland visit was arranged under the auspices of the Men's Equal Suffrage League, conveniently sidestepping the awkward tension between MWSA and Florence's group. While leaders from all four of Portland's suffrage leagues sat on the platform with the speakers, Robert Whitehouse presided over the ceremonies for the evening. Governor Milliken came from Augusta to urge a yes vote on suffrage, lending an added dignity and importance to the occasion. Missing from the lineup was Portland's Mayor Chapman, who was attending a competing event sponsored by the antis the same evening in the City Council chambers.[226]

The City Hall event was a grand affair. The meeting was preceded by a parade of automobiles bedecked with yellow banners that traveled down Congress Street to the accompaniment of Chandler's Band. The dignitaries arrived at the great stone building at the same time as the parade, and twenty attractive young women dressed in white and holding yellow suffrage banners formed an aisle through which Governor Milliken escorted Mrs. Catt into City Hall auditorium. The Chandler's Band led the remaining dignitaries into the hall and up onto the platform, followed by an audience of about 1,800 people.[227]

The audience that evening included a large number of men as well as women, and when Robert introduced Catt, they gave her a standing ovation out of respect for all that she had done for suffrage. Once the applause quieted and the audience had resumed their seats, Catt proceeded to place Maine's suffrage referendum squarely in the context of the war. "Do you know the connection between the great war and the election on Monday next?" she asked the audience. "Democracy and democracy only can save the world from the menace of militarism, so democracy has come to be the aim for which nearly all the world is fighting today. The election on Monday will be the first election on a question connected with democracy that has taken place since the United States declared war..." It was time for the men of Maine to show the world that true democracies included women as voters; continued rule by men alone could only be termed an autocracy. "There is no democracy where one class or one sex is barred from a voice in government," she declared-- and the audience broke out in applause. She then related an anecdote that showed how the soldiers understood what it was they were fighting for.

An anti group had given an American flag to a regiment that was about to ship out for the front. Some of the men wrote to acknowledge the gift but added that, if it were up to them, they would refuse to accept the flag from an anti-suffrage association. Regimental rules required them to accept a gift of a flag from any source, but it troubled the men that while they were "going to France to fight for democracy, you ladies are going to stay at home to fight against it." The men noted with distaste the role the liquor interests played in funding the antis, and concluded by saying, "The presentation of the Flag under which we fight by your association is a sham, and in order that we may not share in this hypocrisy, we make this statement from our consciences."

In closing, Catt urged the men of Maine not to be swayed by the actions of the pickets in Washington, and declared that in all of history there had never been such a demand for the vote as there was among American women today. Following her remarks, Robert read a telegram he had received from former President Theodore Roosevelt, which said simply, "Accept my hearty good wishes for success for suffrage on Monday." He next introduced Katherine Reed Balentine, who spoke briefly to how women had proven their worthiness for the vote through their war work.

Governor Milliken, whose speech concluded the evening's program, agreed with President Wilson that "we must make the world safe for democracy" but argued that it was equally vital to "make democracy safe for the world." Enfranchising women was the key to establishing a wholesome society that would prevent men from holding office "for selfish purposes alone" and ensure that democracy would be safe for people at home and abroad. He warned that the women of Maine could not be held responsible for the actions of the women in Washington. It would be as unfair to blame the women of Maine, he said, as it would be to blame men throughout the country for dubious actions taken by Congress. Finally, the governor urged the men of Maine to vote yes in Monday's referendum, declaring again that it was "not a question as to whether we shall have equal suffrage, but when we shall have it."

Democracy, patriotism, expediency, justice. These words, varying in emphasis and rhythm and intensity, had resounded throughout the campaign and were now raised to a crescendo in the great hall packed with suffrage supporters. Through a long weary summer, amid the anxiety and sacrifices of war, the suffrage forces had labored to persuade the men of Maine to enfranchise their women. In two days they would know whether they had been successful. This bold step that Maine might take, leading as it had led the country in prohibition and countless other elections, would end the suffragists' struggle and free them to turn to other interests long neglected for their cause. Yet the suffrage battles in Maine stretched back decades, as many in the audience knew all too well. That history was littered with broken promises and pledges unfulfilled. The vote on Monday could go either way. A yes vote would be an affirmation of woman's worth, of her very right to individual existence apart from men. A no vote would effectively deny her citizenship and extend the battle for suffrage that would end only when, through state or federal action, she at last won the franchise.

****

The suffragists presented an optimistic front going into the final days of the campaign. Encouragement flowed into the state from around the country, with even President Wilson sending a letter to Deborah Knox Livingston urging a yes vote. Florence arranged for a special wire to be installed at the Suffrage Referendum League office on Congress Street, which would allow her to receive returns from around the state once the polls closed at 5:00 p.m. Visitors to the office throughout election day would be treated to tea and refreshments prepared by League members. Katherine Reed Balentine kept a lower profile, receiving people at her home on Deering Street.

September 10th dawned clear and fair. There were no driving rainstorms, no extraordinary heat or cold that might keep voters away from the polls in large numbers, yet turnout was light. Perhaps it was true, as some observers speculated, that the fine weather kept farmers in the fields for the harvest. In the Referendum League office, the mood was hopeful until the first election returns began trickling in from Cumberland County towns. Standish, one of the first towns to report, defeated suffrage with only 41 votes in favor and 123 opposed. Sebago followed quickly with a vote of 16 for and 45 against, and Cumberland narrowly defeated the measure at 43 to 47. Results from several other small towns were equally gloomy, but when South Portland and Westbrook both defeated the measure by significant margins, the suffragists must have known they were in serious trouble. Still, they clung to the hope that voters in more remote towns would stand by them. Balentine refused to concede defeat until the following morning, when enough towns had reported that the results were undeniable. When the final vote was recorded, 19,428 men voted for equal suffrage and 36,713 opposed it. The suffragists had lost the referendum by a depressingly large margin.[228]

In Portland, home to many of the state's suffrage leaders, 5,095 voters opposed it to only 1,997 supporting, and the results were equally dispiriting in almost all the state's other major cities. Bangor returned 1,875 votes against suffrage to only 503 supporting, and Lewiston was 1,315 opposed to 654 in favor. There were a few bright lights in this dismal picture; just across the river from Lewiston, Auburn voters approved suffrage 823 to 652, and Rockland voters also passed the measure. Still, there was no denying that Maine men had dealt suffrage a crushing defeat.[229]

In the immediate aftermath of the election, Maine's newspapers supplied a number of reasons for the anti victory. A *Portland Evening Express* editorial suggested that men were genuinely reluctant to burden women with the added responsibility of voting, and that they feared equal suffrage would cause women to abandon the home. The writer went on to say that if women had proven that they truly wanted the vote, men would have given it to them since "men as a rule are not likely to deny anything to women which they want." This, however, the suffragists had failed to do, so it was clearly their fault that they had lost the vote. Finally, the editors detected a hint of obstinacy in the voters, who disliked being told what they should do. They were as disgruntled by the tactics of the women picketing the White House as they were by the exhortations of Governor Milliken, Theodore Roosevelt, President Wilson, and various other luminaries.[230]

In an interesting twist on the old "as Maine goes" adage, some newspapers viewed the election results as evidence that the nation as a whole was not yet ready for woman suffrage. The *Daily Eastern Argus* pointed out that the defeat came after "the Suffragists used their strongest arguments, brought in their most brilliant advocates from other states, and secured endorsements from the most eminent publicists, including President Wilson." If that combined pressure failed to achieve the desired results, then women would simply have to accept that a majority of men were opposed to the idea and wait until they changed their minds. It would be paternalistic and wrong for the federal government to impose equal suffrage in Maine over the clear objections of the voters. The newspapers generally agreed that the suffragists were in the right and would eventually gain the franchise, but at some point in the future.[231]

Within a couple of days, however, blame for the referendum's defeat began to be laid squarely at the feet of the White House pickets. In an article prominently situated below the masthead of the *Portland Sunday Telegram*, Maine's Congressman Hersey praised the courage and spirit of the banner holders, but declared unhesitatingly that they had caused the defeat of suffrage. An editorial reprinted from *New York World* was considerably less respectful but arrived at the same conclusion. In that paper's view, the Maine results could be seen as the first referendum on the pickets. Far from building momentum for equal suffrage, the NWP had managed to "decrystallize" support that had appeared to be solidifying in favor of the franchise. The "... wild women who were nagging the President and shrieking for a constitutional amendment" in wartime had only succeeded in turning public opinion against themselves and would cause a similar defeat in the upcoming referendum in New York if they were not stopped. Other newspapers came to the same conclusions.[232,233]

Similarly, when MSWA convened its annual meeting the week after the referendum, its members lost little time in passing a resolution condemning the pickets for injuring the suffrage cause. The resolution read:

> Whereas we believe the picketing of the White House by the women's party worked incalculable harm on our campaign, and lost us many votes. And whereas, the Maine Woman's Suffrage Association, affiliated with the National American Woman's Suffrage Association with a membership of two million is in no way connected with the women's party that represents less than

two percent of the organized suffragists of the country, therefore,
be it resolved that we utterly condemn the actions of the members
of this organization who are picketing the White House.[234]

No mention was made of the Suffrage Referendum League in connection
with the picketing; in fact, no mention was made of it at all. Remarkably,
despite the considerable contributions made by Florence and her group
in organizing speakers, gathering petition signatures, and preparing and
distributing literature, the Referendum League was not among those MWSA
publicly thanked for work on the referendum campaign. It was as if Florence
and the League had never existed.

Outgoing president Katherine Reed Balentine also strove to distance
MWSA, and her own leadership of it, from any responsibility for the defeat.
She did not attend the annual meeting in person but wrote a letter that was read
to those assembled, in which she said that everyone knew that the campaign
was doomed from the outset! "Lack of the usual pioneer work, agitation, and
educational campaigning; inadequate organization; and added to all this, the
war...could produce but one result...[W]e have known all along what the result
would be, that this first campaign would be lost...." Evidently she had forgotten
the almost giddy atmosphere of MWSA's annual meeting the previous October
at which the women had convinced each other the campaign could be won,
that the "good old state of Maine" would not let them down. Balentine made it
clear that she could not, "under any circumstances," continue as president, but
encouraged them not to despair. Instead, she recommended that they turn their
hands to war work until NAWSA could get the Federal Amendment through
Congress and they could secure its ratification in Maine. She claimed that
NAWSA was "actively working" on the national strategy, apparently forgetting
that the board had suspended work on that until the war was over. There was
no suggestion from Balentine or anyone else that Maine should attempt another
campaign to win suffrage by state referendum.[235]

Florence did not attend the MWSA meeting. She and Robert, along with
sons Brooks and Robert, left for Ohio three days after the referendum. They
were off on an automobile trip to visit Penn, who was stationed in Akron.
Penn was one of twenty American men who were among the first to receive
training from Goodyear to fly dirigibles, and he was expecting to ship out
for France at some point in the next couple of months. They wanted to visit
him before he went overseas, and also planned to celebrate his engagement to

Dorothy Case, an attractive young woman from an affluent New York family. The engagement offered a good excuse to take a family vacation that was long overdue and sorely needed, but following the suffrage defeat it must have felt like a particularly good time to get out of town.

Why did the men of Maine vote overwhelmingly against the suffrage measure? It was true that the White House pickets provided an excuse for some men to vote no. Maine was staunchly conservative and patriotic, and the image of women insulting the president and brawling with mobs in the name of suffrage surely offended some voters. The relatively light voting turnout lends credence to the claim that many people were simply indifferent to the issue and could not be bothered to go to the polls at all. The war certainly exacted a toll; without its distractions, suffragists could have accomplished much more organizing and educational work. Maine's relatively lean suffrage organizations could not spare the funds and volunteers they lost to supporting the war effort.

The extent to which the "whiskey interests" actively influenced the outcome is unclear. Most cities voted overwhelmingly against suffrage, likely due to the higher prevalence of bars and taverns. However, despite strong suspicions, the suffragists were unable to document that funding from bar owners, distributors, or distilleries was fueling the anti campaign.

Finally, it appears that Carrie Chapman Catt had accurately predicted that Maine simply did not have the organizational strength and capacity to succeed in a referendum campaign. And Florence had complained throughout that the MWSA leadership, outside of the highly competent Deborah Knox Livingston, did little to manage and build support for the campaign. Balentine seems to have considered it a lost cause from an early stage, and wasted precious time and energy maneuvering against Florence and the Suffrage Referendum League that would have been better used in winning over more voters.

Florence and Robert wagered their reputations and a substantial amount of their money on the campaign and could not have been pleased with the results. Florence emerged from the experience convinced that the only way to enfranchise women was through national action, and was newly determined to devote all her energies to Alice Paul and the NWP. Robert also continued to support the Federal Amendment and remained chairman of the Men's Equal Suffrage League until suffrage was won. He was less supportive of the White House pickets, however, and this would cause hardships for Florence going forward.

Despite the blow dealt to suffrage forces in Maine, the NWP was making steady progress in winning Congressional support for the amendment. Although it received scant coverage in Maine newspapers, the US Senate's Suffrage Committee unanimously issued a favorable report on the Federal Amendment on September 13th, and Senate leaders promised to bring it to the floor for a full vote in the upcoming session.[236] It was too soon to tell whether the amendment could garner the necessary two-thirds support. About ten days later, the full House voted 181–107 to create its own Suffrage Committee, an action the Democrats had been stalling for years. President Wilson had written Representative Pou, Chairman of the Rules Committee, to urge the House to waste no time in naming the committee, so it appeared the suffragists had been successful in enlisting the president's active support as well.[237] Prospects for securing a favorable vote in both houses of Congress had never been brighter, and NWP state affiliates would be in the front lines of pressuring their congressional delegations to support equal suffrage. In Maine, with a verdict squarely opposing voting rights for women, the battle would now be much harder. Florence would regret not having heeded Alice Paul's warning that once a state voted against suffrage, members of its congressional delegation might seize on this as an excuse to vote against it as well.

VI   Picketing and Politics in Conservative Maine

Florence returned from her two-week vacation to find a telegram from Alice Paul urging her presence on the picket line, and letters from other NWP central office staff asking for help in other matters. Responding to Paul's telegram first, Florence unequivocally refused to come to Washington, citing first and foremost the fact that Penn had been ordered to France "to fight in this hideous war," and might receive a few days' furlough before he went. "You can understand," wrote Florence, "that nothing must interfere with that possibility of companionship." Beyond that, she continued, "...you have yet to convince Mr. Whitehouse of the advisability and wisdom of the picketing." Florence herself had tried many times, but admitted, "I am almost discouraged attempting to." Robert agreed with the predominant view that the pickets had hurt the Maine campaign, "...and therefore he would be very much distressed if I should picket, and disgusted if I should be arrested while doing so."[238]

This letter reveals for the first time that it was her husband's opposition to picketing, not just her own concern about the effect it would have on the Maine referendum campaign, that had prevented her from joining the picket line. Florence was frustrated by Robert's continued disapproval, but he had invested a substantial amount of time and money in the unsuccessful referendum campaign and she did not want to picket against his wishes. Despite his feelings about the pickets, she declared, he still believed in "the fundamental ethics as well as policies of the Woman's Party." Rather than complain about him, she challenged Paul to help her change his mind. Paul was proposing to send Doris Stevens to Maine to help organize, and Florence hoped Stevens might be able to help Robert see the value of picketing.[239] Still, much to her chagrin, Robert remained opposed well into the fall. When Paul and others at NWP headquarters appealed to Florence to join them for a November 10th demonstration, she refused again, saying that if she did, "there would be trouble in the family."[240]

If she was bitter about the results of the referendum, Florence never put those words in writing, nor was she at all apologetic about her decision to ignore Paul's advice and back Maine's doomed campaign. In her letter, she appeared quite recovered from the defeat and ready to plunge back into the battle. She eagerly offered to host Stevens while she was in Portland and "co-operate in every way possible" with what she proposed. She also discussed planned visits to the editors of Portland's *Daily Eastern Argus* and the *Lewiston Journal*, two papers that had been most sympathetic to suffrage, to persuade them to print news from the Woman's Party.

Florence would soon disband the Suffrage Referendum League, she told Paul, since that had been organized only to work for the state referendum. She and Louise Freeman also intended to resign from MWSA and thought others would follow suit. Carrie Chapman Catt had made it abundantly clear that the women "trying to ride two horses should make their choices." NWP members were no longer welcome in NAWSA, and Florence had decided to work full-time for the NWP. While she was willing to accept her own husband's continued reservations about the pickets, she had nothing but scorn for her former colleagues at MWSA. "They have been willing to take the condemnation of the pickets by the National as final, which is nauseating. They have elected a state president who will not amount to anything and they have elected the same board so we have nothing to fear from them," she wrote dismissively. "They are all deadly. We call them the 'Morgue.'" This was in part because NAWSA leaders were still urging women to demonstrate their patriotism and value by supporting the war effort rather than campaigning for the Federal Amendment. MWSA members took this to heart and were working full-time on war relief, doing almost no suffrage work at all.

Symbolizing the renewed vigor she brought to the NWP, Florence rolled out her new stationery in late 1917, most likely designed with the help of Frederic Freeman. On the left side of the stationery Florence listed the names of the NWP's National Executive Committee and its National Committee of State Chairmen, and the Maine branch's officers were in the top right-hand corner. Centered under the title of National Woman's Party at the top of the page was a small cartoon graphic. This consisted of a rectangular box with a man and woman standing facing each other. The woman, bearing a strong resemblance to a youthful Florence, leans slightly toward the man and smiles

confidently, chin up, inviting a reply. In her hands is a paper ballot that she
is holding behind her back, out of view of her companion. The man, clearly
meant to be a politician, is balding and somewhat older. He is standing with
one hand stroking his chin, looking indecisive as if considering what she has
offered. The caption beneath the cartoon reads "A fair exchange is no robbery,"
suggesting that women as well as men could exchange their political support
for action taken.

Treatment of the pickets continued to dominate national suffrage news
during the fall of 1917. NAWSA had ceased active campaigning for the Federal
Amendment before the US entered the war in April, so the NWP appeared
justified in claiming that its picketing had won the recent victories in Congress.
NWP correspondence stressed, for example, that the unanimous favorable
report from the Senate's Suffrage Committee came immediately after its
chairman, Senator Jones of New Mexico, had visited the suffragists serving
60-day sentences in the Occoquan Workhouse. He was sufficiently moved by
this visit to schedule the vote the following day. The NWP particularly rejoiced
in this because Senator Jones had previously made numerous public statements
to the effect that he would *never* schedule a vote while the picketing continued.

The pickets paid a steep price for these advances, however. The women
imprisoned in the workhouse were exposed to harsh treatment and miserable
conditions. Their cells were damp and cold, full of the stench of unwashed
bodies and sewage, and populated by rats. Their meager rations were either
undercooked or half-burned, the meat was generally spoiled, and all the grains
had weevils. Many were forced to do hard labor that they found difficult in
their weakened, half-starved condition. Any who protested this treatment were
put in solitary confinement and fed just bread and water, with an open bucket
for a latrine. Age was no protection; Mary Nolan, a 73-year-old suffrage picket,
spent several weeks in solitary confinement when she told a prison matron
that she was too weak from lack of food to complete her work assignment.
The prisoners were frequently denied visitors and the right to either receive or
send mail, and were forbidden to speak at all when they gathered at mealtimes.
Nevertheless, with the help of sympathetic guards and the occasional visitor,
they managed to smuggle out messages describing their appalling treatment,
and the NWP wasted no time in publicizing their plight.

Paul and her staff appealed to the District of Columbia authorities to
intervene, and encouraged NWP state affiliates to write letters to their
congressional delegations decrying the treatment of suffrage pickets. The

NWP even sent out the "Suffrage Prison Special," a train car decorated like a prison cell and staffed by women who had been jailed for picketing. The women wore exact replicas of their rough prison clothes, and they toured the country giving speeches about the horrific treatment they had received in pursuit of their democratic rights.[241]

In the face of all evidence to the contrary, Wilson administration officials still hoped that they could intimidate the women into giving up and going home, but the crackdowns had the opposite effect. Many women who had been arrested and imprisoned returned to the picket line as soon as they were released. Other suffragists, inspired by the heroic examples set by the women who were jailed, were willing to take their places on the picket line. Some of the mail the NWP received opposed the pickets, but the majority was encouraging. Paul and her staff patiently responded to the negative letters, explaining why they believed the policy had yielded positive results and reframing the issue as the Wilson administration violating women's civil rights.

Things took an uglier turn when Alice Paul and three others were arrested again on October 20th. In an attempt to make an example of her, Paul was sentenced to seven months at Occoquan, the harshest sentence anyone had yet received. Within days of arriving at the workhouse, Paul and another suffragist, Rose Winslow, began a hunger strike. Prison officials fumed and threatened, and after a week of failing to coerce the two women into accepting food, began force-feeding them three times a day. This procedure involved snaking a flexible tube through the nose or mouth and down the throat into the stomach and pouring milk, raw egg, and other ingredients through the hose. Since the women fought the feedings, the hose was often jammed in with no regard for their safety, and the sores they subsequently developed in their throats made the feedings even more painful. In a note smuggled out of the jail, Winslow reported that she and Paul both vomited frequently during the feedings, their stomachs unable to cope with the quantities of food they received. The forced feedings continued for three weeks.

Perhaps even more frightening, Paul was secretly transferred to the prison psychopathic ward at the District jail. There, prison psychiatrists, in hopes of getting evidence of mental illness, encouraged her to say that Wilson was persecuting her. This would justify committing her to a psychiatric hospital and claiming that she was not a political prisoner at all, but merely unhinged. Despite her weakened state, Paul retained sufficient presence of mind to avoid this trap. For ten long days, prison officials refused to tell anyone her location, not even her attorney, Dudley Field Malone, and her anxious colleagues at headquarters telegrammed NWP state chairmen and other organizers around the country urging them to publicize this new abuse. Malone finally filed a writ of habeas corpus in order to locate her; by the time he found her and was able to get her transferred to the prison hospital, she weighed a mere 65 pounds. A short time later, following widespread reporting of these and other horrific incidents at Occoquan, President Wilson pardoned all the suffrage pickets and they were released.[242]

Against this backdrop of long prison sentences and harsh treatment of prisoners, it is somewhat surprising that Robert Whitehouse finally relented and agreed to Florence taking her place on the picket line. Precisely when and why that happened is unclear, but it is likely that a number of factors contributed. NWP organizer Abby Scott Baker, when she stayed with the Whitehouses in Portland during an organizing visit that fall, may have managed to convince him that picketing truly was winning votes in Washington. Baker had served as treasurer of the Congressional Union, then later as the NWP's press chairman and its political chairman, and was on its national executive committee. She had been in the thick of the suffrage battles for some time. She also had three sons, all of whom had volunteered for active duty when the war broke out. Baker and Florence connected immediately around their shared devotion to their sons and anxiety over their safety. Baker may have been able to reassure Robert that picketing was just the sort of thing Florence ought to be doing and that it was an effective strategy for moving the Federal Amendment through Congress.

NWP headquarters continued to exert steady pressure on Florence to join the picket line, sending her frequent telegrams and letters. Lucy Burns pleaded with her to come and picket at a large demonstration on November 10th. Burns, who had herself just been released from the DC jail, appealed to Florence because "there are always so few women who are ready to stand for their convictions through thick and thin" and "we urgently need the help of every brave woman in the United States." She tried to reassure Florence that any sentences meted out would be short, since they were hoping large numbers of women would participate in the November 10th action and the administration found it embarrassing to jail lots of women at once for the crime of asking for political freedom. As for Robert's concerns about the pickets, it was only natural that he would want to spare his wife the ordeal, Burns wrote, but once Florence picketed, Robert would see that she did it from the purist motives and would be proud of her. Indeed, Burns had observed that other husbands, equally reluctant, had experienced a complete turnaround once their wives picketed, and had become staunch defenders of the practice.[243]

Finally, following the reports of abuses at Occoquan, public sentiment was beginning to turn in favor of the pickets. Their courage and spirit in the face of brutal treatment from prison guards won them grudging respect from the general public, and forced people to recognize the irony of the US fighting a war for democracy abroad while abusing the women who called for it at home. The picketing had helped convert President Wilson into a vocal supporter of equal suffrage, even if he was not quite ready to work hard for the Federal Amendment. In another promising development, in early November, five members of Wilson's cabinet released statements of support for equal suffrage, marking an important shift in the attitude of his administration on this issue.[244]

It seems likely that Florence traveled down to DC to take her place on the picket line in December or early January. Penn had come home on several weeks' leave in October, awaiting the orders that would send him to France. They had had a lovely family reunion. Dorothy Case, Penn's fiancée, traveled to Portland to stay with the family, and various friends stopped by to wish him well. When Bob came home in early November from the eight-week aviation course he was attending at the Massachusetts Institute of Technology, the whole family retreated to the rustic camp on Panther Pond.[245] Penn played guitar, and Bob was skilled on the piano tucked into the corner of the living room, so there were surely music and singing to pass the time. At the end of the day, as the late autumn sun slipped below the horizon, the family gathered around the great brick fireplace in the snug log cabin, storing memories of closeness that would sustain them in the months ahead.

Florence was in a grim humor after Penn left, and picketing the White House might have been the perfect outlet for expressing her rage and anguish at sending her eldest son off to a war she did not believe in and had no power to stop. In October she had written a letter to the editor in which she made her strongest statement yet in favor of the pickets. She was moved to write by the odd coincidence of receiving, on a single day, a letter exhorting her help in organizing a week-long food drive for war relief and a note from the NWP informing her that four women had been arrested and sentenced to six months in Occoquan. They and others already sentenced were being held in appalling conditions, simply because they asked for the vote. While willing to do her bit "to bring this hideous war to its righteous conclusion," Florence wrote bitterly that;

...in my heart there is a deep resentment against my Country—
that at this time when it is demanding the greatest sacrifices from
me—and from hundreds of thousands of mothers the country
over—that democratic principles be advanced in Europe, it refuses
to recognize women in that democracy at home; a resentment that
in all President Wilson's splendid oratory upon human liberty there
is no inclusion of women as human beings; that women who are
responding with sons, money, and service to the Government can
be mobbed without protest, arrested, and sentenced and placed in
prison, by the Government which is taking their sons, and their
money, and their service to wage its wars.

The treatment of the Washington pickets will forever be a blot
upon the United States Government; whether or not we believe
their action is wise, there is no question but they are within the law
under the first amendment of the Constitution...

The shame of the treatment of the pickets rests upon us, if we
allow the Government at Washington to enforce its maximum
penalty upon American women who demand justice, without
registering our protest.[246]

Florence's anger may have swept aside any final objections Robert
had about whether it was right for her to picket. She probably missed the
November 10th demonstration to which Burns had invited her, but timed her
visit to coincide with a large banquet that NWP headquarters organized at the
Belasco Theater in honor of the suffrage pickets, especially those who had
been imprisoned in Occoquan. As it happened, Robert's fears of her arrest and
imprisonment were, if not groundless, at least never realized. Florence appears
to have picketed during a period in which the Wilson administration called off
harassment of the NWP demonstrators, and she was never arrested. Even the
jostling crowds seemed to have quieted, as all she noted was President Wilson
nodding and bowing to the pickets as he drove by.[247,248]

Still, the experience strengthened Florence's resolve to support publicly
both the pickets and the other strategies employed by the NWP. As part of a
national NWP strategy to educate the public about the picketing, she arranged
for Mabel Vernon (see Figure 14) to come to Portland in early January 1918 to
speak about her experiences. Vernon was one of the five suffragists who had

unfurled the banner in Congress in December 1916, and she had been arrested and jailed for picketing on a number of occasions. The lecture took place in Portland's Frye Hall and occasioned another exchange between Florence and a local newspaper on the topic. This time it was the *Eastern Argus*, which had been so supportive of suffrage during the referendum campaign the previous year that lashed out at the NWP. In a half-page editorial, the *Argus* charged that the pickets were persecuting the president, and claimed that "[e]verybody can see their injustice, and recognizes they are unlawful."[249]

In a lengthy response the following day, Florence challenged all the arguments the editorial had employed. Again she asserted that the right to picket was upheld by both the US Constitution and the Clayton Act, and noted that many reputable papers around the country (*The New Republic* and the *Boston Journal* among them) had supported the NWP policy. "Instead of 'leaving a blot upon the history of the movement' as you so confidently prophesy will be the case when the cause is finally won, there are people…who feel that the 89 women who have been arrested for picketing—many more have picketed, including your humble servant—and suffered for the cause through prison sentence will be honored by later generations as faithful soldiers who made possible the enfranchisement of women through their unswerving courage and steadfast loyalty at a time when the cause was threatened with submersion beneath the horrors of a world-wide war."[250]

If it were true, the *Argus* editor wondered in his follow-up the next day, that the Constitution upheld picketing, why was it so many women had been arrested and jailed? This exchange was interrupted by news that President Wilson, just prior to a full House of Representatives vote on the Federal Amendment, had for the first time publicly supported adoption of that measure "as an act of right and justice to the women of the Country and of the world."[251] The president's change of attitude was evidently a big surprise to many people, although not the NWP, and for the first time it seemed likely that the House would pass the Federal Amendment. During the House debate, Representative William Gordon of Ohio tried to condemn the pickets for attempting to coerce President Wilson into supporting the amendment. A chorus of "They did it and they got him!" arose from the Republican side of the aisle, rising to a roar in which many Democrats joined. On January 10, 1918, the US House of Representatives produced exactly enough favorable votes to gain the two-thirds majority needed to pass the Federal Amendment. Suffragists all over the country rejoiced at this breakthrough.[252]

The *Argus* interviewed several of Maine's suffrage leaders for their responses to the victory, and Florence was quick to point out that the threat of political action had moved the measure through the House. If the House had not passed the Federal Amendment, the NWP would have held the Democrats responsible for its defeat, and they did not want to have that against them going into the 1918 elections. Irrepressibly, she added, "There isn't the slightest doubt but the picketers had much to do with the passage of the bill; they have kept it daily before the President and Congress and have advertised it from one end of the Country to the other."[253] To this sally, her former colleague, Mrs. Augusta Hunt, responded indignantly, "I am one of the group of women who has been working for suffrage for 40 years, and to me it seems absurd that the Woman's Party, headed by English militants, should claim the victory." Even in victory, the two suffrage organizations could not put aside their differences.

Next the measure had to win approval in the US Senate. MWSA's Helen Bates, when interviewed, announced her belief that Maine Senator Frederick Hale would now change his mind and vote in favor of the Federal Amendment. Bates would prove to be wrong about Senator Hale, and this quickly turned into a major dilemma for the Maine suffragists. Prior to Maine's statewide suffrage referendum, Senator Hale had told Florence that he would be bound by the outcome of the vote on September 10th. In a statement much publicized in the local papers, Hale declared that if the matter came to the Senate for a vote during the upcoming session he would follow the lead of the men of Maine. Since the measure was decisively defeated in Maine, Senator Hale felt that he had no choice but to honor his word and vote against it, at least during the session immediately following Maine's referendum.

Both national suffrage organizations, for NAWSA was once more pushing federal action, canvassed all 100 US Senators to determine how each stood on the Federal Amendment. The initial results showed that they were still well shy of the necessary two-thirds majority; at least seven more men would have to be persuaded to change their votes.

Despite his avowed intention to vote against it, Senator Hale was on the short list of Senate holdouts that suffragists thought might yield to persuasion because he was generally supportive of suffrage. All the other members of the Maine delegation were pro-suffrage, so Florence and her fellow NWP members wrote to encourage them to persuade Hale to change his mind. Representative Ira Hersey replied that the Maine delegation had "…done all we could to make him see that he should change his attitude but without success."

FIGURE 14 Mabel Vernon, one of the National Woman's Party organizers.
Women of Protest: Photographs from the Records of the National Woman's Party, Manuscript Division,
Library of Congress, Washington, D.C.

Hersey had a suggestion of his own: the women of Maine should convince Hale that suffrage had such momentum that by the time he next ran for office they would be in a position to vote. They could either vote for him, grateful for the memory of his support at a crucial moment in suffrage history, or they could vote against him for failing to come to their aid.[254]

Florence thought this was good advice and got a chance the next day to act on it. Hale had returned to Portland for a visit, so she telephoned him to make an appointment. He was busy, but agreed to see her at his hotel if she came immediately. There was no time to pull together a delegation, so she left word for Louise Freeman and Helen Leonard to come if they could and hurried off to Hale's hotel. There she found him with Senator Joseph Frelinghuysen of New Jersey, whom he introduced as a recent suffrage convert. After some preliminary chat, they got down to the business at hand.[255]

Hale reiterated that he felt bound by his promise to stand by the verdict of the state referendum. Because suffrage had become such a nuisance, he said he would prefer to vote for it in this session to get it "out of the way," but felt comfortable assuring her that he would vote for it in the following session. Florence told him graciously that since he had first made that promise to her personally, she would gladly release him from it, but this left him unmoved.

Florence next tried impressing on Hale the number of Maine women, some 38,000, who had signed petitions asking for the right to vote. While Senator Frelinghuysen was impressed by that number, Hale was not, pointing out that he did not owe his election to women. "But if this thing goes through in Washington and is ratified by the states, you may want the women's help four years from now," Florence persisted. The veiled threat in this remark prompted Hale to tell Senator Frelinghuysen, "Mrs. Whitehouse believes in picketing." Frelinghuysen said he didn't like picketing. "Of course you don't, Senator" replied Florence warmly. "No man does who has a political position. You like the ineffective way the National [NAWSA] has of saying 'please,' but that is not what is bringing lawmakers over. We are playing politics…"

Florence told Hale it was rumored that Governor Milliken planned to run against him in four years, and as a strong suffrage supporter, Milliken would be more likely to have the women's endorsement. This seemed to interest Hale, but he made little response until she offered to get the 38,000 Maine suffragists to write letters to him or sign petitions asking him to change his vote. Hale threw up his hands. "Call off the letter writing," he said. "I'm sick to death of it now!" Florence thought that he genuinely regretted the bind he was in but was not ready to change his mind. He believed that the measure would fail in the current session but that it would pass if it came up in two years. She left the meeting convinced that the only solution lay in persuading Hale that the amendment would go through in 1918, with or without him, and that if he voted against suffrage it would be a blot on his record for the remainder of his political life.

The very next day, Florence sat down to write Hale a letter, pointing out several errors in his thinking about his stance on suffrage. In the first place, she reminded him, when he had made his promise to her that he would abide by the results of the state referendum, he was already an elected Senator and thus did not owe his election to men who voted for him because of his position on suffrage. Therefore, he should not feel bound by that promise. Secondly, she encouraged him to think about his long-term political interests. While he expected suffrage to lose in the Senate this year, she wrote, "Have you thought about your position should we win?...[S]uppose you do not have another chance and your record in opposition to the great democratic movement, which is not only sweeping over America but the whole world, is registered for all time, do you not think you will have a more difficult explanation to make upon why you did not vote for it...?"[256]

As a fallback position, she suggested that if he could not vote for the amendment, "[W]hy don't you take Senator Wadsworth and go on a 'much needed rest' the day the vote is taken." Senator Wadsworth was from New York, and was an active and vocal suffrage opponent. She was referring here to the practice of "pairing," in which legislators voting on opposite sides of an issue agree to form a pair and absent themselves from the vote. Their votes are thus not counted, and they are not on record as having supported or opposed a particular piece of legislation. Florence closed the letter by urging Hale to consider her ideas carefully. "I may want to vote for you in 1922," she said playfully.

Senator Hale was not to be budged. He denied that he was "playing politics" on the issue of suffrage; on the contrary, he was honorably "trying to keep my word in a matter where doing so is distinctly to my political disadvantage." If he sounded slightly aggrieved, it was because Florence and her fellow NWP members had called upon any man they believed might influence Hale to write, telephone, or send telegrams asking him to change his mind. In addition to private citizens, she lined up support from the state political parties and from state legislators who would eventually ratify the amendment once it passed through the Senate, to pressure Hale to vote for it. Women's groups, county political chairmen, local unions, and others also responded to the call and began lobbying Hale.[257]

February saw a flurry of letters and telegrams passing between Florence and the NWP office in DC, sometimes several each day, as they sought ways to increase the pressure on Hale to change his mind. A critical component of this strategy was to convince conservative Mainers that picketing, far from being a treasonous and unjustifiable activity, was an honorable exercise of fundamental democratic rights. To that end, Alice Paul proposed sending Dudley Field Malone to Portland to give a speech on suffrage and defend the pickets. If Maine could afford it, the national office could send up an organizer to help prepare for the event. Florence was both thrilled and alarmed by this; she had been unsuccessful in drumming up much interest in talks given by other NWP organizers who had traveled to Maine in recent months, and the image of Malone speaking to empty chairs in a vast hall terrified her. At the same time, Malone was one of the great champions of suffrage and she wanted very much to have him come. Yet funds were so tight that the Maine branch could not afford Malone's travel expenses along with the $100 monthly salary the NWP paid its organizers.[258]

Malone was a lawyer and a Democrat who had been a staunch supporter of President Wilson, helping him win election and serving in his administration as the collector of the Port of New York. In the 1916 election, he had traveled to the equal-suffrage states in the West, promising women there that Wilson was a friend to suffrage and would help push it through if they reelected him. Malone's promises were instrumental in thwarting the NWP's campaign against Wilson in that election. In the first half of 1917, when Wilson evidenced lukewarm support for the Federal Amendment and pursued a policy of increasingly harsh treatment of the pickets, Malone met with Wilson to protest his actions.

In September of that year, convinced that the Wilson administration was abusing the pickets' civil rights and that he could no longer support his administration, Malone resigned his commission at the Port of New York. By that time, he had already begun serving on a pro bono basis as the National Woman's Party's attorney, defending the suffrage pickets in court when they were arrested. He also made fundraising speeches on their behalf, and in early 1918, though battling illness, traveled to several states including Florida, Georgia, Illinois, Connecticut, and Massachusetts before arriving in Maine in late March. He had not wanted to come to the Northeast at all and only agreed to do so if he could be guaranteed large audiences to make the trip worthwhile. This added to the pressure on the Maine branch to deliver an audience at a time when they were having extreme difficulty recruiting new members. In early February, the Maine branch's treasurer, Helen Leonard, hosted a meeting at her house to which they had sent out 200 invitations. Only 14 people showed up, and of these just three or four joined the NWP. The prospect of turning out a huge audience for Malone was making the Maine branch feel a bit shaky, Florence told Paul.[259] Maybe they had better call the whole thing off.

****

Anxious to convert Senator Hale, Alice Paul opted to have the NWP bear the expense of sending Julia Emory, one of the young national organizers, to help organize for the Malone meeting. Emory was the daughter of a Maryland state senator. She was attractive, optimistic, and cheerful, possessing a youthful "gee whiz" determination that won converts and helped overcome any obstacles in her path *(see Figure 15)*. In contrast to many of the organizers who seemed to emulate Alice Paul's spare, professional style, Emory's notes were full of bounce and humor, the latter as likely to be directed at herself as at the letters' recipients. In particular, she seemed to think Paul was in need of some direction, and though Emory was several years her junior, she often lectured Paul in a humorous way to encourage her to pay more attention to her personal needs. She closed one long note to Paul with a series of mock orders. "Have you had a good light put in your room—apologies, I mean 'cell'—and if not, please won't you do so immediately? Please write me that your room is fixed up just like you really, honestly like it and that your new dress is altered and ready to be worn. Please have it made shorter. You are plenty tall enough and it's entirely too old for you the length you have it now."[260] Paul never responded in writing to her teasing, but it is clear she liked young Emory and thought highly of her organizing talents.

Young as she was, by the time she arrived in Maine, Emory was already a veteran of the picket line and of the Occoquan Workhouse, and had been deployed in several cities as an organizer. Maine was her first solo assignment, however, and she was initially intimidated by creaky, frigid Portland, and very homesick for DC.[261] Yet Florence and Robert insisted she stay with them, and within a short time, her natural optimism reasserted itself. She and Florence

FIGURE 15 Julia Emory, one of the National Woman Party organizers.
Women of Protest: Photographs from the Records of the National Woman's Party,
Manuscript Division, Library of Congress, Washington, D.C.

got along famously, and her letters back to headquarters were soon filled with praise for her and for a few of her NWP colleagues. "You certainly made a wise choice when you picked your State Chairman for Maine. She and Mrs. Freeman (and Mr. Freeman too) are the only live wires I have come across in Portland." Emory was not so impressed with the other Portlanders she met in the course of her work, however, and she offered fresh observations as to why Maine was so difficult to organize.[262]

> Portland is great, but the people—Gosh—they resemble mahogany furniture. They are so damned dignified. They are conservative, conceited, self-centered, self-conscious, and fifteen years behind times, narrow to the limit and are ready to forgive most anything before they would condone the dreadful sin of youth and enthusiasm. They criticize Mrs. Florence because once when she made a speech she 'gesticulated,' which wasn't lady-like and 'Mrs. Catt never would, you know.' Lord, how I hate the name of Catt. One-third of the population are antis and one half are Catt-ites. The others are nothing at all or else indulge in the Woman's Party as a secret sin.[263]

Florence's relations with her former colleagues at MWSA had been deteriorating steadily, and Emory's chatty letters reveal just how petty and spiteful the other women could be. Florence's friend Anne Gannett had resigned from the NWP in October 1917, citing the pickets as the reason. "To me the things they are doing are perfectly awful," she wrote Florence. "...I can't be a part of it even in the smallest way because to me it is all wrong." She closed by hoping, rather primly, that Florence would not travel to Washington to join the picket line as she had been talking about doing. Anne Gannett's disavowal further distanced Florence from respectable Maine society. Gannett, as a member of a wealthy, political, and socially prominent family, was in a position to influence public opinion, and her support might have gone a long way toward transforming public attitudes toward the pickets. Instead, her resignation spoke volumes about the unseemliness of such behavior.[264]

In late 1917 or early 1918, Katherine Reed Balentine and Mrs. Holman led a successful effort to amend MWSA's bylaws to explicitly prohibit joint membership in MWSA and the NWP. They claimed that Carrie Chapman Catt had instructed them to do so, though NAWSA denied this. Florence wrote Nettie Rogers Shuler, who was then Catt's personal secretary and with whom Florence had struck up a friendship, to inquire whether Catt had indeed issued the order. Shuler responded that she was positive Catt had not done so. "I know the correspondence that passed between Mrs. Catt and Mrs. Holman…and also between Mrs. Balentine and Mrs. Catt, and I know that Mrs. Catt realizes fully that instead of helping with the [1917 referendum] campaign in Maine, both Mrs. Balentine and Mrs. Holman acted as a deterring influence." Shuler promised to have Catt reply to Florence directly in regard to this issue. She closed the letter, "With best wishes for you always, and with great sympathy for you for the foolish action of those more foolish women in Portland…"[265] Even the NAWSA national officers appreciated how difficult their supporters in Maine could be.

Despite MWSA's ongoing efforts to discredit the NWP, with Emory's help six influential people joined the rival organization after attending a suffrage meeting at Florence's house in early March, where they heard firsthand the story of the pickets and what the NWP was trying to do. MWSA immediately began hounding them to win them back, pleading with them not to join "those women" until they could be shown the light. Sentiment was tipping toward the pickets, although Emory noted philosophically that simply defending the pickets "takes as much courage for the girls up here as picketing seemed to be to others." She was openly frustrated by the conservative pack mentality she encountered in Maine, even among the younger set. "That is one of the terrible things about the people here. So few of them have the grit to buck up against the rest and be individual." For the time being, however, MWSA was unsuccessful in winning back its lost members and its leadership was furious.[266]

In the face of the new gains the Maine NWP was making, it might have been expected that MWSA would redouble its efforts to convert Hale and win the day for the suffragists. The reverse appeared to be true, however. In early March, MWSA leaders told Florence that they had "done everything there was to be done" and had decided that Hale was "impossible to convert and there was no use trying anymore." Following this, Florence told Paul gleefully that she had effectively assumed direction of the local MWSA affiliates around the state. "It is a huge joke but they are all at my command as if they were Woman's Party organizations." Florence explained how she had sent a letter to all suffragists statewide, regardless of their suffrage affiliation, encouraging them to enlist men in their area to write Hale telling him to support the Federal Amendment. One of these was Florence's friend Mrs. George (Abbie Ann) Peaslee of Lewiston, who, while she remained a MWSA member, was still on speaking terms with Florence. Peaslee told Florence that she had acted immediately on her request and that very evening, a flood of letters and telegrams left Lewiston directing Senator Hale to change his vote.[267,268]

****

Anyone capable of comparing self-righteous Portlanders to mahogany furniture was sure to find a warm spot in Florence's heart, and during the roughly six weeks Emory spent in Maine, the two made a splendid team. They had two challenges to solve immediately. The first was to raise money to support the NWP's activities, including renting the hall and developing publicity materials for the upcoming Malone speech, and the second was to recruit new members to bolster the NWP's thin ranks. Emory wanted to bring in younger women who might be more willing to do some work and be less constrained by social conventions. As a member of the younger set herself, Emory was perfectly positioned to appeal to other young women, and she had arrived in Portland armed with the names of some Vassar College graduates she hoped to enlist in the cause. One of her young converts invited 25 of her friends to an NWP informational meeting in her rooms at which Emory spoke. Many of these did join and were eager to be put to work. A common complaint leveled against MWSA was that there was nothing to do; one of their only activities in early March, for example, was to hold a suffrage tea at which the agenda was dominated by a musical recital and very little else.

The fundraising remained a challenge. Emory noted with some exasperation that "[t]he people really have the money, if we can just make them come across with it…"[269] Between the war and the picketing, the climate was so difficult that the Maine NWP had come to rely on either Robert Whitehouse or Frederic Freeman to write a check whenever money was needed, but Emory was determined to get others to dig into their pockets as well. She met personally with every existing Maine NWP member, asking her to enlist one new member and one new subscriber (or donor), vowing to follow up with each to make sure they completed this small but vital task. She arranged to speak at a local socialist meeting, where she issued an appeal for funds. She and Florence also organized a large suffrage meeting one weekday morning, and planned an afternoon tea several days later. By the end of February, they had succeeded in recruiting a grand total of three new dues-paying members, and had received a few donations and several pledges of support toward for the Malone meeting. In early March, Helen Leonard, the Maine NWP treasurer, sent a report to headquarters listing the donations received since the first of the year. Donations in response to Mabel Vernon's speaking tour through Portland in late December amounted to a paltry $100.00. Altogether, Leonard listed 13 donors, including herself, Florence, and Louise Freeman, and as usual, these three were responsible for almost half of the $79.50 raised since January 1st.[270,271]

Things improved somewhat in early March, but Emory was clearly worried she had lost her fundraising touch. "Please tell me, dear, what is wrong with the way I go about it for I do it the best way I know how," she wrote Paul plaintively. Again and again, she would get people excited about the NWP to the point where they would insist on giving a donation, and then they would open their purses and extract only one or two dollars. Her biggest contribution to date, she reported sadly, had been $10. "You know one time you told me that the reason Mrs. Lewis could get so much was because she inspired people with confidence in herself and her ability to use their money. Do you suppose I inspire these people to the extent of only one or two dollars?" This was asked half in jest, but the problem was a difficult one. Emory thought Mainers were naturally tightfisted, but since they routinely exceeded their fundraising goals for war stamps, war bonds, and the Red Cross, they were clearly willing to be generous when sufficiently moved. Paul reassured Emory that she was an effective fundraiser; one generous donor had sent the NWP $100 in response to an appeal Emory had made prior to arriving in Maine.[272] She would just have to keep trying to figure out how to untie Mainers' purse strings.[273]

Despite these difficulties, Florence was typically ebullient when she wrote her own note to Alice Paul apprising her of their activities. Julia Emory was doing great work, she reported, and she thanked Paul several times for making her available. In particular, meeting Emory was helping people see that the pickets "were not amazon Carrie Nations out for a row, but ladylike, gentle, enthused women who were willing to sacrifice for a cause in which they devoutly believed."[274]

Organizing for both the upcoming meetings was going well, Florence reported. In addition to Dudley Field Malone, now scheduled to speak in Portland on March 25th, Paul had recently proposed that Beulah Amidon swing through for a quick tour on March 13th and 14th. Amidon, from North Dakota, had been in the thick of the picketing for many months and was one of Paul's trusted lieutenants. She had been arrested on many occasions and imprisoned at Occoquan. Her Maine appearances were intended to educate people about the democratic principles involved in picketing and to help stimulate further fundraising. There was reason to hope that she might get a better reception in Maine than previous NWP speakers had received, because in early March the Washington, DC, court of appeals, after mulling over the case for months, finally ruled that all of the pickets had been unjustly arrested and jailed.[275]

Naturally, the NWP gave widespread and vocal publicity to this positive development, and almost overnight the pickets assumed an added stature. Critics such as the *Argus*'s editor and the MWSA leaders could no longer vilify them as treasonous criminals; all they could fall back on was that their behavior was unladylike. This claim now rang hollow as the pickets seemed more and more like heroines who had been ill-used by their country. Florence and Emory were quite pleased to have Amidon coming to town, even though her arrival added to the pressure of fundraising and publicity, because it helped build interest and momentum. Besides, it was just plain fun; as Florence wrote to Paul, describing all their activities, "Hooray! I love something doing and something is certainly doing in this war mad town."[276]

****

The Federal Amendment had been given a further boost in February when the national Democratic and Republican parties met in convention. For the first time ever, both parties adopted the Federal Amendment in their party planks, which further exposed those Senators wishing to vote against the measure. They could no longer hide behind their party platforms. Since Hale had not been using that as an excuse, he was able to shrug off this new development, but it still provided another avenue for bringing pressure to bear.

The concentrated lobbying directed to Frederick Hale in Maine was being repeated in other states across the country where there appeared to be some hope of changing a wavering senator's no vote to a yes. The pressure intensified on March 1st when newspapers reported that Senator Gallinger of New Hampshire, the leader of the Republicans in the US Senate, pledged to vote in favor of the amendment. In the wake of this announcement, several other senators were said to be considering a similar move. Nevertheless, in mid-March the Federal Amendment remained stalled in the Senate. The

Democrats, having successfully maneuvered the amendment through the House, seemed to think their record so superior to that of the Republicans they were inclined to rest on their laurels. Neither President Wilson nor congressional leaders were exerting pressure on the party's holdouts to change their votes. The Republicans saw no point in making any extra effort either. The tension for the suffragists lay in the fact that the Senate's approval had to be secured within the same legislative session in which the House had approved it. Otherwise they would have to begin all over again in the next session to get the amendment approved by both the House and Senate, and that might prove more difficult. Women all over the country were stretched to the breaking point, between war work and suffrage, and if they lost the momentum they had gained so laboriously in the House, it might set the movement back years.[277]

With Democrats still in control of both houses of Congress and the presidency, the NWP executive council vowed to continue holding them responsible for passing the amendment. Since there was no election campaign on the immediate horizon, they chose instead to remind the Democrats of their culpability in the unlawful arrest and imprisonment of the suffrage pickets and their subsequent mistreatment in Occoquan. Pressing for a congressional inquiry would continue to shine a spotlight on the Democrats' role in those events, and would make them feel they needed to "do a little more in order to make up for the black record of the past." They had to be made to feel that passing the Federal Amendment was the only way to compensate for past actions. Paul called on all state NWP chairmen to have letters and telegrams sent to President Wilson, to the senators from their states, and to Senate Democratic and Republican leaders demanding an inquiry into the arrests. "We are all harried and worried because of the Senate situation," Paul admitted to Florence, displaying what was for her an unusual amount of emotion. "I hope you will do whatever you can."[278]

On the plus side, a $10,000 gift from a wealthy supporter named Colonel Thompson allowed the national NWP to pay off $3,000 in overdue bills that remained from getting the amendment through the House, and would help finance the campaign under way in the Senate. The timing could not have been better, as it removed the worry of paying off past creditors and allowed Paul to focus all her attention on the Senate.

Now firmly committed to passage of the Federal Amendment as a "war measure," President Wilson began lobbying wavering senators in an effort to change their minds. He met with them privately and wrote them letters, assuring them that his ability to win the war depended in part on passage of the amendment. The world was watching to see if the United States would live up to its democratic ideals and enfranchise its women who had done so much to support the war. Still, the stubborn senators continued to resist, and the attention of the entire country became focused on the fact that only two votes stood between women and the resolution of their 70-year campaign for enfranchisement.

****

"My dear, I just <u>wish</u> you could be up here. You would love it," wrote Emory to Paul. "War has been formally declared on us by the other suffrage organization and everybody is being urged to boycott the Beulah Amidon meeting." Incredibly, in the face of the mounting pressure to convert Senator Hale, MWSA was continuing to focus virtually all of its energy on discrediting the Maine branch of the NWP. In an effort to generate news coverage and stimulate interest in Amidon's talk, then just days away, Florence and Emory had sent a "small army" of young girls along Congress Street. The girls were decked out in the NWP's purple, white, and gold colors, and handed out free tickets to the event. They created such a spectacle that the shops and hotels that had previously refused to display posters or leaflets advertising the talk immediately reversed their decision and agreed to post them. It helped, as Emory noted with satisfaction, that the posters carried a picture of Amidon, who was generally agreed to be one of the most attractive suffragists, and "...people were quite smitten with 'Beulah the Beautiful.'" Before the end of the day, however, the posters began to come down, and after grilling several shopkeepers, Emory and Florence were quite confident that MWSA was behind their disappearance. Undaunted, Emory immediately wrote up two stories about the incident that she hoped to get printed in the morning papers.[279]

Unfortunately, Emory's stories were not the only ones swirling through Portland. The antis were circulating a rumor that the Whitehouses had purchased their gracious new home at 108 Vaughn Street with money from the NWP, no doubt because they hosted so many of the organizers who came to town. Not to be outdone, MWSA began telling people that the Maine branch of the NWP was receiving substantial contributions from the Germans! "You can hardly realize what it means in this war crazed burg to start a story of German money…," wrote Emory.[280] Portland was still so gripped by Red Cross fever that women even carried bags made of red cloth, in the shape of a cross, when they went to the market. The irreverent Emory was delighted to observe "chicken feet and celery tops sticking out of a Red Cross!" and even drew Paul a little picture of it *(see illustration in Figure 16)*.

Still, said Emory, MWSA had to be desperate to resort to a rumor of German money. And their plan seemed to backfire almost immediately, as already one woman had stopped by to offer a donation of $20, a generous sum for tightfisted Portland.

Despite MWSA's efforts, or perhaps even because of them, Beulah Amidon's speech was quite successful. With an attendance of over 300 people, it was the NWP's largest meeting ever in Maine. They received $30 in donations and gained 20 new and energetic members. Attendance was even more remarkable considering that Portland was still in the grip of winter, with two feet of snow on the ground and temperatures so frigid that Amidon reported she had had to don Penn Whitehouse's overshoes and full-length coonskin coat to go outside, and snuggle under fur robes even when riding in Helen Leonard's enclosed car.[281]

The local press were quite taken with Amidon, who was every bit as lovely as her picture on the posters promised she would be. The *Argus* described her as "truly a beautiful woman, with a magnetic personality, [and] a voice with a bewitching drawl that made her quite irresistible…" They also took her seriously as a suffragist, however, noting that her great-grandmother, grandmother, and mother had all traveled to Washington, DC, at some point during their lives to ask Congress for the vote. Her suffrage lineage enabled her to hear firsthand how politicians had avoided action literally for generations, and thus Amidon understood that suffragists could only move the issue forward by harnessing women's political power. This she had done by campaigning in 17 states, lobbying Congress directly, and picketing. During her speech, she told a number of amusing anecdotes revealing how Democrats had tried to delay action on the Federal Amendment. Senator Thomas Taggart of Indiana was among those she singled out as being particularly squirrelly. On one occasion, when his was the lone vote needed on the Judiciary Committee to move the amendment forward, he was nowhere to be found. The frantic NWP lobbyists combed the Capitol for him, knocking on his office door and even telephoning his home to see if he had taken refuge there. Finally, they we can get more over. At first, the war and Red Cross had completely put suffrage in the shade. The women had such a Red Cross bug that they even went to market with bags made of red cloth in the shape of a cross. It was a scream to see chicken feet and celery tops sticking out of a Red Cross!

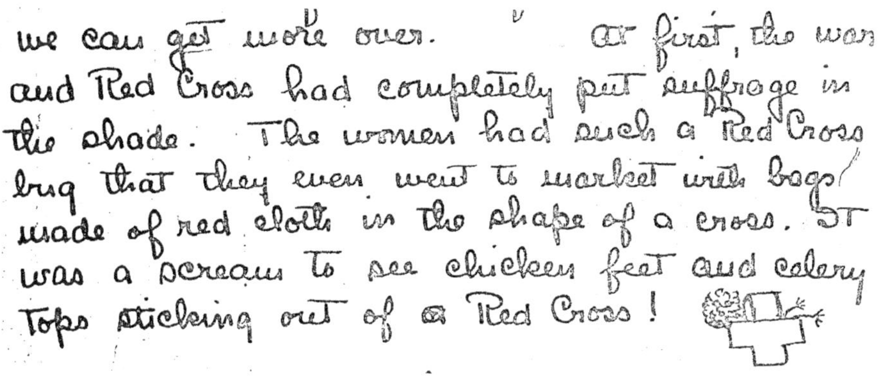

FIGURE 16 Detail from letter written by Julia Emory to NWP Headquarters. Maine Historical Society Collection.

thought to peek through the keyhole in his office door, and there he was, sitting at his desk. "We see you, Senator Taggart" the women shouted through the keyhole, and he finally opened up the door and let them in. They were trying to rush him off to the committee room to vote when a page informed them the committee had adjourned. This story and the many others she told helped the audience understand why the women had been driven to picket, and increased their sympathy and admiration for the NWP.[282]

Amidon reported back to NWP headquarters that Emory was working "remarkably well," especially in reaching out to working women who had not previously joined the NWP in Maine. She concurred with Emory's view that it was best to allow Florence to remain in the role of both the Maine NWP Chairman and the 1st District chairman, as she had from the beginning. Paul had been anxious to recruit someone else to fill the 1st District position, to fill out the NWP's list of volunteers and free up Florence to do other activities. Amidon observed that Florence, "with her remarkable energy," would probably direct the work in the 1st District anyway, so any committee that was formed would likely just exist on paper. Instead, she suggested that the Maine branch of the NWP concentrate on reestablishing committees in Augusta, Lewiston, and Biddeford, as these committees had languished during the previous year's referendum campaign.[283]

Both Emory and Amidon, accustomed to more spartan living arrangements (especially when traveling on the NWP's dime), very much enjoyed their time in Portland. Portland's core NWP members may have been few in number, but they were all affluent, and they rolled out the red carpet for the organizers who came to town. As Amidon wrote to her peers at headquarters, "The meeting was stunning, and everyone was nice and amusing, and seemed to have a large and luxurious home, and I had many good meals, and lived in general maidedness and walked on oriental carpets."[284] One evening, Helen Leonard hosted a dinner party for Amidon, the Whitehouses, and the Freemans, and the whole party went off to the Jefferson Theater afterwards to enjoy a performance of *Pollyanna*.[285] Emory also appreciated her cushiony surroundings. "Your little organizer is being spoiled to death everyone is so good to her," she wrote Paul. "You should see me now in all this luxury!"[286] She claimed she had gained fifteen pounds since arriving in Maine, and Amidon teased that her next assignment would be in Nebraska, where she could find out what life as an organizer was really like![287]

With the Amidon meeting out of the way, the Maine NWP turned to making the final arrangements for Dudley Field Malone's appearance later that month. There was some drama developing around this, as Malone had been ill off and on for weeks and had had to cancel several of his engagements, so there was some doubt that he would make it to Maine. In addition, the speaker Florence had arranged to make the "money speech" at the Malone meeting was incapacitated, so ten days before the meeting, they were scrambling to find someone else. It was critical to have someone in that role capable of whipping up the crowd's enthusiasm to the point that people would dig deep into their pockets and give freely. Mrs. Toscan Bennett was supposed to have traveled up from Connecticut, but due to an accident was now in a plaster body cast in which she would have to remain for some weeks. Mrs. Hepburn (the actress Katherine Hepburn's mother), who was the other speaker Paul had recommended, was also ill, so Florence put in a plea for Mabel Vernon, who had been to Maine several months before, to replace Bennett. Since Vernon's previous speech had not been well attended her remarks would still be fresh to most of the audience, and Florence knew she was a powerful and compelling speaker.

As Vernon was doing the collection speech for Malone in Boston the day before he was due in Maine, Paul arranged for them to travel up together. Florence and Emory were jubilant at this news. Emory requested that NWP headquarters send 500 pledge cards to Maine for the meeting; clearly they were hoping that the fundraising would go over the top this time.

****

In February 1918, Florence and Robert's son Bob received his orders to sail for France. Following completion of his eight-week aviation course at MIT, Bob had been learning to fly at a naval air station in Pensacola, Florida. By early February, he had acquired the nine hours of solo flying time that qualified him for his commission. He described flying as "wonderful sport," but was not wholly enthusiastic about flying bombing missions. He tried to remain stateside by applying for work as a flight instructor, but this effort was unsuccessful so he came home for a brief leave on March 1st and departed just after the Amidon speech. With the Amidon and Malone meetings to prepare for, and continued efforts to pressure Hale to change his vote, there was little opportunity for the full family reunion that had launched Penn off to war four months earlier. The Whitehouse residence at 108 Vaughn Street served as the

NWP's Maine headquarters, and, as a result, saw a steady stream of visitors and volunteers, stacks of mail, telegrams, and suffrage teas and luncheons. Bob had plenty of opportunity to witness how hard his mother and father, Emory, and many others were working to gain the vote, and he was sufficiently moved by this to add his voice to theirs. Writing Hale from Pensacola on the eve of his departure, Bob said he was writing on his own initiative but echoed many of his mother's sentiments. "It seems to me most unfair to expect women to fill in a man's job at home, give up their cherished sons, and suffer the greatest torment of war, namely uncertainty, without giving them at least a voice in the government of which they are proving themselves to be a most vital prop. Furthermore, I cannot see why America preaches Democracy abroad, raising its third gigantic loan to support the tremendous offensive force she is preparing, and still withholds from a large part of her women that which nations across the seas, heretofore always considered far more autocratic than we, have already gladly given."[288]

Hale was as unmoved by this appeal as he was by all the others pouring into his office around this time, and Bob sailed for France without receiving a reply. During this period, the intensity of the American involvement in the war was reaching its height, with war coverage crowding most other stories off of the front pages of newspapers, and much of the news was horrifying to read. The Germans were attempting to drive straight through to Paris and were shelling it daily with long-distance weaponry. The Allies were concentrating their troops and fighting fiercely to halt the German advance, with casualties mounting on both sides.

With the men living in mud, exposed to the elements and disease, and at much greater risk of being in the enemy's sights, the war in the trenches was grim indeed. Yet aviation had its own perils. Prior to entry into WW I, the US possessed virtually no air force; there were only a handful of planes and not many who knew how to fly them. Planes were still of a rudimentary design, ground-to-air radio communication was in its infancy, and there was a meager body of knowledge to support the increasing numbers of personnel entering the aviation service. They were literally making it up as they went along. Both pilots and maintenance personnel received intensive training, but it was for a much shorter period than what they would receive today. Pilots had only a brief period of supervised flying before they flew solo, so it was hardly surprising that the papers reported frequent air crashes in training camps. There were scores of deaths even before servicemen encountered the enemy.

After a particularly disastrous series of crashes, Portland's *Daily Eastern Argus* noted in a gloomy editorial that "[h]ardly a day passes that reports of fatalities do not come over the wires from the training fields." The editors were of the opinion that "only a minority of birdmen will come out of the war alive," a comforting thought for the Whitehouses, who had two sons in the aviation service.[289]

In one letter home, Penn described returning from a convoy patrol in which they had dropped a bomb on a German sub just as twilight set in. On the trip back to base, the dirigible engine began shooting red sparks. "Cheerful as hell!" Penn remarked lightly. "Half a dozen bombs around us, a box of detonator fuses under our feet, mitrailleuse before and behind and engine sparks coasting all the length of the hydrogen filled bag." Despite these dangers they made it safely back to Painbouef, landing the big airship after dark. Even though Penn and Bob sought to allay their parents' fears, and generally wrote of their "adventures" in a lighthearted way, reading between the lines it was clear that some of these incidents could easily have ended in disaster. Between their letters and the daily newspaper reports, it must have been a very anxious time for Florence and Robert.[290]

****

With concerns about her sons always present, Florence continued to prepare for the Malone meeting. The plan was to drum up such a tremendous interest in Malone's speech that they could easily fill the 1,200 seats at Portland's Frye Hall and would have to turn latecomers away, the ultimate suffrage coup. An organizing strategy used successfully in filling the Belasco Theater in Washington, DC, for Malone was to distribute many more tickets than there were seats available; for that event (which Emory had helped organize), they had given out about 80,000. Paul suggested that they use this approach in Maine, and recommended sending out somewhere between 75,000 and 100,000 tickets! Though they decided to distribute far fewer tickets, both Emory and Florence were optimistic they could pull off a successful event. At the last minute, Anne Martin agreed to travel to Portland to share the billing, making the evening one of the most exciting events of the season.

Martin was from Nevada. She was a key advisor to Alice Paul and served as the NWP's legislative chairman. She had recently announced her intent to run for the US Senate seat of a Nevada senator who was retiring and had been her mentor for many years. Her supporters in Nevada affectionately referred to her as "Little Governor Anne," a tribute to her role in engineering Nevada's successful state referendum giving women the vote. As the first-ever woman Senate candidate, Martin was a national curiosity and would be sure to draw a crowd. She might also serve as a backup speaker if Malone, still canceling or rescheduling some of his engagements, was too ill to speak, but Emory was determined that Malone come as planned. Two days before the event, she scribbled a hasty note to Paul on a scrap of paper, alarmed that an inquiry from Malone about the projected size of the crowd in Portland meant he might be trying to beg off. "Do you suppose he means to drop out if the crowd isn't large enough? Because we have Miss Martin and Miss Vernon doesn't mean he can get off and for God's sake don't let him do anything like that. It would ruin us."[291,292]

Interest in the event was running high despite the fact that both Emory and Florence complained the papers were refusing to print any publicity material the NWP submitted regarding the meeting. This was a slight exaggeration. They did manage to insert short notices in the society pages announcing the arrival of the speakers, and brief descriptions of all three speakers, the latter typically buried in the back pages of the paper. It is true that their attempts to connect local suffrage events to what was happening nationally, or to feature national suffrage news, were generally suppressed. In order to get the word out about the upcoming event, NWP members were forced to canvass Portland from one end to the other, talking up the speakers and handing out free tickets, but they had succeeded in building great excitement about what promised to be Maine's most impressive suffrage event ever. In the space of a few weeks, Portlanders went from asking indifferently, "Who is Malone?" to being thrilled that he was coming to town and eager to hear what he had to say. Canceling his speech would have been a serious setback, even though Vernon and Martin were effective speakers in their own right. "You know how to handle Malone so please make him come," Emory pleaded to Paul. Whether or not Paul had to intervene, the following day all three invited speakers arrived in Maine as scheduled, Mabel Vernon staying with Helen Leonard and Anne Martin and Malone hosted by the Whitehouses.

The evening's program was set and every possible detail planned in advance. An orchestra played as people arrived, and they were escorted to their seats by dozens of young women attractively dressed and sporting sashes with the NWP's colors of white, purple, and gold. Banners with these colors also filled the room. Following a rousing rendition of the "Star-Spangled Banner," Florence opened the meeting by briefly describing the work of the NWP on behalf of the Federal Amendment, after which she introduced Dudley Field Malone. Malone was a witty and engaging speaker who at the same time conveyed an absolute sincerity in his belief in woman suffrage. He expounded at some length on the injustice of demanding women's sacrifices in war while denying them liberty at home, and then turned to the subject of Senator Hale. Hale, he said, was clearly a man of integrity who was popular in Washington and who seemed to have a promising career ahead of him. Malone found it surprising that a young man with such a bright future would risk voting on the wrong side of suffrage.[293]

Following Malone's remarks, Mabel Vernon took the stage and made the pitch for money to keep the work going. The ushers circulated throughout the hall collecting cash donations, while members of the audience called out pledges, some directed to a particular purpose. Herbert Brown responded first, pledging $25 for general support. Frederic Freeman, a generous and frequent suffrage donor, pledged $25 in honor of Julia Emory, who had done so much to help bring the meeting about. Other pledges followed; $10 in honor of Anne Martin's Senate campaign; a total of $100 in $5 increments in honor of Malone; $5 from Malone toward the conversion of Senator Hale, which encouraged others to follow suit, and so on. Part auction, part revival meeting, this section of the program was designed to get competitive juices flowing and stimulate ever higher pledges that the NWP suffragists would redeem in the days following the meeting.

Anne Martin was the last to speak, her brief remarks focusing on the hard work that went into just gaining a hearing in the House of Representatives, and the activities of the NWP in the months since the House had approved the Federal Amendment. The evening's program also included Mrs. John Hupper Turner singing "The Women's Marseillaise" and the Woman's Party version of "Alive, Alive, Oh." (The words to the latter had been written by Beulah Amidon when she was imprisoned in Occoquan Workhouse.)[294] By the evening's end, Portlanders had pledged close to $500 and donated another $38 in cash—not over the top, but a respectable amount given their previous unwillingness to fund the cause. They had also succeeded in attracting a very large audience of nearly 1,000 people, not quite filling Frye Hall to overflowing, as they had hoped to do, but leaving relatively few empty seats.[295]

The following day, the Portland papers provided detailed and thoughtful coverage of the program. Florence sent the clippings up to the *Kennebec Journal*, and was thrilled to see it publish a fine editorial reviewing Malone's major points and urging Hale to "identify himself with progress" by supporting the Federal Amendment.[296]

Scarcely able to draw breath once the Malone meeting was over, the NWP plunged into its next challenge: to persuade the 1,400 delegates to Maine's Republican convention to pass a resolution calling on Senator Hale to vote for the Federal Amendment. The convention itself would be held in Portland's City Hall Auditorium; an unusually large attendance was expected since the headline speaker for the event was former President Theodore Roosevelt. Governor Carl Milliken also attended the convention along with Maine's entire congressional delegation. The party headquarters were set up in the Falmouth Hotel, on the corner of Middle and Union Streets, just a few blocks from City Hall.

Roosevelt was decidedly pro-suffrage and had been for some time. It was in large part at his instigation that the Republican presidential candidate Hughes had veered from his party platform and come out in favor of the Federal Amendment in the 1916 election campaign. Florence had written Roosevelt earlier in March asking him to work similar magic in converting Hale. She hoped to meet with him to discuss strategy when he came to Portland, but unfortunately his letter back to her went astray and they never connected.

Prior to the convention, Florence had written many of the delegates to encourage their support for a resolution calling on Hale to change his vote, and had asked other suffragists around the state to do the same. She had been hesitant to call for the resolution, fearing that if the delegates passed something with weak language that gave Hale an out or, worse yet, advised him to oppose the amendment, they would lose any slim chance they had to convert him. Alice Paul had pressed hard for them to secure a resolution, however, and with Emory's help and the excitement generated by the Malone meeting, Florence decided that perhaps it could be done after all.

Since one of the objections to women voting was the unseemliness of women mixing with men at the polls, it is not surprising that women were discouraged from attending political conventions. But when Florence heard that MWSA representatives planned to be there, she "corralled seven of the loyal ones" and headed off to the Falmouth Hotel. Delegates and well-wishers showed up in such numbers that the hotel was packed; as one reporter noted,

"[T]he average man had to carry a shoe horn in order to get through the crowd." The congressional delegation and the governor all had rooms on the second floor in which to receive visitors, and, as befitted the occasion, the rooms were draped with banners, flags, and other patriotic decorations. Despite the late-winter chill outside, the throng of closely packed bodies generated a great deal of heat, so that Senator Fernald's room, where he was dispensing Poland Spring Water by the gallon, was the most popular stop. Music was supplied by an orchestra and by a group of Milliken supporters (the "Milliken Club"), who led a parade up and down Congress Street before setting up near his headquarters in the hotel.[297,298]

Robert Whitehouse met Florence and her colleagues at the door and ushered them in, bringing them first to see Governor Milliken. The governor received the group of women very warmly, chatting with them until it was time for him to go and make the welcoming speech, and urging them to use his receiving room as their headquarters. This they gladly accepted, and from there launched themselves on a "triumphal tour" of the congressional delegation. To Florence's utter joy and satisfaction, as they approached each receiving room, the congressman would invariably spot them and wave. At this, the men surrounding him would turn and make way for Florence's procession, the sea of men parting so they could sail through unimpeded. Florence introduced Emory as the picket who had been imprisoned for "obstructing traffic on Pennsylvania Avenue," offering many vivid details of her arrests and imprisonment. The men were impressed that such a charming and vivacious young woman had been so greatly mistreated merely for demanding political freedom; Congressman Peter, in particular, insisted several times that it was a "great honor" to meet her.

They saw Senator Fernald, who was in a celebratory mood as he had just heard his only opponent had withdrawn from the Senate race. Fernald welcomed them with open arms and assured them he would talk with Hale, all night if necessary, to make him change his mind. Hale was considerably less pleased to see them, looking rather confused and red in the face, and trying to derail them by saying that he had read in the papers the nice things Malone had said about him and they were all true! They agreed, but reminded him of Malone's other point, namely that it would be a pity to see a rising young star such as Hale have his political career prematurely ended by voting on the wrong side of an issue whose passage was imminent and unstoppable.

While Florence and her entourage plunged through the crowd in the

Falmouth Hotel, their progress was watched with veiled envy by the handful
of women representing MWSA. As Emory noted with delight, the MWSA
representatives sat on the stairs for half an hour, looking "scared to death, pale
as ghosts." They withdrew for a short time, possibly to repair their frayed
dignity, and when they returned, the husband of one of them escorted them
to the door, telling them firmly "this is no place for ladies." They had spoken
to no one, although through prior arrangement had managed to get some
resolutions introduced.

Robert Whitehouse had also prepared several resolutions for the
convention, calling on Hale to vote for the Federal Amendment, the president
to increase pressure on Senate holdouts to support the measure, and the
Maine convention to adopt national suffrage as a plank in their platform.
Just prior to the convention, he had met with a number of influential men,
including Governor Milliken, to get their help in pressuring the Committee
on Resolutions to adopt the measures. Yet as the convention unfolded, the
suffragists watched in frustration as the delegates passed resolutions on good
roads, sheep raising, agriculture, and water power, while woman suffrage
receded ever further into the background. Not one of the influential men
whose support they had sought prior to the convention referred to the issue
directly. Following several hours of private meetings with Senator Hale,
Governor Milliken reneged on his promises to speak in favor of suffrage to
the Resolutions Committee and in the party caucus, and the resolutions Robert
introduced failed narrowly, by a 7–8 vote, to make it out of the committee. In
his convention speech, Milliken spoke passionately in defense of prohibition
but failed to mention suffrage at all. Roosevelt did only slightly better, twice
referring to "men and women" in his speech, and stating, "[Y]ou know I
believe in universal suffrage."[299]

This fell far short of the suffragists' goal to use the convention to force
Senator Hale to change his vote, and they were bitterly disappointed. They
learned later that Hale, during his meetings with Governor Milliken, had
"advised against" introduction of the resolutions. Florence and Robert could
have asked supporters to offer them from the floor during the convention, but,
if rejected, they were certain they would never convert Hale. Once again, the
men who claimed to support them had failed to live up to their promises, and
they had lost a critical opportunity to pressure Hale to change his vote. Emory
wrote Paul with bitter humor that "I would have gladly smashed windows if it
would have done any good." She wondered how Paul had managed to keep her

temper all these years. "You must have felt terribly hot at times when you were completely fooled and—worse—ignored!"[300]

Perhaps the biggest achievement of the convention was that the NWP had roused their rivals at MWSA, who had previously given up on Hale, into a brief flurry of suffrage activity. In contrast to the highly politicized, action-oriented focus of the NWP, MWSA meetings through this period resembled social clubs in which affluent women met for tea and discussed a number of good works, suffrage being just one of them. In mid-March, for example, the Augusta Equal Suffrage League held its annual meeting to elect new officers and plan its agenda for the coming year. After electing Anne Gannett their new president, the members heard from the treasurer, who reported that the two biggest expenditures of the last 12 months had been $10 to purchase yarn to make articles for the Red Cross, and sending $10 to the suffrage coffee house at Camp Devens in Massachusetts. Owing in large part to the fact that they had done little actual suffrage work, the League's funds were healthy enough that the members enthusiastically voted to "adopt" a French orphan for one year. Toward the end of the meeting, discussion at last turned to suffrage, and considerable time was spent on the new membership book and on strategies for raising funds. Only after these important matters were dealt with did talk turn briefly to the legislative work.

After being outmaneuvered at the Republican convention, Florence and Emory almost despaired of ever converting Hale. They pondered their options for a day or two and then hit on the notion of trying to influence the state's Democrats at *their* convention to be held in early April. Democrats were upbraiding the Republicans for having failed to support suffrage, and boasting of their own party's superior record, and it seemed to Florence and Emory that they might turn this political rivalry to their advantage. If the Democrats vigorously supported the Federal Amendment at their convention, it would reflect poorly on the Republicans, they reasoned, and the Republicans might feel compelled to call on Hale to change his vote. In the end, though, the Democrats proved no more forthcoming than the Republicans, so those hopes were soon dashed.

Hoping that Roosevelt might come to their rescue, even from afar, Florence wrote him in Oyster Bay and urged him to use his influence with Hale. Since Roosevelt seemed puzzled as to what he might do in this matter, Florence laid it out for him quite bluntly. "We need only two more votes in the Senate, and we frankly are indifferent whether they come from Democrats or Republicans," she told him, "but whichever party gets it through will get the credit." Since Hale was still on the list of senators believed capable of changing their votes if subjected to enough pressure, Roosevelt should work on him and help secure the everlasting gratitude of the women for the Republican Party. It is unclear what, if any, steps Roosevelt took to persuade Hale, and Florence eventually abandoned attempts to use him as a political fulcrum.

Paul was anxious to expand the Maine branch's leadership by setting up active committees in other towns and counties, particularly in the 2nd and 3rd congressional districts, and proposed sending Mrs. Toscan Bennett to Maine to help spark interest in Lewiston or Augusta. Florence and Emory both thought this premature. In the first place, Florence pointed out to Paul, there was plenty of work to do in Portland establishing working committees and engaging the new recruits secured by the Malone meeting.[301] Furthermore, it did absolutely no good to whip up enthusiasm elsewhere in the state if they lacked the resources to follow it up. There appeared to be no one outside of Portland as yet who had an interest in leading a local committee or who possessed the courage to stand up to the harpies at MSWA. The Augusta women, now led by Anne Gannett, were perhaps the least receptive audience for a Woman's Party pitch. "[T]hey are benighted there, and as narrow as toothpicks," Florence told Paul. She promised Paul that when time permitted she would go and stay with her mother in Augusta for a few days to see if she could rouse some interest, but until they could follow it up with some intensive organizing, it was probably a waste of time. While Paul and Vernon still hoped meetings in other towns would uncover suffrage talent and enthusiasm not previously known to exist, Florence was able to prevail on this point.

Florence's resistance stemmed in part from the knowledge that the Maine branch would soon be doing without Emory's help, as Paul had already decided to deploy her elsewhere. While the Malone meeting had helped raise $500 in pledges, most of those funds had yet to be collected and the branch had incurred other expenses that still needed to be paid. Maine was not in a position to take on Emory's salary of $100/month. Since the national organization was also short of funds, Paul decided to send Emory to Pennsylvania, where the local branch desperately needed an organizer and could afford to pay her salary and expenses. Senator Penrose of Pennsylvania was on the list of Republican "hopefuls," and the state branch wanted help to convert him. Emory would have preferred to stay in Maine straight through ratification, and the suffragists there would have loved her to remain. She was a great favorite of all the Maine NWP members, who had christened her "Dixie" in honor of her southern roots. She was a cheerful and optimistic presence at the end of a dreary Maine winter amidst the worry and privations of war. With the finish line in sight, she had brought new energy and optimism to Maine's suffrage work during a period when it was desperately needed. Above all, she was a hard worker who made the work fun, and she had connected with the younger generation and with working women in a way that the Maine branch had not previously managed to do. They would be sad to see her go, but when Paul proved adamant on this point, they accepted her decision with little fuss. The Maine branch was able to muster enough funds to hold on to her for another week or two, just long enough to help collect on most of the pledges. Then she packed her bags, said goodbye to her Portland friends, and headed south to take up her new post in Pennsylvania.

VII   Divided Loyalties

W hile continuing to call publicly for Senator Hale to change his vote, by the end of April, Florence was admitting privately that it might be impossible to convert him. Neither local and state pressures nor the influence of powerful friends such as Theodore Roosevelt appeared to have swayed him in the least. Since only four of the twelve New England senators had announced their intent to vote for national suffrage, Catharine Flanagan, an NWP organizer in Massachusetts, proposed that they hold a regional conference in late May to consider how they might bring some of the other votes into the "yea" column. Paul enthusiastically supported the idea, and within a month they pulled it together. Suffrage activists from the New England states gathered in Hartford, Connecticut, on May 29th to report on their efforts and see if they could come up with new avenues of persuasion. Florence, Louise Freeman, and Helen Leonard were the Maine representatives on the organizing committee, although only Florence actually attended the event. She stopped on the way down to take part in an open-air meeting on the Boston Common on the evening of the 27th, one of several speakers addressing a crowd of about 2,000 people. The Boston City Band provided the musical entertainment, but although the crowd was large, they managed to raise only $7.50.[302]

The Connecticut meeting was not a huge success, either. Vermont had virtually no NWP organization and was not represented at all, and the speaker from Rhode Island also failed to show. The program announcement had pointedly invited suffrage supporters, whether or not they were members of the NWP, but no NAWSA members deigned to appear, and apart from a large group from Connecticut, the attendance was quite low. Alice Paul hosted a planning session on how to persuade Republican senators from New England to vote like their more moderate counterparts elsewhere in the country. The upshot of the meeting seemed to be that they should simply work harder to bring pressure to bear on the recalcitrant senators through letters and telegrams, and raise more money to pay for speakers and organizers—in other words, more of the same.

Throughout the spring of 1918, the national NWP worked intensively to keep up the pressure on the handful of wavering senators, with no more success elsewhere than they were having in Maine. In response to frequent urging from NWP headquarters, local branches kept up a steady stream of petitions, letters, telegrams, and delegations to encourage committed senators to stand firm for suffrage, and request their support in converting their colleagues who were opposed. Despite this unrelenting lobbying, no new votes were pledged, but since Senate leaders had not yet scheduled a vote, there was no immediate alarm. The impasse continued for several months until suddenly, in early May, Senator Jones of New Mexico did his own private poll and must have thought that he had enough votes to squeak it through. On Monday, May 6th, after a hurried early-morning conference with Suffrage Committee members, he moved that the suffrage amendment be made a special order of business before the full Senate the following Friday at 1 p.m.[303] Due to his lack of advance planning, 19 Senate members who were pledged to vote for the amendment were not even present, and the motion failed by one vote. Trying to salvage the situation, Jones announced that he would bring the issue up again the next Friday and advised all supporters to be present. When Friday came, he was forced to concede that he did not have the votes to pass it after all and he would not move that it be considered.[304] Suffragists were almost as irritated by his inept handling of the matter as by the continued lack of support for the amendment, but there were some useful side benefits to the event. For one thing, it helped to flush out who were the committed supporters, who was still opposed, and who might waver. The Republicans could point to as many as three-quarters of their members who were pledged to vote for it, while many more Democrats were shown to oppose it. Once again, responsibility for failing to pass the amendment seemed to rest with the Wilson administration, and the majority Democratic Party. But it now appeared they needed three more votes to win, not just two as they had thought.

At the NWP headquarters in DC, the suffragists were increasingly frustrated by the intransigence of both political parties. Democratic leaders assured them that Wilson had wrung every possible Democratic vote out of the Senate and told them to go talk to the Republicans. Republican leaders said there were no more votes coming from their side and the Democrats would have to supply them. Once again, an impasse reigned and the suffragists had to find a way to break through it.

It had become a war of attrition, with both sides dug in and grimly waiting for the other's resolve and funds to run out. Suffragists hoped that the deluge of mail, phone calls, and in-person lobbying would convert the few remaining senators they needed to pass the amendment through the Senate. Suffrage opponents, on the other hand, hoped to hold out long enough that the suffragists would conclude it was futile to pass the amendment in the current session. In the next session, with the war over and the country returning to business as usual, it might be possible to muster enough votes to prevent its passage in either house of Congress. In fact, they were dangerously close to being successful in this. The constant fundraising for war bonds and the Red Cross was making it nearly impossible to collect funds to support suffrage work. As one state worker observed dryly, "If there is such a disease as ingrown patriotism, some of our people have it."[305] At NWP headquarters, they had been into deficit spending for several months, and by mid-June were nearly $10,000 in debt.[306] Without funds they could not pay organizers, send telegrams (now used frequently as a means of communication with the field, as the mails were slow and erratic), travel, or rent halls, all things they had to do to keep the struggle in the public eye.

In response to this, Paul exhorted the state branches to continue their fundraising drives, and toured the Northeast herself to solicit funds from wealthy individuals who had given generously in the past. The money trickled in slowly from all over the country, though not from Maine. After a flurry of activity through the winter, the suffragists there seemed to be taking a breather. This was a common pattern; in ordinary times it was difficult to sustain the intensity of the state campaigns, particularly in states where there were relatively few committed women to carry out the work. The war exacerbated this, of course, by demanding an equal or greater expenditure of time from the suffragists.

From the war's outset, Florence served as the public relations coordinator for the local Red Cross, though during the months of active campaigning to change Senator Hale's mind her Red Cross work had taken a backseat. Then in April 1918, the Portland chapter created an Information Bureau and appointed Florence the chairman. The ten-member committee included both Louise Freeman and Helen Leonard, who were also two of the most active members of Maine's NWP branch.[307] The Information Bureau's charge was to help manage communication between the federal government and servicemen and their families, as there was no other locally based infrastructure through which the government could deliver information about service pay and benefits. With so many Maine men enlisted in the war, there was a huge need for a local organization that could answer questions about benefits, particularly when they were delayed. Families who were dependent on the income from servicemen were devastated when expected payments failed to arrive.

At first the all-volunteer committee focused on providing information about the benefits draftees and their families could expect to receive. It proved so capable and efficient, however, that it soon expanded its duties to include case management for families to help them track down and correct benefit delays, and a revolving fund that provided short-term loans to families until their benefits arrived. Finally, they became the information lifeline between the government and the servicemen around pay and insurances. In her final report for the chapter, Florence noted that between April 29, 1918, and April 21, 1919, the Bureau had provided a tremendous amount of assistance, including:

Information cases	1,636
Form letters written	713
Cases	59
Bureau of Communication	250
Draftees	1,011
Inquiries sent out	523
Bonus letters written	457
Total Activities	4,649

During that period alone, the committee averaged 136 information cases a month, along with a host of other critical letters and communications. A typical case might require several letters as well as face-to-face sessions, phone calls, and general discussions and planning time to sort through the issues and arrive at a solution that met the family's needs. This required hours and hours of labor on top of the Red Cross publicity work that Florence was still managing. In total, this section of the Red Cross assisted an estimated 7,000 families during the war. In its report, the Portland chapter recognized Florence and Louise Freeman, among a handful of others, for volunteering nearly full-time at the chapter office during the war.[308] It is small wonder that through the spring of 1918, Maine dropped out of sight of the suffrage battle: its principal agitators were committed elsewhere.

Despite the apparent stalemate in Washington, there were some hopeful signs. Wilson appeared to be working more vigorously for suffrage and was rumored to be considering an address to the Senate in which he would urge passage of the Federal Amendment as a war measure.[309] The pro-suffrage forces now believed victory was imminent, and President Wilson indicated that the final vote would be scheduled as soon as he had lined up the last few supporters.[310]

Then, on June 20th, Senator Hollis, the acting chairman of the Senate's Woman's Suffrage Committee, announced plans to bring the amendment up for a vote the following week. In anticipation, the NWP went into overdrive, calling on suffragists all over the country to mail or wire their senators to hold firm to pledges they had already made, or calling on those who were wavering to back the amendment. Recognizing the vote's historic nature, the NWP also reserved 100 seats in the gallery and invited supporters to travel to DC to witness the end of their struggle with Congress. Rooms at NWP headquarters were at a premium as women scrambled to reserve a place to stay. Florence arrived at the train station in DC early on the morning of the 27th to take her place in the gallery, eager to be present when the amendment cleared the last Congressional hurdle and rounded the turn into the home stretch.[311] So confident of victory were they that NWP organizers in some states were already turning their attention to the ratification campaigns. There was widespread faith that the administration would not be bringing the issue to a vote if it were unlikely to pass.

On the morning of the 28th, the women assembled at the Capitol early, filling all the available seats. As they settled in, they knew that several opponents were absent, giving the pro forces enough votes to pass the amendment, and spirits were running high. Debate went forward in the usual manner for nearly two hours, and then the Army Appropriations bill came up. At that point, Senator James Reed from Missouri led the Democrats in a filibuster that threatened to derail not just the suffrage amendment but the Army Appropriations bill as well. Incredibly, the Democrats were willing to delay voting on funds to resupply troops fighting in Europe in order to ensure that suffrage did not come to a vote. They would only permit a vote to occur if a pro-suffrage senator paired with an opponent, which would defeat the measure. Suffrage supporters were unable to hold together long enough to carry the day, so the motion to vote on the amendment was withdrawn. Once again, suffrage was defeated, this time by the Democrats, whose leader, President Wilson, had assured suffragists that he was doing all he could to support the bill.

Florence returned to Maine as bitter and frustrated as everyone else. They were so weary of fighting the measure through Congress. It was inconceivable that they could have worked as hard as they had over the six months since the House voted for suffrage and still be two votes short in the Senate. The state ratification campaigns that signaled the end of the decades-long suffrage battle were so close they could taste them, and yet they could not turn to them until they secured those remaining votes. Which senators were the most likely to turn? With a substantial block of opposition coming from southern Democrats worried about the "race question," it looked as though northern senators might offer greater opportunity for conversion. Senator Hale still seemed absolutely immovable on this issue, but Alice Paul thought some opportunity might remain to change his mind.[312]

She proposed sending Dora Lewis and Abby Scott Baker up to Maine in mid-July to do a two-week automobile tour of the state with Florence in order to publicize the Senate situation and the consequences of Hale's continued refusal to support the suffrage amendment. Suffragists based in DC were always pleased to travel to Maine in the summer months, and Baker, who had struck up a close friendship with Florence, was particularly eager to make the trip. With sons in the service, the two mothers had even more to share than just their suffrage interests. Baker had already booked her train berth to Maine when Paul decided that, as the NWP's Political Chairman, she was needed in DC for a while longer. "I hope I am not going to miss the great pleasure of being in Maine with you," Baker wrote Florence. "I am going to look forward to it hopefully until I hear it is quite impossible." Then she added, mother to mother, "I hope you hear good news from your boys. We have had four cheerful interesting letters from Henry. I believe, though, that the letters make me feel worse even than the silence."[313]

A few days later, Paul telegrammed Florence asking if it would be acceptable to have Mary Winsor replace Baker as the organizer on the Maine trip.[314] Florence responded promptly that she would prefer to wait for Lewis and Baker, in part because a military draft had been moved up to occur earlier in the summer, and no one could focus on anything else when those were under way. The papers would publish almost nothing else. "We make a lot of it…," wrote Florence. "It is the boys time public meetings and R.C activities fill all our hearts and mind and we would not get anywhere with suffrage." Then, too, summer brought staffing shortages at the Red Cross as volunteers left for vacations, making it impossible for Florence to be gone for any length of time. Louise Freeman's maid had suddenly announced plans to go on vacation for a month, which would tie Freeman to her house, and Helen Leonard's mother had to have an operation that would require several weeks of convalescing and nursing care. Thus, the only other two able and committed Red Cross volunteers would be unavailable to cover for Florence on her tour of the state, so she thought it best to wait until later in August.[315]

On top of everything else, the doctor in charge of her son Brooks's care had decided it was time to operate. The procedure would entail breaking the bones in his foot and resetting them, a very painful procedure that would require extended nursing care afterwards. Florence needed to travel to Boston to meet with the doctor in advance of the surgery. "This all sounds 'weak sistery' to you I am afraid," she wrote Paul, "but unfortunately for suffrage, none of us can give our undivided time and attention to it. We all have other duties which are pressing, and at times absorbing."

From the outset, Florence had juggled her family responsibilities and her commitment to suffrage, but now the Red Cross also tugged at her loyalties and demanded her time. As usual, her competence had made her indispensable to that organization, and now that she chaired the Information Bureau it was difficult for her to drop Red Cross work for extended periods in favor of suffrage. The work she may have taken up initially for political expediency, to win favorable sentiment for the Suffrage Referendum League during the 1917 campaign, had become another passion. Trying to explain all this to the single and childless Alice Paul, who never wavered from her focus on passing the Federal Amendment, clearly made Florence a bit defensive, but she was stubbornly convinced she was doing what she had to do. While the statewide tour would have to be put on hold temporarily, Florence described to Paul a number of other things she would do for suffrage, including bringing organizers from nearby states up for meetings, and trying to persuade a "radical" young woman she had heard about in Augusta to take over the congressional district chairmanship there. This Miss Presson was well known in Augusta, her father being the Adjutant General for the State of Maine, and Florence hoped that she would be able to get things moving. They also planned to keep up the letter-writing campaign directed at President Wilson and

Maine's two senators.

Since Paul was receiving similar mail from her workers in other state branches around the country, she had no choice but to accept Florence's reasons for postponing the automobile tour, but pressed her to plan for a definite time later in the summer, either at the end of July or in August. She thought Abby Scott Baker, whom she had decided to deploy in New York at that state's Republican convention, would be free to come to Maine then. In the meantime, she urged Florence and Maude Neal, who was the Maine NWP's membership chairman, to keep the focus on recruiting new members. At this point, Maine had a paper membership of 301 women, 100 of whom had joined in the previous twelve months. This was significantly more than either New Hampshire (47) or Vermont (124), but still fell short of where Paul thought they should be. Paul believed new recruits brought added credibility to the state branches, created an impression of energy and momentum, and provided more hands to share the workload. Consequently, she sent out regular missives encouraging them to set and achieve new goals. If Maine had 300 members, could it not get to 500 with a little more effort?[316]

While the state branches appreciated her reasoning, there was some evidence that they viewed new members less enthusiastically, as in the short term new recruits actually added burden. In order to get them engaged, they had to be given work to do, which required planning and supervision from more experienced volunteers. While there were some tasks such as routine office work that could be delegated easily, lobbying, giving speeches, or doing organizing tours of the state required people with more skills. In Maine, Florence was both the most skilled public speaker and the person with the clearest grasp of the organizational work that needed to be done. It was impossible for her to be simultaneously in the field and in the office, and with her Red Cross responsibilities, it was hard to find the time to train someone else, even if women with the proper skill set could be found. National organizers such as Julia Emory could be very helpful in recruiting and training new members, but for the moment, Maine was not able to afford these services so it fell to the core volunteers to do what they could. Other states were experiencing identical problems; in response to a similar request from Paul, the New Jersey NWP chairman, Alison Turnbull Hopkins, wrote that the war had made serious inroads into both fundraising and volunteer recruitment. Workers who had previously been very active for suffrage were devoting all their time to the Red Cross, or found themselves tied to home or family businesses for lack of hired help. Nor was the state's NAWSA affiliate any great help. "The members of the State Association tell us reproachfully that 'they are too busy to work for suffrage, they must give all their time to war activities' and they really are quite passive, as far as I can make out," Turnbull complained to Paul. "I consider it quite as unsatisfactory as you do, but it seems impossible to stir up much enthusiasm this season," she concluded.[317]

In mid-July, Paul tried to gather all the forces she could for a final push to get the missing Senate votes. She and her staff believed that Congress would stay in session through the middle of October, giving them roughly two and a half months to get the measure through before Congress recessed. Paul was particularly anxious to keep suffrage a central issue because of the upcoming fall election campaigns; if they could make suffrage a campaign issue, they might win the two votes they needed. If they were unsuccessful in this, it might still be possible to get it through in the short session of Congress between December and March, but if they failed, they would have to reintroduce it in the House of Representatives and get it approved there again before returning to the Senate. This could mean a loss of momentum that Paul wished to avoid at all costs.[318]

Paul decided it was time to for a new action to ratchet up the pressure on Congress. Quietly, she began planning a demonstration she would hold across from the White House, under the statues of Rochambeau and Lafayette, to evoke memories of the American struggle for freedom in the Revolutionary War. Her plan was to surround the statues with suffragists holding the purple, white, and gold tricolor banners, and to feature the NWP's most prominent and effective speakers. In recognition of the work a number of NWP members were doing for the Red Cross, she suggested that these women attend wearing their Red Cross veils and be clustered in their own group.

The plans for the demonstration were somewhat complicated by the fact that for several months the DC police department had been refusing to issue the NWP permits for open-air meetings, except at two out-of-the-way places that would not give the suffragists the visibility they required. As a result, Paul was forced to hold the meetings without a permit, which would almost certainly result in police interference and arrests. "Our lawyer informs us that we have the constitutional right to do this...and states that if we are sentenced at all it would probably be for a very short time, and the longest sentence could not be for more than six months,"[319] she wrote Mrs. Toscan Bennett, asking her to be one of the speakers. Anticipating that the prospect of arrest might not be too appealing, she suggested that, if she felt speaking would be too risky, perhaps Mrs. Bennett could simply come and hold a banner. This type of appeal was issued to other state chairmen and supporters, and by early August, Paul could count on at least 52 women who would carry banners.

In typical fashion, she used these numbers to leverage commitments from women who were more hesitant to jump in at first. "Fifty-two banner bearers pledged for Tuesday demonstration. Wire whether you can come," Paul telegraphed to Florence on August 2nd, just four days before the demonstration. "Impossible for me to come. Good luck and loads of success," Florence wired back promptly. She gave no excuses, but the cost and time required to travel to DC were certainly impediments. During this period, the majority of suffragists participating in the demonstrations were from Maryland, Pennsylvania, Virginia, and New York, all of which were within easier striking distance of DC. A handful of long-time activists traveled down from Boston, but few others from New England were able to. The women participating also tended to be young and unmarried, and those who did have husbands either had no children or were older so their children were adults and no longer dependent on them. With her family and Red Cross responsibilities, Florence simply could not afford the two days round-trip travel time to DC, and risk arrest and imprisonment on top of that. If Robert was opposed to her participation in the demonstrations at this time, she did not mention it as an excuse. Despite the 100 or so new members the Maine branch of the NWP had gained in the last year, including many younger women, Florence could find no one else to take part either.[320,321]

The August 6th demonstration resulted in 48 arrests, though the women were released on bail until the prosecution could decide on what grounds they could be tried. In the meantime, Paul began organizing a new demonstration for August 12th, the day before the women arrested were due back in court. Once again, she appealed to a broad number of women, including Florence, to take part or to send someone else who could. "Must be prepared for imprisonment," she warned. Since Paul had been among those arrested on August 6th, she fully expected that she would receive a prison sentence that would take her out of the office for some time. As a result, when not planning the following week's demonstration, she caught up with her correspondence, sent new directions to her field organizers, and prepared for the fall election campaign.[322,323] Along with her appeals for participation, Paul also wired NWP state chairmen to inform them of the arrests and ask for their help in publicizing them. In particular, she wanted letters and telegrams sent to President Wilson and to each state's US senators to protest against women being arrested for "conducting a peaceful and lawful open air meeting" in DC. Since she had again declined the invitation to demonstrate, it is likely that Florence did comply with this request, although there is no record of what she accomplished. It was getting harder to generate public sympathy for the suffragists, as the demonstrations had moved from silent picketing to more brazen actions. The general public had come to some grudging acceptance of the pickets; even if the tone of their banners had been shrill at times, the women at least stood modestly in front of the White House and let the banners speak for them. The courts had subsequently upheld their right to be there, and the suffragists had exhibited a steadfastness and courage in the face of attacks that was truly admirable.[324]

At the Lafayette Park demonstrations, on the other hand, the women burned President Wilson's speeches and denounced his failure to persuade enough Democratic senators to vote for the Federal Amendment to get it passed. In every other public policy sphere, they maintained, Wilson had prevailed when he threw his weight behind a measure. If the president was failing to get the same results for suffrage, then it could only be because he was not working hard enough to gain the needed votes. These accusations rankled since Wilson had come a long way from the early years of his administration, when he told delegations of women that he had not paid much attention to suffrage and had no opinion on whether or how it should be achieved. From that inauspicious beginning he had later been moved to announce his support for suffrage, but only if it came through state adoption. He had eventually been persuaded to accept the necessity of the Federal Amendment and had been instrumental in maneuvering it through the House of Representatives; in the summer of 1918, he even urged the Senate to adopt it as a war measure. Many suffragists subscribed to the popular opinion that Wilson's support for suffrage was so strong that he could no longer be held responsible for his party's failure to pass the amendment. Even some very staunch NWP supporters, including the chairman of the New Jersey NWP branch, Alison Turnbull Hopkins, and Mrs. O. H. P. (Alva) Belmont, who had been the NWP's primary financial supporter since its inception, urged Paul to shift her focus from Wilson to those "willful men" in the Senate.[325]

Paul declined to accept this advice and maintained pressure on President Wilson. The action held on August 12th resulted in 38 women arrested; when they were charged and released that same afternoon, they went straight back to Lafayette Park, where all but two of them were promptly arrested again. They received much rougher treatment as the police seized their banners, with the result that quite a number of women were injured, including Julia Emory, whose wrist was sprained in the melee. To prevent further demonstrations, the authorities sentenced the suffragists to up to 15 days in an old abandoned jail where sewer gas leaks, cold, and dampness almost immediately made them seriously ill. Except for two of the women who were too old and frail to attempt it, all of those imprisoned immediately went on a hunger strike. The public outcry caused them to be released after five days, but they were in such a wretched state that NWP headquarters immediately cancelled plans to hold another demonstration and a welcoming dinner for the women after they were released from jail. Paul decided to wait until September 16th to hold another action.[326,327]

Again she wrote to all state chairmen, organizers, and friends of the NWP to take part in the demonstration, issuing the most strongly worded appeal yet. This time she specifically took aim at the women who had not been willing to step up and put themselves on the line for suffrage.

> We earnestly hope that you will join in this demonstration yourself and bring others. You undoubtedly realize the importance of our having numbers. The protests of many women will bring quickly what the protests of a few will take long to accomplish. Do not force other women to bear the burden of this fight for you. Your failure to help will make more difficult, and less effective, the protests of those who have been actively carrying on the fight in Washington, and upon whom the burden will continue to fall unless you and the other millions of women who have not helped will take their share in the battle.[328]

She also urged them to send money; fifty cents or a dollar if that was all they could spare, five, ten, a hundred, or a thousand dollars if they had that. Once again, Florence refused the call to participate, although the summer was over and women were back from vacation to help with both the Red Cross and suffrage work. No one else from Maine volunteered to go, either, and there is no record of whether the Maine branch was able to find a few dollars to send to support the work. Once again, suffrage seemed to be at a standstill in Maine.

Despite NAWSA's continued claims that the NWP's antics caused them to lose ground in Congress, the September 16th action produced a flurry of suffrage activity and hopes were rekindled once again that the Senate might approve the amendment before it adjourned for the fall election campaign. Although it had no other pressing business in the several weeks prior to adjournment, its members had showed little interest in acting on suffrage; the Democratic chairmen of both the Senate Rules Committee and the Suffrage Committee specifically told NWP lobbyists that suffrage was not on their agenda and that President Wilson had not asked them to act on it before the elections. Then suddenly, the day after a demonstration at which a large and enthusiastic crowd applauded the burning of Wilson's speeches and spontaneously contributed almost a hundred dollars to the organizing effort, Senate leaders reversed their decision and announced suffrage would be considered after all. They set September 26th as the date, and the NWP appealed to state branches and organizers to pressure their senators to vote for it. Both politicians and suffrage activists seemed anxious to bring the issue to a close, but the NWP organizers, having seen their hopes dashed before, did not issue broad invitations to attend the vote and seemed skeptical that it would pass. Their cynicism seemed well founded when on the 26th the Senate postponed deliberations to Saturday the 28th. When debate resumed, two things were clear—that they lacked at least one vote necessary for passage, and the Democrats keenly understood the political predicament that confronted them. Any outcome other than passage of the amendment would be blamed on the Democrats, whether it was a referral back to the Suffrage Committee or an outright defeat, and holdouts were warned that the NWP would come after them in the fall elections. At stake were not only the political fates of individual senators but the Democrats' political control of Congress.[329,330]

At the last minute, President Wilson sent word that he would address the Senate in person, as he had the House the preceding January, and ask that they approve suffrage as a war measure. Approval of suffrage was not only a matter of justice, Wilson told the Senate, but was also critical to his efforts to conduct the war and to win the peace.

> I tell you plainly, as commander-in-chief of our armies and the
> gallant men in our fleets...that this measure is vital to the winning of
> the war and to the energies alike of preparation and battle. And not
> to the winning of the war only. It is vital to the right solution of the
> problems which we must settle, and settle immediately, when the war

is over…The problems of that time will strike to the roots of many things…and I for one believe that our safety in those questioning days will depend on the direct and authoritative participation of women in our counsels…That is my case. This is my appeal…The executive tasks of this war rest upon me. I ask that you lighten them and place in my hands instruments, spiritual instruments, which I do not now possess, which I sorely need, and which I daily have to apologize for not being able to employ.[331]

Wilson was obviously weary of having angry women carrying banners and burning his speeches outside his front gates and was anxious to put that behind him, and he had genuinely come to respect the contributions of women to the war effort. Yet despite the intense lobbying from all over the country and from the president himself, the Senate defeated the measure when it finally came to a vote on October 1st. It lost by two votes. Senator Jones, as he had promised the suffragists he would do in the event of a defeat, quickly changed his vote from "yea" to "nay" so he could move to have it reconsidered at any point prior to the end of the session. For now, though, the Senate was adjourned and the suffragists were left to plan their next move.

Within a day of the vote, the NWP executive committee met, and Paul and her colleagues committed to being active in the upcoming Senate races, targeting the senators who had opposed the amendment. As usual, they would work on several different levels simultaneously. On October 7th, suffragists began picketing the Senate, protesting the 34 "willful men" who voted against the measure. This would keep the issue in the public eye, as the arrests that occurred would help generate news coverage and shine a spotlight on the actions of those senators. The NWP would not limit itself to the Senate, however; in the coming months, other demonstrations would be held to protest the Democratic Party's record, and might even target President Wilson if he did not follow up on his recent speech and do what was necessary to secure the votes they needed.

Four of the "willful men" included Senators Baird of New Jersey, Drew of New Hampshire, Benet of South Carolina, and Guion of Louisiana. All of these men had been appointed by their governors to fill vacancies created when the previous officeholders died. These were temporary appointments until elections could be held to fill the seats; they would be filled permanently in the general election on November 5th. If these seats could be filled by pro-suffrage senators, the suffragists would have enough votes to win in the current session of Congress once it met again in December. Since primary elections had already been held in South Carolina and Louisiana, the NWP decided to zero in on the races in New Hampshire and New Jersey.[332] In both those states, the Democratic candidates had publicly stated their support for the amendment while the two Republicans opposed it. While it posed some awkwardness for the NWP's "keep the party in power accountable" policy, Paul urged women in those two states to campaign and vote for the Democratic candidates. She reasoned that the NWP policy was not really applicable in this case because the current campaign would just fill vacancies for a short stretch and would not affect the party majority in the Senate. Paul also urged suffragists across the country, especially those in states where women were already enfranchised, to vote against Democratic candidates in their state elections.[333]

Finally, she appealed to all suffragists to "give now as you have never given before." There were just 100 days to reverse the vote and get suffrage passed before the session was over, she told her members bluntly. After March 1st they would have to begin all over again to win passage in the House and then the Senate, and there was every likelihood that the House would stall as long as it could to avoid acting on the measure. All the momentum they had gained could be lost if they failed to win passage by March 1st.

Poised to launch into her all-out assault on the Senate, Paul came up against an even more powerful obstacle: the influenza pandemic of 1918. Known as the "Spanish flu," though it may have originated in Kansas, it had begun around March 1918 and swept around the world in a relatively mild form. By August it appeared to have spent itself, without having been much more than a nuisance, and was virtually forgotten. But a month later, the virus struck again with much greater intensity. Soldiers at Camp Devens, a military training camp outside of Boston, began coughing and running high fevers. Within days of getting sick, their lungs would fill up with fluid, and many men died despite every effort of the medical staff. Soon 2,000 cases of the flu were reported at Camp Devens alone, and soldiers going home on furlough carried the virus with them. Before long, it had spread throughout the United States and health officials scrambled to respond. Since transmission occurred through sneezing and coughing, local officials were considering shutting down all mass gatherings, including suffrage rallies. This threatened organizing efforts in New Jersey and New Hampshire, and elsewhere in the country as well.[334]

Paul issued her suffrage "call to arms" on October 12th, but four days later she had to admit that the flu had defeated them. She had planned to flood New Jersey and New Hampshire with NWP organizers, but "...nearly everyone in our headquarters has been ill, and those who have not been sick have had to look after those who were. Three are ill in bed at present," she wrote Alice Turnbull Hopkins. Paul promised to send as many people as possible, but warned that "[t]he same situation seems to prevail with regard to our workers outside of headquarters."[335] In desperation, she began wiring every worker she could think of, including Florence, who had not left Maine to organize since the fall of 1916. The same day she wrote to Hopkins, Paul telegrammed Florence;

> "WIRE WHETHER YOU CAN GO IMMEDIATELY NEW JERSEY
> TAKE PART ELECTION CAMPAIGN AGAINST SENATOR
> BAIRD NEED YOU URGENTLY WE WILL PAY EXPENSES
> OF TRIP IF NECESSARY CAN YOU BRING OTHER HELPERS
> ALSO."[336]

Then the National Health Department, which had been threatening for weeks to shut down large gatherings in an effort to prevent mass transmission of the virus, decided to act. For the next two weeks, no public meetings of any sort could be held anywhere in the United States. If the virus continued to spread, the ban might be extended to a month. Paul immediately abandoned plans to organize in her usual fashion and instructed workers to canvass house to house, distribute literature, and do whatever they could to get suffrage material into the newspapers.[337] It was slower and much less efficient, especially since the ranks of organizers were already depleted by the flu, but there was no alternative.

Florence did not respond to the first telegram, so several days later, Paul sent another message.

> "WIRED YOU SOME DAYS AGO ASKING WHETHER YOU
> CAN HELP IN ELECTION CAMPAIGN. CAN YOU GO
> IMMEDIATELY TO NEW HAMPSHIRE REMAINING IN
> CAMPAIGN UNTIL ELECTION IS OVER. WE WILL BE
> RESPONSIBLE FOR EXPENSES OF TRIP IF NECESSARY."[338]

Florence finally wired her back the next day.

"IMPOSSIBLE FOR ME TO GO TO NEW JERSEY. SON JUST RECOVERING FROM OPERATION NECESSARY FOR ME TO BE HERE VERY SORRY ARRIVED HOME LAST NIGHT SO COULD NOT WIRE BEFORE."[339]

Doctors at Children's Hospital in Boston had organized the first polio clinic in the country and were generally acknowledged to be the most expert in providing care for victims of the disease. They pioneered procedures to help polio victims who suffered from muscle weakness and contractures to regain the use of their limbs. To get Brooks the best possible care, Florence and Robert had been bringing him to the Boston clinic. Over the summer, the medical team had decided it was time to operate, and Florence had traveled down from Maine to learn more about what it would entail and the kind of care and therapy he would require afterwards. The surgery involved breaking and resetting some of the bones of his foot and leg. This would be a painful procedure for any person, but later research has demonstrated that polio survivors are more sensitive to pain and take longer to recover from surgeries than those without a history of the disease.[340] Now back in Portland, Brooks would need ongoing care and physical therapy, and there was no one Florence could entrust with this responsibility. Once again, family duties prevented her from doing what Paul asked of her, as much as she would have liked to. Had she not been bound at home just then, Florence might very well have been happy to join the fray in either New Hampshire or New Jersey.

Paul, who frequently lost workers to family emergencies, gave up on Florence for the moment and continued trying to find more funds and more workers to throw into the campaign. After the setbacks of earlier in the month, hope was renewed when Senator William Pollock of South Carolina quietly indicated to the NWP that he would vote with the suffragists next time the measure came before the Senate. Pollock would take his seat in November, filling a vacancy created by the death of his predecessor, Senator Tillman, who had opposed the Federal Amendment. He swore the NWP to secrecy about his intent because he wished to avoid the negative pressure and lobbying that would ensue if the anti forces learned he was pro-suffrage, but they felt comfortable that he was sincere. Publicly, they continued to say they needed to convert two more senators, but they were now within just one vote of passage.

Throughout October, the NWP staged daily demonstrations at the Capitol to protest the actions of the 34 "willful men" in the Senate. The women were arrested every time they picketed, but they were never charged with a crime; the police simply held them for a few hours and then released them. The authorities were mindful that previous harsh treatment had merely increased the public's sympathy for the protesters, and at least initially the arrests were almost perfunctory. Still, they gave Paul an opportunity to communicate with her state chairmen and field workers, and she encouraged everyone to give the protests wide publicity. By month's end, the police were tiring of the pickets and began treating them much more roughly, making the events even more newsworthy. The pickets stubbornly clung to their banners as the police tried to wrench them from their hands, and in the process the women were thrown to the ground, some of them suffering arm and back injuries.[341]

As the weeks dragged on into November with no visible progress toward winning the remaining vote they needed, the suffragists discovered that a new hurdle had emerged. Their allies told them that the anti-suffrage leaders in the Senate planned to prevent the amendment from being reconsidered—at all—in the current Congress. Even if they were successful in gaining the last vote, the Senate could refuse to consider the question. "I do not think there is a single senator who believes it is possible that, even if the additional vote is won, we can force the Senate to consider the measure again," Paul admitted bleakly. "There is no question but that if it is put through during this Congress, it will be only by a terrific struggle on our part."[342]

To add to the twin woes of political stalemate and the national influenza epidemic came a third, almost insurmountable problem: the NWP was again completely out of money and had plunged into debt to finance its activities during the final weeks before the fall elections. Paul pulled together the NWP's executive committee to plan the strategy, and they agreed that the final push would require a war chest of $50,000. This was an extraordinary sum for the suffragists to raise, and they needed to do it quickly. The armistice ending WW I had just been signed, but the Red Cross still urgently needed funds and supplies to care for the wounded, so there would be competition from that quarter for the foreseeable future. And the NWP membership was weary; for 18 months they had either been juggling Red Cross and suffrage work, or they had been working overtime for suffrage because so many women were occupied elsewhere. They were within one vote of passing the Federal Amendment, but the rank and file was almost too tired to care.

Paul called a national conference. She and Elizabeth Selden Rogers, the NWP advisory council chairman, wrote separate letters to the state chairmen and national advisory council members appealing to them to set aside other work for the next 100 days and focus solely on winning the final vote in the Senate. Rogers was fairly diplomatic in her appeal, but Paul, as usual, drove straight to the heart of the matter. She pointed out that workers at headquarters were bogged down in fundraising when they should have been planning and implementing the campaign to win the vote. "If all of the states will make as determined an effort at money raising as they have made during the past year in raising funds to obtain self government for the peoples abroad, the money which is so urgently needed at this time would be forthcoming," she observed crisply. Paul had been patient with members who had transferred their allegiance to the Red Cross over the preceding months, but now she was calling them back. The NWP itself was in crisis, and she needed their help as never before. "Will you not for the sake of all the women of this country and all the women who come after us, put all other things aside at this time and make a supreme effort to raise a substantial contribution from your state to make this campaign possible?"[343]

This letter put Florence in a quandary. She was definitely in the camp of state chairmen who had been distracted by Red Cross and family responsibilities at various times in the last year and a half. The call for help from Paul and Rogers must have struck a chord, but the timing was very difficult for her. The conference was scheduled for December 14th through 16th in Washington, DC. While Brooks would be well on his way to recovery at that point, the operation itself had been very expensive, and between that and money they had given to the Red Cross and for war bonds, the Whitehouses were strapped for cash. Much as she wanted to go, she decided she could not afford it, and for several days she hesitated, not committing herself one way or the other. Then the follow-up appeals started rolling in. Would she make sure that each congressional district in Maine sent a representative to the conference? On Monday the 16th, delegates from every congressional district across the country would march to the Capitol and present a resolution to Congress urging passage of the Federal Amendment. Would she head her state delegation? They needed her presence in DC for this last appeal to Congress.[344,345]

Finally Florence decided she had to break the news that she was not going to make it for the conference, nor would Maine be contributing its $1,000 any time soon. She directed her letter to Dora Lewis, probably hoping to avoid a confrontation with Alice Paul. "[You] simply can't know how I would love to go to Washington for the 16th, but I just cannot," her letter began. "I have been on twice this year, as you know, and I have used up all my money in the loans and the Red Cross &c as everybody else has and I cannot afford it." Furthermore, Florence reported, the state branch had only $19 in its treasury. As usual, following a period of relative inactivity on behalf of the NWP, Florence was full of plans. When the Maine NWP branch met the following week, she would beg donations from them, and hoped to "have some kind of a 'rumpus'" soon afterwards to try to raise more funds. "People are low in their purses from all the war activities and I am afraid it will be a bit like pulling teeth, but I am going to try very hard to get something," she promised. She also still hoped to have Abby Scott Baker come up after the conference to tell everyone about it. "Won't you explain to Lucy Burns and Miss Paul how terribly disappointed I am not to go and yet that I simply cannot."[346]

Alice Paul would not let her off so easily. As soon as she heard this news, she sent off a terse night letter to Florence. "Please make every effort to come to Washington for conference beginning Saturday morning December fourteenth. It is most important that the Senate is impressed by leading women coming from every State demanding action. You are the only one we can count on from Maine. Please make utmost effort to come."[347]

Dora Lewis responded more kindly, but was no less adamant that Florence needed to come. "We really cannot let you off. Of course you must be with us for the conference, and we hope you will stay with us at headquarters as a guest." All Florence had to do was come up with the train fare, she said, and the NWP would cover the rest. "I gave Miss Paul and Miss Burns your message, but they refused to be disappointed for we feel sure that you will come when you know how much we need and want you." She finished the letter, "Much love to you as always."[348]

Florence telegrammed back to Lewis on the 10th of December:

> IMPOSSIBLE FOR ME TO GO TO WASHINGTON MUCH
> DISAPPROVED HAVE MEETING TOMORROW TO PLAN
> LEGISLATIVE PETITION FOR RECALCITRANT SENATOR
> ACCORDING TO MISS YOUNGER'S SUGGESTION HAVE
> WRITTEN TWO OTHER MAINE WOMEN IN WASHINGTON

AND HOPE THEY WILL REPORT TO YOU MY HEART
WILL BE WITH YOU.[349]

Florence's response suggests that there were other obstacles to her participation than just the money. "Much disapproved" could only mean that Robert took a dim view of the NWP's latest demonstrations and asked her not to take part. While it is likely that her fellow Portlanders denounced the NWP's latest antics, Florence had shown her independence from their criticism in the past. If Robert had supported her attending the DC conference, she most likely would have gone.

Still, when Florence sat down to write Paul a lengthy letter, she did not use Robert as an excuse, emphasizing instead that the expense of Brooks's operation kept her from participating in the conference. The influenza was also a factor, as another local outbreak had everyone fearful of crowds and train travel. She went to some lengths to reassure Paul that in refusing to come to DC she was not abandoning the NWP; in fact, she was able to report on a successful meeting of the Maine branch (their first since the summer). Her group had decided to renew efforts to convert Senator Hale, initially through having his more influential supporters write to him, and also by laying the groundwork for the upcoming state legislature to pass a resolution calling on him to change his vote. Florence had canvassed the state legislators who would take their seats in January, and early results suggested there were sufficient votes to ratify the Federal Amendment once Congress passed it. Finally, she discussed plans for fundraising and for expanding the NWP's presence in Augusta and Bangor. Paul had been pressuring her for some time to establish NWP branches throughout the state and Florence had resisted doing so, primarily because she lacked the time and resources to keep them going. In reciting all of her renewed activity, Florence seemed anxious to convey that she still belonged to the NWP and would be stirring things up in Maine. "Good luck to you, you wonderful little woman, and try to feel that I'm not deserting but am only the victim of circumstances," she concluded.[350]

Paul did not waste any more time trying to change Florence's mind, hardly surprising since by this time the conference was upon them. Florence was not the only state leader who was lost to competing interests from time to time. What separated the suffragists who were active primarily at the state level from the national staff was not their skills or their passion for suffrage, but their freedom to commit themselves to a single cause. The national organizers as a group were younger, unmarried, and without children. Florence was closely tied to her family and to her community, and she was unable to turn her back on them when she was needed most and could make a difference. Real misery, such as that endured by families whose breadwinners were in the war, or within her own family, she simply could not ignore.

But the war had ended in November and Brooks was recovering nicely from his operation. Once again, Florence was free to lead the Maine branch of the NWP back into the fray. If she could turn Hale and make his the final, deciding vote in the Senate, perhaps she and the Maine branch could redeem themselves.

VIII   Congress Passes the 19th Amendment

Florence had plenty of opportunity to be active again as the NWP started off 1919 with a bang, creating many opportunities to generate more publicity. On New Year's Day, Paul and her colleagues set a watch fire in one of the urns in Lafayette Park, across from the White House, and announced they would keep it burning until the Senate passed the Federal Amendment. The demonstrations would include ceremonial burnings of speeches that President Wilson, who was in Europe to help negotiate the peace accords following the end of the war, was delivering on the themes of peace and justice and democracy.[351]

Alice Paul and Dora Lewis received five-day jail sentences for the charge of "lighting a fire after sunset"; Julia Emory and three others were sentenced to ten days for the same offense. The NWP then changed its strategy slightly; rather than trying to keep watch fires burning in Lafayette Park, they would set a lighted torch on the balcony at headquarters around the clock. Whenever President Wilson delivered a speech in Europe, they would ceremoniously march with the torch to Lafayette Park, use it to light a fire, and consign his words to the flames. Since in all probability they would be arrested every time they did this, they would need reinforcements, and NWP headquarters issued a call for help. Women everywhere were urged to send telegrams to their senators protesting the treatment of the suffragists and demanding that the Senate pass the amendment. Florence did her best to get these dramatic events covered in the Portland papers, though she continued to have difficulty getting them to print news of NWP actions.[352,353]

At the same time, she was busy persuading the Maine legislature to instruct Senator Hale it was time he voted for the Federal Amendment. There was general agreement that this strategy might work; in North Dakota, Senator

McCumber had openly stated that the only reason he had voted for the amendment was because the legislature told him to do it. In New Hampshire, Paul now had seven organizers in the field, as Senator Moses had promised he would vote for the amendment if the legislature told him to. If the Maine legislature would pass a similar resolution, then Hale could legitimately claim that it was a new yardstick by which to measure public opinion and would be relieved of his promise to be bound by the result of the 1917 referendum. Hale denied such instruction would move him at all, and suggested he would issue a statement to that effect. This temporarily deflated the suffragists, but then they reasoned that Hale might be just saying that to put them off. If the legislature could be corralled into instructing him, perhaps he would be glad to change his vote. But would the legislature act? Everyone agreed that if the resolution failed, it would end any chance of winning Hale over.[354]

The Maine legislature had to be canvassed very carefully. While there appeared to be sufficient votes to ratify the amendment once Congress approved it, the legislature had no precedent for instructing the state's US senators how to vote, and some people showed a marked lack of enthusiasm for establishing one. Paul sent Betty Gram, another of her capable national organizers, to help Florence measure the strength of legislators' support for the idea. Gram came to Maine by way of New Hampshire, where her efforts to convince the legislature to tell Senator Moses to support the amendment had not been successful. The New Hampshire House passed the resolution calling for his favorable vote, but the senate refused to follow suit and Moses announced he would remain opposed. Gram was convinced that he had never intended to change his mind. "Maud, dear," she wrote back to headquarters, "we were beat before we started—that man Moses is the most detestable dog alive today—for I have not one doubt in my mind that the plot was laid immediately after our interview—and in the words of an unscrupulous politician, 'He slipped one over on the women that time alright.'"[355]

New Hampshire would clearly not be supplying the missing US Senate vote. Maine, along with Louisiana and Idaho, remained one of the few states where there was any hope of bringing a senator into the "yea" column. Fresh from the New Hampshire debacle, Gram agreed with those who counseled against asking the Maine legislature to pass a resolution. If one or both bodies failed to pass it, any chances of converting Hale would be doomed. A petition signed by a majority of the legislators would have the same effect on Hale as a resolution, she and Florence decided, and carried less political risk. They would frame the petition to Hale as the latest expression of the state's sentiment regarding the Federal Amendment. The suffragists contended that, since the September 1917 referendum defeat, sentiment in Maine had shifted. The crucial role women had played in mobilizing the country for war had earned them new respect, and with that came acceptance that the world's leading democracy should grant them voting rights. Florence and Gram collected some signatures from the Portland delegation to start off the petition drive and traveled up to Augusta, where they stayed with Florence's mother while they collected the other signatures they needed.

In Augusta they found confirmation from the other legislators that the petition was the correct strategy, although the consensus seemed to be that it would have absolutely no effect on Hale. Still, in relatively short order, they had collected 75 of the 100 signatures they sought, and had hope of getting the remainder. Hale was expected back in Maine in two weeks, and they were anxious to gather all the signatures before his return so he could be presented with them. Gram also met with the president of the American Federation of Labor, who agreed to get resolutions passed at two upcoming conferences calling on Hale to change his vote, and they encouraged any individuals they met to shower Hale with telegrams and letters.[356]

Senator Hale remained unperturbed by all this attention, which was absolutely maddening to the suffragists. Whether in Maine or in DC, whenever NWP organizers approached him, they invariably reported that he was amiable, even chuckling when asked if he had experienced a change of heart, but he steadfastly maintained that he was honor-bound to vote against the Federal Amendment, at least in the current Congress. He always managed to sound a shade regretful, and to imply that he might change his mind when the next Congress was installed in April, but stopped short of a full promise that he would do anything of the sort.

After interviewing 180 men, some as many as ten times, Florence and Gram got 92 of the 100 signatures that had been their goal. A majority of state representatives signed, but they did not persuade a majority of the state senators, so it was wise of them to have pursued a petition rather than a resolution. The petition read:

> We, the undersigned members of the Seventy-ninth Legislature of the State of Maine, believing that in response to the demand for a more complete and consistent democracy in this country inspired by

the ideals of the world war, there has been a change in the attitude of the people of Maine toward the question of the enfranchisement of women since the referendum submitted in 1917, and that the proposed Federal Amendment to the Constitution granting the franchise to women, would, if submitted, be ratified by the legislature of this State, do hereby, without assuming the right in any way in our capacity as legislators to dictate what your course of action would be, respectfully request you to give your vote and support to secure the passage of that measure.

The diplomatic wording was necessary since Maine had no precedent for state legislatures telling US Senators how to vote. While 12 other legislatures around the country had already done so, at least one Maine lawmaker was apoplectic when he thought that was what Florence and Gram were asking him to do. A number of the men were reluctant and required several meetings before they could be convinced to sign. While some were simply opposed to suffrage, other reasons the legislators gave for not signing were simply inane. The presiding officer said it was unethical for him to sign the petition; another said he never signed petitions and would have preferred a resolution; in one case a man said his wife was opposed; and one was peeved because he viewed himself as a good suffragist and they came to him last, so he refused to sign. A few did not want to do anything they thought would keep Hale in office. "He is dead if he does not vote for it but I won't help keep him alive," was the sentiment. A few were also concerned that the petition would only make him more obstinately opposed, and there was some concern that signing it would prove costly politically. "Ye gods, one would think that the rotation of the earth on its axis depended on whether or not one of those ge–rand hicks writ his name on a little piece of paper…," wrote Gram to headquarters in some exasperation. "O it was a scream and dear Mrs. W and I had one great time doing it." There was substantial agreement, even among those signing, that the petition would have no effect whatever on Senator Hale. The exercise was not completely fruitless, however; it gave the women another chance to assess the strength of the sentiment for ratification, and they were quite cheerful about its prospects.[357,358,359]

Alice Paul wanted Florence to lead a delegation of Maine women down to DC to present the petition to Hale in the Capitol; she said she thought it would have more effect on him in DC, but she likely hoped she could persuade them to take part in the watch fire demonstrations while they were there. Florence flatly refused. "We cannot send on a delegation," she wrote Paul. "[W]e have no money and nobody who has is sufficiently interested to go or pay for us who are." Florence suggested that Doris Stevens present the petition on Maine's behalf, since Hale had spoken favorably of her in the past. She doubted the petition would have the desired effect, though. "Everyone agrees that Senator Hale is hopeless and that we are wasting our time, but all the work we are doing would help in ratification if we should be able to ratify this winter." Feeling guilty that she was once again refusing to come to DC to work, Florence ended the letter, "I feel like a slacker, not being there to help, but my work must be done from this end. The bonfires are extremely unpopular among the legislators but I think they are quite partial to the Woman's Party per se."[360]

In the midst of all this, Paul sent Florence a letter exhorting her to recruit some new members. With a paper membership of 303, Maine was still outperforming both New Hampshire and Vermont, but while Paul applauded her effort, she wanted more. Yet when Florence hosted a meeting at her house, it netted just one new member, so she and Gram decided to use a stealth approach to recruiting the younger set. Gram, of course, was staying with the Whitehouses. Florence would invite a number of young women to tea on the pretext of meeting her guest Miss Gram; then, when they were all assembled, they would spring the trap. Instead of idle chit-chat, Gram would talk about the Woman's Party and why their help was urgently needed, and proceed to "recruit a lot of very necessary talent." On the face of it, this ploy seemed unlikely to work. Gram's photo, accompanied by a story of why she was in town, had been featured in the Portland papers the preceding week, and Florence was certainly well known as a suffrage leader, so anyone going to the grand house at 108 Vaughn Street for tea might suspect that suffrage would be a topic of conversation. Still, the standard organizing approach was not yielding many new members, so plotting this "clever camouflage" must have seemed a better strategy, and it was certainly more fun. Gram was clearly tickled by the plan. "It is nice of Mrs. Whitehouse to put such faith in me, isn't it?" she wrote back to headquarters.[361,362]

Like all the other organizers, Gram very much enjoyed being in Maine. Living with the Whitehouses was "more than delightful" she reported back to Paul. "They are charming hosts treating me exactly like one of the family— such a contrast to that granite state of New Hampshire." Even if Maine was conservative, hard to organize, and had a stubborn senator who refused to change his mind, it was not exactly a hardship post. Living in the Whitehouses' home was far more comfortable than living in a cheap hotel such as Gram had just left, and it came with amenities such as good food, maid service, and hosts who were attentive to her every need. They certainly worked hard, but the weariness of the labor was softened by the comfort of their surroundings and the energy, competence, and humor the Whitehouses and the handful of other NWP stalwarts brought to the work.[363]

They would need all the humor they could find because a new calamity was emerging. Just before Gram arrived in Portland, MWSA had quietly introduced a presidential suffrage bill into the state senate, where it was referred to the Judiciary Committee. The bill was introduced by Senator Guy Gannett, whose wife, Anne, was now chair of MWSA. Florence found out about it only after the fact and was utterly stunned by this fresh evidence of their lack of political savvy. For 18 months, MWSA and its local affiliates had done very little but raise money for the Red Cross. The published account of the Portland Equal Franchise League's recent meeting in December, for example, demonstrated that it was still functioning more as a general woman's club than as a suffrage organization. Members attending this meeting had heard presentations on the "canteen work" of the local Red Cross; the accomplishments of the Senior War Council; accounts of the Junior War Council's organizing of the Girl's Patriotic League; what the Liberty Loan drive had netted; and work under way to assist French orphans. According to the newspaper, suffrage was not even on the agenda. What is more, half of the biweekly meetings planned for the coming months would be devoted to "sewing for Devastated France." In contrast, the agenda of the Maine branch of the NWP, which met the same day, had no mention of the Red Cross at all; the meeting was devoted entirely to reviewing the status of the national suffrage campaign, listening to Florence's analysis of the state legislature's readiness to ratify, and planning upcoming weekly business meetings.[364]

It is unclear what MWSA thought it could accomplish with the presidential suffrage bill. Even if passed, it would give women the right to vote only in presidential elections; the next one of those was still almost two years away, and by then, national suffrage might very well be enacted. As long as the legislature alone passed the bill there was little chance of it damaging the chances for ratification. The danger was that the presidential suffrage bill would be sent to the voters for approval, either through direct action by the legislature or through a petition drive by the antis. It would be particularly alarming if a referendum took place before the legislature had the chance to ratify the Federal Amendment. Despite their claims that the war had shifted public sentiment in favor of suffrage, the NWP activists were not anxious to try their case in the court of Maine's public opinion. As they had in 1917, the voters might very well vote it down. If that occurred, the legislature might be more likely to follow suit and refuse to ratify the Federal Amendment.

Florence and Gram were gathering petition signatures in the State House when the Judiciary held a hearing on MWSA's presidential suffrage bill, and many lawmakers asked them if they supported it. When Gram replied in the negative, she was asked, "Oh, we see, you believe in going to the limit or not at all?" That was a pretty clear characterization of the difference between the NWP and MWSA, and many pro-suffrage legislators were surprised that the state association was willing to settle for less when full victory was plainly within their grasp. The presidential suffrage bill sailed through Maine's Judiciary Committee on a vote of eight to two, and prospects looked good for passage.[365]

It is true that MWSA had precedent for trying to obtain presidential suffrage, and plenty of company, even at this late date. Illinois had pursued this strategy successfully in 1913; North Dakota, Nebraska, Rhode Island, and Michigan had followed suit in 1917; South Dakota in 1918; and Maine was one of eight states with such bills before their legislatures in 1919. It had seemed a reasonable strategy for those states when passage of the Federal Amendment looked to be several years away. But this was 1919. At the federal level, suffrage was through the House and just one Senate vote stood between it and the final ratification campaign. Successful presidential suffrage campaigns in 1919 may have helped keep woman suffrage in the public eye, yet with full suffrage around the corner, NWP activists were frustrated that NAWSA members would consider asking for anything less. If MWSA had joined forces with the NWP and leaned harder on Senator Hale, it is possible that the single missing vote for the Federal Amendment could have come from Maine.

****

Back in the US Senate, Jones of New Mexico, the Suffrage Committee chairman, announced on February 3rd that he would bring up the Federal Amendment for debate in the Senate the following Monday. Both parties were agreeable to voting on the amendment, but the pro-suffrage forces knew that they had not yet obtained the final vote they needed. They had a week to do it.[366]

So again, telegrams poured out from headquarters to the state chairmen and organizers in the field, urging them to come themselves and lead delegations of women from their states to join a massive demonstration in DC on Sunday, the day before suffrage would be brought up in the Senate. They set a goal of bringing 100 women to participate in yet another watch fire demonstration in Lafayette Park, but this time they planned to burn more than the president's speeches. They would burn Wilson himself in effigy to symbolize women's anger at his failure to campaign vigorously for suffrage. They hoped to have a line of banner-holders that stretched the length of the White House grounds; the large numbers would be both evidence of strong approval for such a daring act and protection against the inevitable wrath of the police and watching crowds.[367]

Florence declined to attend; if simply picketing the White House was shocking to conservative Mainers, consigning the president's image to the flames would be more than they could stand. Paul managed to keep her plans relatively quiet until Saturday evening, February 8th, when an NWP member she had asked to participate in the demonstration broke the news to Maude Wood Park. Park was NAWSA's chief lobbyist and was well connected in Washington. Without hesitation, she telephoned the chief of police, tracking him down at a dinner party, and revealed to him the NWP's intentions. At dusk the following day, the women marched out from NWP headquarters carrying their banners, including one that read, "Only fifteen legislative days are left in this Congress. For more than a year the President's Party has blocked suffrage in the Senate. It is blocking it today. The president is responsible for the betrayal of American womanhood."[368]

As the marchers assembled, they were met with a large force of police officers determined to keep them from carrying out their plan. Mindful of this, the suffragists initially just lined up with their banners, making no attempt to light a fire. Drawn by news releases Paul had sent to all the major papers, a crowd of thousands also showed up to watch the spectacle, waiting patiently through two hours of speeches for the suffragists to make their move. Finally the women kindled the watch fire and ceremoniously dropped a black-and-white sketch of President Wilson into it—not quite as dramatic as the life-size puppet they had planned, but still expressive of their contempt.

The police would certainly have confiscated a puppet long before it could be torched. Despite the milder gesture, the police still arrested Mrs. H. O. (Louisine) Havemeyer, and then pandemonium ensued. Any woman standing near the demonstration was at risk of being seized, whether she was actively participating or not. So many women were taken into custody that they filled the waiting patrol wagons as well as others that the police hastily sent for, and the officers still had to commandeer nearby cars. Some of the women were released, but dozens more went to the abandoned jail that had made them so ill the previous summer.[369]

No one was surprised when the NWP melee failed in its desired effect, and the following day the Senate once again defeated the measure by one vote. NAWSA was furious with the NWP for pulling this outrageous stunt during such a precarious moment in the Federal Amendment's history, but future events proved that the outcome of that particular attempt at passage would have been no different even if the NWP had adopted the more decorous approach of its sister organization. As the weeks had stretched into months following the House's approval of the amendment, the women had turned the senators one by one toward suffrage using every means at their disposal. Each vote had been more difficult to gain than the last, and this final one, this prize, was the most difficult of all. The Senate was simply brought to a standstill, each side straining to force the other across the line that divided them. The presence or absence of women demonstrating in a nearby park on a winter afternoon was not what would obtain the needed vote. The NWP's actions helped shine a spotlight on an issue that many senators must have wished would fade quietly into the background.

Beyond that, though, suffragists needed to find the right combination of pressures on the right senator at the right moment that would cause him to yield and change his vote, and then convince the Senate to consider the measure one more time before it adjourned. They only had days in which to do this; the session of Congress would adjourn on March 4th, and the legislators had other business to complete by that deadline, which complicated the effort to bring suffrage up again. After March 4th, they would have to start over to get the Federal Amendment through both houses of Congress, a step backward no one wanted to take. The NWP kicked into high gear, ratcheting up public pressure all over the country to keep the measure before the Senate until the final vote could be secured.

NWP sent its "Prison Special," the train car it had outfitted to resemble a prison cell staffed with women who had been arrested for picketing, to help dramatize what was happening in the nation's capital. From DC, the train car traveled down to Florida, across the south to New Orleans, through Texas to Los Angeles and San Francisco, then back through Denver to Chicago, up to Syracuse and over to Boston. Paul asked Betty Gram, who was still in Maine, to help organize the reception for the Prison Special when it arrived in Boston.[370]

With work on the postwar peace accords largely completed, President Wilson was sailing back from Europe, and his ship would dock in Boston Harbor on February 24th. Boston planned a huge parade for him and Paul decided that the NWP should be there as well to remind him of the unfinished business he had waiting for him in DC. Paul deployed four organizers to Boston and traveled up herself the day before to help organize the protest. Mindful that the world's eyes were upon them during this historic occasion, Boston officials were "hysterical with anxiety" in arranging the ceremony, and patriotic fervor ran high.[371]

Florence came down from Maine to help with the demonstrations. The day before the president's arrival, the NWP planned an open-air meeting from the bandstand on Boston Common. As they always did, they requested a permit from Boston Mayor Andrew Peters and were told that they could not receive one because the president "might want to speak there." The suffragists then asked if permission to have a meeting was refused, and were told no, that the mayor would get back to them later. He never did, and it was clear to the suffragists that once again they were being denied their civil rights merely because of the cause they represented. They held the meeting as planned, and Florence watched as for over two hours a crowd of 600 people stood and listened, in frigid temperatures, to what the women had to say. Despite the fact that the meeting was orderly, with no hecklers, the police arrested two of the speakers and hustled them off to jail.[372]

The following morning, Florence accompanied 22 women as they marched out from the NWP's Boston headquarters, though once again she was there as a witness and not a participant. As an observer, she managed to get printed a lengthy—and highly indignant—letter to the editor of the *Portland Evening Express* describing the events in Boston. The marchers held banners that carried the now familiar wording: "How Long Must Women Wait for Liberty?" and "We demand an amendment to the Constitution enfranchising women." A second banner, throwing the president's words back at him, read, "You said on September 30, Mr. President, 'We shall be distrusted, and we shall deserve to be distrusted, if we do not enfranchise women.' You alone can remove that distrust now, by securing the one vote needed to pass the suffrage amendment before March 4th." Others carried the tricolored banners of purple, white, and gold, bright splashes of color against the stark backdrop of a New England winter sky.[373]

The women marched over and stood silently with their banners near the reviewing stand where the president would watch a welcoming parade. They stood there for 40 minutes undisturbed, whereupon a police officer told them they had to "move on," they could not "loiter" there. Eyeing the crowds of thousands who were also standing around "loitering," though not being harassed for doing so, the women refused and were promptly arrested and escorted to the waiting patrol wagons. Betty Gram told the police she was not breaking any law and if they wanted her in the patrol wagon they would have to put her in bodily. They did so, and then all "these liberty lovers," as Florence termed them, were hustled off to the city jail, where they spent an uncomfortable night. City officials quickly discovered their mistake in trying to silence the protesters. The following morning, hundreds of supporters, Florence among them, lined the corridors of the courthouse demanding to know where and when the women would be tried. Afraid that the rowdy crowd might disrupt the proceedings, officials announced that the courtroom would be closed to spectators. Another storm of protest arose: How could the women expect a fair trial if it occurred behind closed doors?

Furious at their treatment, when the hearing began, the prisoners refused to provide their names or cooperate in any way with the court. In response, the judge assigned them fictitious names such as Jane Doe and fined them each $5. Of course they refused to pay the fine, so these largely middle-class women were sentenced to eight days in the Charles Street jail with drunks and streetwalkers as their cellmates. Ten of them immediately began a hunger strike and demanded that as political prisoners they be allowed to wear their own clothes rather than the clothing issued by the jail. Reporters were allowed into the jail to interview the prisoners, and quickly broadcast their stories across the country. This was turning into a much bigger circus than local officials had bargained for, and within a few days a mysterious "Mr. Howe" came and paid their fines, earning them an early release. When the Prison Special arrived a few days later, the Boston NWP chapter held a huge meeting at which those recently jailed for freedom received their prison pins, a badge of honor.[374]

In Portland, the papers were full of news of the president's arrival. "President Lands as Guns Roar, Whistles Shriek, Crowds Cheer; Boston Gives Him Deafening Welcome" ran the headline in the *Evening Express* the day of his arrival. No conquering hero could have had a more triumphal return, and readers got an enthusiastic description of the pomp and circumstance that greeted the president and his party. Nor could readers have missed the less admiring story printed alongside the article about his arrival. "Suff Lifted Bodily into Patrol Wagon" said the headline, disapprovingly. "22 Arrested in Front of State House in Boston; They Were on Hand Early to Heckle the President and Refused to Move on When Ordered to Do So by the Police."[375] The article was short, but noted that it was Betty Gram whom police had to physically throw into the police wagon. While it did not mention the fact that Gram had been staying with the Whitehouses in Portland just days before, many readers would have known this to be the case so there was more censure in store for Florence.

As Florence had not joined the banner-holders in Boston, she could have ducked this one, making no public comment on the events and waiting for the fuss to die down. Yet she was clearly stirred by what she had witnessed, and she could not stay silent in the face of widespread disapproval of what the suffragists had done. When she wrote to the *Express* editors to give her version of the events, she unequivocally allied herself with the NWP, heaping scorn on NAWSA. She noted the irony that as the women were being sentenced in a closed courtroom in violation of their civil rights, in the same city President Wilson had given a speech about men dying for liberty and making the world safe for democracy, and "prettily dressed" NAWSA leaders had thanked him for his support of suffrage while condemning their sisters who were suffering for freedom. And yet, Florence continued, the NWP's so-called militancy had really been of a very mild sort. "We have never destroyed property, we have never menaced life, we have simply refused to pretend that we are duped, for a moment, by the politicians who pass out bouquets to us with one hand and hit us with the other." The watch fires in DC were necessary to keep pressure on the president and Congress because without this, history showed that the political rights of women would be ignored again. "And we burned him in effigy because we knew that he knew, and the men in Congress knew, that there was no hope of the suffrage amendment passing when it was voted upon on February 10…and we knew they were going to vote upon it just to 'hit us again.'" It was time for President Wilson to throw his full weight behind the amendment, and until he did, "we will continue to consider all his wonderful eulogies upon freedom for women as airy camouflage fitted only to throw dust into the eyes of the National American Woman Suffrage Association."[376]

There was little public response to this broadside, but it was a gutsy stand for Florence to take at a time when virtually no one else in Maine had anything kind to say about the NWP. In taking aim at NAWSA, she was also ridiculing MWSA, whose membership included some of the most prominent women in the state. It would have been easy for her to claim, as some of her own members wished to, that the outrageous actions of the NWP in Boston, DC, or anywhere else had nothing to do with her. In truth, she herself was not very happy with the effigy incident, as she would tell Paul later on. Still, it appeared that the NWP's agitation was having the desired effect.

After months of doing little to support it, on his return to DC, President Wilson appeared to make securing the passage of the suffrage amendment a top priority. Part of his motivation was that in the elections the previous fall the Republicans had picked up several new seats, so when the 66th Congress took office, the Democrats would lose their majority in the Senate. In the last days of this lame-duck session, Democratic leaders were suddenly anxious to have the political benefits of passing the Federal Amendment accrue to them, rather than their political opponents, since the Republicans would almost certainly manage to get it through in the next session. Wilson and Senator Jones, who was still chairman of the Suffrage Committee, met to strategize how they would win the single vote they needed and maneuver the measure through the Senate in the time they had left.

On March 1st, with three days left in the session, Senator Edward J. Gay of Louisiana announced that he would vote favorably on the Federal Amendment. There was no time for celebration, since they still had to bring it to a vote in the Senate. Florence received this breathless telegram from Alice Paul, sent just before midnight on March 1st:

VOTE LACKING TO PASS SUFFRAGE OBTAINED TODAY WHEN
SENATOR GAY LOUISIANA ANNOUNCED WOULD VOTE
FAVORABLY NECESSARY TWO THIRDS NOW PLEDGED IN BOTH
SENATE AND HOUSE...SENATE PLANNING ALL NIGHT SESSION
PLEASE HAVE TELEGRAM SENT PRESIDENT URGING HIM NOT
TO LOSE THIS LAST OPPORTUNITY.[377]

Florence responded quickly, along with thousands of other women, and such a flood of telegrams poured in from all over the country that Congress dredged up an old rule that prohibited them from getting printed in the Federal Register. Despite this pressure, and intense lobbying from the president, Senate leaders were unable to secure a vote. Senate rules required unanimous consent to get it on the agenda, and two eastern senators, Weeks of Massachusetts and Wadsworth of New York, worked together to ensure at least one of them was present at all times so that if anyone proposed a vote they could object. Passage of the Federal Amendment would have to wait for the 66th Congress, which by order of President Wilson would be seated in special session on May 19th.

The mood in NWP headquarters was grim but determined. The good news was that they had the necessary vote in the Senate, and support in the House was stronger than ever, so as long as nothing else happened, the prospects of victory in the next session were excellent. The Senate support was so fragile, however, that the suffragists would have to continue organizing and demonstrating in order to keep the senators they had won, and perhaps convert a few more.

Florence proposed to Paul that Maine hold another mass meeting, similar to the Malone meeting, to inform Portlanders of the events in DC and keep the pressure on Senator Hale. Paul was enthusiastic, but demurred when Florence wanted Lucy Burns or someone of her stature to come deliver the speech. Burns would be needed in DC into the spring, she told Florence, and suggested that she try to get the state chairman from either Massachusetts or Connecticut, or Mrs. Toscan Bennett, who was a member of the advisory council. Part of the issue was money, once again. Even with Gram's help, the Maine branch had been able to raise very little, and so despite being nearly bankrupt itself, the NWP headquarters had picked up the cost of having her there. It would be less expensive to bring in a speaker from a nearby state, and Paul thought the Maine branch could afford to cover that expense itself.[378]

Paul then asked for an update on the presidential suffrage bill that MWSA had introduced into the Maine legislature. Since Maine's lawmakers were largely pro-suffrage, it had easily won approval, but its supporters had just barely mustered the votes to block it being sent to referendum. Paul wondered whether the fact that the legislature had passed presidential suffrage so handily might encourage Hale to reconsider his opposition to the Federal Amendment, but Florence assured her that while she would keep after him, he would likely "forever be an anti."[379,380]

The real problem, Florence admitted to Paul, was that "suffrage is at a standstill in the state." It was true that NWP fundraising was hampered by the fact that champions of other causes were trying to raise money at the same time, but once again the actions of the women in DC had made Florence's job more difficult, and she told Paul so at some length. "It is just as I wrote you, you set the state by the ears with the 'insult to the Pres' when you burned him in effigy—It may be stupid of them—tho I confess I was very much disturbed—but it is the truth," she wrote bluntly. "If we want money from the state we cannot keep antagonizing the state people—It may help in Washington but it reacts on the states and after all it is quite important to keep the state alive." One of the Maine branch's most influential members, a Mrs. Charles (Edna) Flagg, had withdrawn from the NWP after the banner incident complaining that "I cannot belong to a Party I have to apologize for all the time."[381]

Florence was certainly not alone in complaining to Paul about the effects on the states of the NWP's actions in DC, but she was unusual in that she remained loyal even in the face of enormous family and local pressure to renounce her support. Her own husband had lost patience with the NWP, confirming that her absence from demonstrations in DC had much to do with his disapproval. Other state chairmen faced similar opposition within their organizations. Anne Martin, the Independent candidate for governor of Nevada who had traveled to Maine the year before with Dudley Field Malone, had severed ties with the NWP completely, taking the Nevada NWP branch with her. Yet despite the deluge of criticism, Florence was not ready to quit, nor had she quite lost her sense of humor. There might be ways to whip up enthusiasm, "...but many of the suffragists say they would rather have suffrage put off for 25 years than have it come thru such Bolshevist methods— Everything is Bolshevism now, you know." Florence then discussed ways she might raise money and get more publicity, but noted that all the papers were angry with the NWP as well and were refusing to print much of anything to do with them. Nor was sentiment any better elsewhere in the state. "I suppose you thought this all out before you burnt the President and concluded that the sacrifice is worth the result, but these are the results as I have seen them," Florence said in closing. It had gotten to the point—once again—that she would have to stay quiet for a little while until people got over their anger toward the NWP. "I love you all—but alas—that does not fill your coffers—or make the public realize how wonderful you are...Write me and tell me what to do."

Paul did not respond to this letter. What could she have said that would have made a difference? What strategy might Florence have employed that she had not tried already? Maine was still difficult to organize, politically conservative, and bound by a rigid sense of propriety. The small group of women still willing to be active for the NWP had been isolated and cast almost as members of a lunatic fringe. Their stories were censored by the local press; they were reduced to introducing suffrage news covertly into the society column. For example, several of the young national organizers had gotten married in the last year. One of these was Beulah Amidon, who had made such a hit in Portland the year before, so at the prompting of headquarters, Florence and Louise Freeman sent a news release to the Portland papers announcing her wedding. These kinds of stories worked on a symbolic level, refuting claims that NWP suffragists were somehow unfeminine or even unmarriageable, but they were a poor substitute for news of women jailed for freedom, or the continued recalcitrance of a certain senator from Maine.[382]

Moreover, as Florence tried to convey to Paul, the agitations in DC that Paul and others insisted were vital to advancing the cause were having the opposite effect in Maine and other states. The DC staff was at this point rather bitter that it was shouldering most of the burden of the suffrage campaign. With some reinforcements from New York City, Boston, Baltimore, and other cities with strong labor unions, it was the suffragists at headquarters who were facing ugly crowds at demonstrations and risking arrest, trial, and imprisonment. On top of this, they were responsible for most of the fundraising as well, a disagreeable but necessary task that no one was eager to do. The most recent campaign in the Senate had left the NWP at least $17,000 in debt, so once Congress adjourned they switched to fundraising almost full-time. Appeals to Maine and other state branches yielded only pocket change, if that. Far from the seat of power and the swirling intrigues that accompanied the legislative process, the average citizen simply could not understand why a small group of hysterical women found it necessary to burn the president and hoist inflammatory banners at the Capitol. It seemed to them highly unreasonable, so in increasing numbers they refused their support and raised their voices in condemnation. Yet the more obstinate and treacherous the lawmakers proved to be, the more grimly determined were Paul and her colleagues to do whatever was necessary to shine a spotlight on what was happening and demand that Congress be held accountable.[383],[384]

This clashing of strategies posed a serious threat to the NWP and the suffrage struggle just as they were on the verge of victory. It is interesting to note that from the time the 65th Congress adjourned until the vote was won, the NWP refrained from the kind of demonstrations that caused Florence and other state chairmen such embarrassment. Perhaps, as Florence had pointed out to her, Paul understood that she could not expect much assistance when the NWP's actions in DC alienated the very people the state branches were trying to ask for money.

The suffragists were certainly not without some provocation to act out again. On top of having to fund-raise a deficit, they were still one vote short in the Senate! While they had for several weeks believed that Senator Gay would supply the remaining vote, a further canvass had revealed they were mistaken in this. They had votes to spare in the House and were hopeful they could get the measure approved there without much drama, but the Senate looked like it would require another campaign.

Senator Hale, still planning to vote against the amendment but (unlike some of his colleagues) not opposed to the principle of woman suffrage, remained on the short list of senators who might be converted. Fortunately for Florence, who must have been pondering how on earth she could move him at this late date, on May 9th William Harris, a new senator from Georgia, declared he would vote in favor. At long last, they could be sure of the two-thirds majority they needed. Nevertheless, mindful that some backroom deal could quietly steal a vote or two at the crucial moment, the suffragists were anxious to keep up the pressure on all senators to prevent backsliding and perhaps win a more comfortable margin of support. When there were indications that Senator Keyes of New Hampshire might come out in favor of the amendment, a series of public meetings were planned for May 26th and 27th; Alice Paul traveled up from DC to speak and encouraged Florence to lead a delegation of women from Maine to participate.[385],[386]

The idea of having another big suffrage meeting in Portland and Bangor was still alive, but no headway had been made on it. The Maine branch was still out of money and the NWP remained in disgrace locally due to the effigy incident, so there was little likelihood of raising the funds needed to pay a speaker's traveling expenses, rent a hall, and manage all the publicity. Without funds, Florence could afford no paid organizing help, and she was down to a small handful of supporters who would do any work. The war had run up a staggering debt of close to $18 billion that officials predicted would cost the American people $700 million a year for 25 years. Thus, even though the war was over, there were still active campaigns urging people to buy bonds for "Victory Loans," and a lot of spare cash went to that cause over the next several months. The NWP national headquarters was still fundraising to pay off its own deficit, so there could be no help from that quarter unless Alice Paul decided it was critical to do so. There was some question as to whether they could even get press coverage of events; as Florence complained, "…the papers are all so reactionary and they froth at the mouth when the Woman's Party is mentioned…"[387,388]

What Maine did contribute when Congress reconvened on May 19th was a delegation of four US Representatives fully committed to passage of the Federal Amendment. The vote took place on the session's third day, and, as expected, the House passed it with a healthy majority, 304–89. Maine was one of 26 states whose Representatives provided only favorable votes.[389] For the second time in history, the amendment had made it through the US House and all eyes turned to the Senate, where once again the battle was shaping up. Seventeen months had passed since the amendment first cleared the House, and in that time, the suffragists had whittled away at the opposition until they finally had the necessary two-thirds majority. The last obstacle was persuading the Senate to act.

Suffragists at NWP headquarters had been assured by Republican leaders friendly to the cause that the Senate would soon follow the House in voting for the amendment, but these hopes were quickly dashed. When they were the minority party in the Senate, the Republicans had loudly decried the Democrats' unwillingness to support suffrage and had assured women that if they were in charge, things would be different. Now that they were the majority party, they were having some difficulty making good on their promises. Senators Lodge of Massachusetts and Borah of Idaho led a last-ditch effort to prevent the amendment from coming to a vote. While individual members seemed as pro-suffrage as ever, the party leadership seemed unable to shepherd the legislation through the maze of parliamentary tricks and hazards that threatened to block its passage. Even more disquieting, there were some murmurings that "there were more important things than suffrage at this time and that suffrage should not interfere with the peace."[390]

The prospect of having suffrage deferred once again due to "more important business" was maddening. Every delay simply bought opponents more time to dream up other ways to block suffrage, but fortunately the Republican leaders were able to reassert control. They agreed to postpone the vote over Memorial Day weekend, but then Senator Watson, now chairman of the Suffrage Committee, brought it up as unfinished business so it would have to remain before the Senate until its members acted on it. Anti forces fought to derail or modify the measure right up until the last minute. Senator Harrison, a Democrat from Mississippi, offered an amendment that would restrict suffrage to white people, but the Senate speedily dismissed this, 58 to 17. Senator Gay of Louisiana tried once again to insert wording that would leave enforcement of suffrage up to the states, claiming that without this amendment 13 states would refuse to ratify, enough to block it from becoming part of the Constitution. This was viewed correctly as an effort to disfranchise black women and was soundly defeated, 62–19. Senator Underwood of Alabama moved to require that the Federal Amendment be approved by Constitutional conventions in each state, instead of by their legislatures. The Constitution specifically offers this as an option for ratifying amendments, and many Senators seemed to think it might be a good idea. In reality, though, a majority of the states would have to call special legislative sessions in order to ratify, which suffragists already considered a significant burden. Requiring ratification through popular conventions that states had no prior experience in organizing would cause further delays and offer endless opportunities for blocking passage. Suffrage supporters watched nervously from the packed gallery until the Senate defeated this amendment by a vote of 45 to 28.

Southern Senators and their sympathizers inveighed against this erosion of states' rights; Senator Borah of Idaho, for example, decried the "Prussianism" by which three-quarters of the states could trample the wishes of the remainder, even though the Constitution's framers had envisioned the need for amending the document and had provided for it in this way. In a more ominous note that presaged the confrontations of the civil rights movement of the 1960s, he pointed out that the southern states had no intention of allowing *any* blacks to vote, women or men. If the suffrage amendment were to be passed and ratified, it would be a "solemn lie" because everyone knew it would not be enforced. Debate continued for four hours, during which Democratic senators filibustered to delay the vote until their absent members could be paired, but eventually they gave up and allowed it to proceed.[391]

So it was that on June 4, 1919, the Senate of the United States finally passed the Nineteenth Amendment enfranchising women. Once it was clear that the measure had the 64 votes required for passage, two Senators changed their votes from "nay" to "yea" so they could be counted among the majority. When the Senate President announced the vote results, the chambers and gallery erupted in applause that stretched into two minutes, as jubilant suffragists celebrated the end of a campaign that had begun in earnest 40 years before.

Attendance at the signing ceremony, which took place immediately after the vote, was limited to a handful of NAWSA leaders. NWP leaders were pointedly not invited to participate, and the gold pen used to sign the amendment was presented to NAWSA. Alice Paul was unruffled by this slight, offering a brief statement to the press in which she expressed her belief that "[t]here is no doubt of ratification by the States. We enter upon the campaign for special sessions of Legislatures to accomplish this ratification before 1920 in the full assurance that we shall win." Women would vote for president in the 1920 elections, she declared.[392]

Congratulatory telegrams addressed to Alice Paul poured into the NWP headquarters from all over the country. Florence wired her:

CONGRATULATIONS AND REJOICING SUFFRAGE VICTORY IS DUE TO YOU AND YOUR UNDAUNTED FATE [sic] SPLENDID VISION AND UNTIRING DEVOTION TO THE CAUSE AM PROUD TO BE THE LOWLIEST OF YOUR DISCIPLES
ADMIRINGLY AND AFFECTIONATELY
FLORENCE BROOKS WHITEHOUSE[393]

It was an enormous achievement to have maneuvered the Susan B. Anthony Amendment through Congress, yet even as they rejoiced, the suffragists knew that much work remained to be done. Suffrage opponents had known what they were doing when they dragged out passage by the Senate into 1919. Had the Senate followed the House and approved the amendment early in 1918, the ratification process would have been far easier because most states were scheduled to have their regular legislative sessions in the coming year. Ratification could take place as part of the other business legislators were already there to transact. Persuading governors to call special sessions in 1919 would be difficult to do. Governors or legislative leaders opposed to ratification could use all types of excuses to avoid an extra session, including the legitimate one that doing so would add extra expense to the state at a time when budgets were lean. If women were going to vote in the next presidential election, 36 state legislatures would have to meet and ratify the Federal Amendment, and they had 17 months in which to do it. There was no time to lose.

On June 5th, the day after the Senate vote, Alice Paul wrote to Florence and the other state chairmen to focus them on the task at hand. Characteristically, she wasted no time exulting about the vote just passed; her lead paragraph referred to it briefly and cut straight to the chase. "Now that Congress has submitted the national suffrage amendment to the state legislatures, we are endeavoring to conduct a most vigorous campaign in order to secure ratification within a year," she wrote. Paul knew how desperately everyone wanted to be done with suffrage and move on to other things. With the focus now shifted to the states, it would be easy to sit back and let each state organization proceed at its own pace, until the legislature got around to ratifying, but if that occurred it could take years to finish the process. It was better to get it done sooner, and by setting an artificial—yet still achievable— target of 12 months, Paul was trying to rally her weary forces to fight through to the end.[394]

Florence and Betty Gram had canvassed the Maine legislature when they were collecting signatures on the resolution for Senator Hale, so the suffragists were confident that Maine would easily ratify the Federal Amendment. Questions remained about how and when this would happen, however. Would Governor Milliken call a special session, adding expense to a state budget that was already stretched thin in the wake of the war? And how would MWSA's ill-conceived presidential suffrage referendum affect the ratification process?

IX Maine's Ratification Battle

If things had not returned exactly to normal for the Whitehouses by the spring of 1919, they certainly were happier than they had been for a long while. The press of Red Cross work had abated and the suffrage campaign had shifted to ratification, putting a stop to the ugly confrontations in DC that had made promoting the Federal Amendment in Maine so difficult. Penn and Bob were back safely from the war, in good health and high spirits, and bound together by an intense loyalty that would last the rest of their lives. Many families were less fortunate than theirs; sons either did not return at all or were spent and broken from their experience and forever changed. The previous two years had been so packed with hard work and grief, so emotionally charged and endured with such grim determination, that it was an enormous pleasure just to be together again.

Just after the historic Senate vote in early June, Florence, Robert, and their three sons gathered at their East Raymond camp for their last weekend together as a unit for some time to come. Bob's graduation from Harvard was scheduled for June 17th, and his work as a salesman for a paint company would keep him traveling through the southeastern part of the United States for long stretches. Penn's long-planned wedding to Dorothy Case would take place on the 21st, and the couple planned to settle in Cambridge while Penn attended Harvard Law School. Brooks, now recovered from his operation and enjoying much greater mobility than he had in the past, would attend boarding school at Deerfield in the fall. Before their sons scattered, the family needed some time together at camp.

On Saturday night, Florence sat down before the big brick fireplace to pen a lengthy letter to Mabel Vernon. "It is wonderful here tonight," she wrote. "A

big open fire and my precious boys all here. After the horror of the past two
years this seems little short of heaven." The peace and remoteness of the log
cabin enabled Florence to gain some perspective on recent events, and while
not directly apologizing for having been somewhat inactive through the spring,
she clearly felt some need to justify her decisions.[395]

She could be active once again for the NWP, but when the DC protests had
been causing such an uproar during the winter, she had thought it best to lie
low. Some of the Maine branch's most influential members had been furious
over the effigy incident, and Florence believed that any additional action on
her part at that time could have triggered mass resignations. Now she could
report that her strategy had worked, as Edna Flagg had recently told her she
had thought it over and would not resign after all. To Florence's delight, Flagg
had decided that she could not reasonably expect to agree with every action of
every organization she became part of, and while she continued to disapprove
of burning the president's image, she fully supported the political actions of
the Woman's Party. Florence wrote happily to Vernon, "It means a great deal
to us to have her belong to it because she is influential and sane and helps give
the party prestige in Maine." If Flagg stayed with the NWP, it meant other
women would, too.

They might need all her influence and then some because Maine was in an
unusual position with regard to suffrage. The MWSA-sponsored presidential
suffrage bill had sailed through the legislature during the winter and all signs
indicated that ratification would enjoy the same support; Florence's own polls
of lawmakers had shown this to be true. The potential wrinkle was that the
antis were collecting signatures on a petition to send the presidential suffrage
bill to the voters. They needed to get 10,000 signatures, which presented a
substantial hurdle, but since they had money to pay signature gatherers, there
was a strong likelihood they would succeed. If the antis managed to force
the bill to state referendum, the vote might be able to piggyback on a special
election tentatively scheduled for early September. Maine voters had soundly
rejected full woman suffrage two years before, and they were just ornery
enough to do the same with this bill. If they voted down presidential suffrage
before the legislature met to ratify the Federal Amendment, antis could claim
with some justification that the state did not want to enfranchise its women and
might persuade lawmakers to reject the amendment. The challenge, then, was
to delay the timing of the referendum vote and bring the legislature back into
special session as quickly as possible so that it could act first.

To make matters worse, Florence noted, MWSA leaders, having acted irresponsibly in the first place by pursuing presidential suffrage instead of throwing their weight behind the Federal Amendment, evidently felt no inclination to oppose the antis in the referendum! "Having set the Presidential suffrage baby adrift on the sea they will undoubtedly sit back and let it drift to shore or sink as Fate and the Antis will," she complained to Vernon. Florence was thoroughly disgusted with them. "You never saw babes newborn so stupid as those women were about it," she wrote. "They never looked ahead a moment. One of the leaders said to me, when I remonstrated with her, 'We had to do something.' 'Well, why didn't you work for the F.A.' I said, 'instead?'" The woman merely looked disconcerted and walked away. Florence promised Vernon that she would monitor the situation closely and make every effort to ensure that the Maine legislature met in special session before the voters considered presidential suffrage.[396]

Despite the hazards the amendment still faced in Maine, Florence was optimistic about its future and pleased to be back working with the NWP. "Lots of love to you my dear," she finished the letter to Vernon. "You will always be most welcome at our house when you come to Maine. I love all [sic] you dear W.P. women—You see I do not make it quite so inclusive as I started to—but many of you are awfully satisfactory and you are one." This was a trifle odd, as it is not clear at all from Florence's correspondence which "W.P. women" she considered unsatisfactory. She had enormous respect for Alice Paul, "adored" Abby Scott Baker, and had spoken highly of all the organizers who came to work with her. Also, it was a little risky; letters of this sort, containing an analysis of a state's political situation, were routinely shared among staff at headquarters, so broadcasting the fact that she had favorites was a potential faux pas. Nevertheless, with this letter, Florence signaled that she was back on the job and would remain there until the amendment was safely ratified in Maine.

The good news was that Governor Milliken was a staunch suffrage supporter and was also closely watching the progress of signature-gathering for a presidential suffrage referendum. Maine had held only six special sessions since the state became organized in 1820, and Milliken was unwilling to schedule one for suffrage alone. If there were other business to be taken care of, however, it would be easy to bring the lawmakers back to Augusta and urge them to ratify immediately. Happily, it looked as if there *would* be other business, and he was planning a special session for either September or October. Florence kept in close touch with Milliken and his staff as they waited to see whether the antis could gather enough signatures to force the presidential suffrage bill to referendum vote, as they would need to move quickly if that occurred.

Maine would certainly not be among the first to ratify the Federal Amendment, as a flurry of states acted in the months immediately following its passage by the Senate. Suffragists were thrilled to see several states compete to gain the distinction of becoming the first to ratify, and on June 10th, Wisconsin succeeded in this, followed within hours by Illinois and Michigan. Eight more states followed by the end of July, and for a brief, giddy period, the NWP staff at headquarters actually thought they could be done by the end of the summer. The ruse they hit upon was to persuade at least one legislator to offer publicly, in each state where a special session was needed, that he would not accept pay or mileage for attendance at the session. If one man did it, his fellow lawmakers would surely feel honor-bound to follow suit, and before long a significant obstacle to calling special sessions, namely their cost to taxpayers, could be removed altogether. That idea did not gain much traction, though, and before long, the suffragists accepted that they would simply have to fight it out, state by state, to get the measure ratified however it could be done. Every state presented unique challenges. In California, for example, there was widespread bipartisan support among politicians for calling a special session. But the governor refused to call one for suffrage alone, and there was other business pending that he was actively trying to prevent bringing to a vote at all. If he called a special session, he would either have to allow legislators to act on the other measures or take the political risk of telling their proponents that they could not bring them up. Under these circumstances, he preferred doing nothing at all, and he was unmovable on this for many months.[397,398]

By early July, Maine's antis had succeeded in collecting 12,000 signatures, far more than the 10,000 needed to force the presidential suffrage bill to referendum. By itself, a citizen's referendum on presidential suffrage might not have stimulated much interest among the voters, but the antis had been very clever. In the last session, the legislature had ratified the 18th Amendment to the US Constitution enacting national prohibition. The antis had joined up with the "wet" forces in the petition drive, attempting to force a referendum not just on the suffrage question but on ratification of national prohibition as well. Joining the two issues together drew enough support for both to succeed.

Many states besides Maine objected to their legislatures ratifying national prohibition, and since the suffrage amendment followed immediately, it fueled this debate. Some people were simply opposed to prohibition, suffrage, or both, but the larger issue was the tension between states' rights and federal rights that had been present from the country's beginning. States' rights proponents did not deny that the US Constitution provided a vehicle for amending it. They simply believed that issues such as prohibition and suffrage were not the proper purview of the federal government; the states should decide on them individually.

Furthermore, the phrase "government of the people, by the people, for the people," uttered by President Lincoln at Gettysburg, had become a rallying cry for many who fought against usurpation of individual rights by state and federal governments. These believers promoted the citizen referendum process as the ultimate expression of true democracy, saying that any controversial legislation ought to be referred to the people to decide, giving legislatures little power to govern. State Senator Alfred Ames articulated this position in February 1919 when he moved to amend Maine's presidential suffrage bill to require a referendum vote. (His motion was defeated, which is why the antis had been forced to gather signatures to send it to referendum.) "This law should be submitted to the people of this State," declared Senator Ames, "and we should not assume the great responsibility of determining so great a question. It was for such determination that the referendum was created—that the people might rule. If we withhold the referendum from this measure we deny to the people the right to determine for themselves how they may perform one of the highest duties of citizenship."[399]

Opponents argued that overuse of the citizen's referendum should be avoided. Senator LeRoy Folsom of Norridgewock, for example, complained that "When no argument prevails, legislators are becoming prone to invoke the referendum….In other words, legislators are liable to become addicted to the habit of a referendum, referendumitis, so to speak." When most voters were not concerned about an issue, or were actively in favor, as Folsom believed was the case with presidential suffrage, the legislature should simply act on it and move on to other business. Still, the importance of "letting the people decide" was the Maine antis' most effective argument in opposing ratification of the federal suffrage amendment.[400]

Governor Milliken made a last-ditch effort in July to head off a statewide referendum by referring the issue to the Maine Supreme Court, asking for a ruling on whether the legislature could act independently on both

Constitutional amendments, or if they were covered by the initiative and referendum clauses contained in Article 4 of Maine's constitution. Maine was one of 22 states whose initiative and referendum clauses permitted sending federal amendments to voters for approval *after* their state legislatures had acted on them. These clauses had never been challenged in court. The issues of suffrage and prohibition prompted the examination of the larger constitutional question of whether states could unilaterally change the process by which the federal Constitution was amended. These challenges were occurring in many other states across the country, and would ultimately be brought to the US Supreme Court for a final ruling.[401]

In the meantime, suffragists across the country watched anxiously to see how the Maine Supreme Court would rule on this issue. If Maine's court ruled that both amendments needed to go to referendum, the pro-suffrage forces could be in for an extended battle for suffrage, as even states that had already ratified the Federal Amendment might be forced into referendum campaigns. Considerable relief and rejoicing followed when Maine's highest court ruled unanimously that prohibition, as an amendment to the federal Constitution, was not subject to Maine's initiative and referendum process. The presidential suffrage measure, however, since it was an action of the state legislature, would have to go before the people of Maine.

MWSA leaders, Florence griped, "proving again how deadly lacking in political acumen they were…" with regard to the whole presidential suffrage issue, had mounted no counter-campaign to dissuade people from signing the petition. Florence had absolutely refused to rescue them, so the state was now stuck with the referendum vote. It was fortunate for the suffragists that Maine's political leadership remained firmly in support of ratification. Governor Milliken, legislative leaders, and none other than Senator Hale himself publicly pledged themselves to ensuring that Maine was among the states that ratified. Ironically, Hale now claimed to be one of woman suffrage's biggest supporters, although his single vote in the Senate could have secured its passage months earlier than it actually occurred. Once the deciding vote had been obtained, Hale had bravely called a press conference to announce his decision to change his vote in favor, wiring Florence the same day, "I shall vote for the Federal Amendment." Ignoring the fact that his vote was superfluous, when it might have been decisive, the local press praised him for his vision and commitment to suffrage. His duplicity, combined with MWSA's foolishness over the presidential suffrage bill, was almost more than Florence could stand, but, on balance, it was better to have Hale with them than against them so she kept quiet about it.[402,403]

Fortunately, Maine state law required, at minimum, a four-month period after the referendum signatures were submitted before the vote could take place, which bought time for ratifying the Federal Amendment. According to Robert Whitehouse, who had met with him on another matter and had seized the chance to discuss suffrage as well, Governor Milliken still hoped ratification could occur at a special session that would take place *if* a transportation bond issue passed at a special election in September. If the bond issue failed, the governor was unwilling to call a session solely to ratify the Federal Amendment. The only way he would do it was if other governors agreed to do the same in their states, or if Maine's vote were critical to gaining the required number of states nationally. Still, he seemed to understand the danger of waiting to ratify until after the presidential suffrage referendum took place, and promised to watch the situation. Based on the relative ease with which the antis had secured 12,000 signatures, Florence was convinced the referendum would be defeated, so she was very anxious that the legislature ratify the Federal Amendment first.

Alice Paul shared Florence's determination that the special session should be scheduled as quickly as possible. She still hoped that it might be possible to secure the 36 states they needed as early as September; if this occurred, women would have ample time to register for the upcoming November elections. One wonders if this was simply a high-pressure tactic on Paul's part to wring greater effort from her staff and state branches, since the resistance in many states to scheduling special sessions suggested that this hope was doomed from the start. Still, it did help infuse a sense of urgency into the campaign and gave suffragists new excuses to hold public meetings and pressure their politicians. Paul thought she could arrange to have a prominent speaker travel up to Maine to help draw crowds. Florence was still holding out for Abby Scott Baker. "I want you and not someone else," she wrote Baker, "and hope you will use your influence to get here. It will be wonderful to see you again and we will get in a little fun besides. Write me when and I will meet you." Florence hoped to tour the state for several days with Baker, going at least as far as Augusta and perhaps up to Bangor as well. While she still doubted it was possible to raise much money or even to draw much of a crowd to meetings, Florence believed that Baker's experience as the NWP's National Political Chairman would bring a fresh perspective to interviews with legislators and, most importantly, with Governor Milliken. "[T]he Governor knows me too well," Florence told Baker. Baker might move him as no one else could.[404]

Baker was detained by some personal affairs until mid-August, so in the interim, Paul proposed that Mary Winsor, who was vacationing at the Islesboro Inn in Dark Harbor from mid-July to early August, could be of some service. Winsor had graduated from Bryn Mawr the year previously and was a veteran of the picket line, having been one of the women sentenced to 60 days in Occoquan back in 1917. She had also been in charge of finances for the "Prison Special" in February 1919. Winsor was very agreeable to making hers a working vacation, offering to speak at meetings in Bar Harbor and surrounding towns if they could be arranged. Paul sent her up some photos of Occoquan so the audience could see as well as hear about that experience. In the end, though, Florence said she was too busy to set anything up for her. The NWP had no local branch in Bar Harbor, so organizing a meeting would have required her to travel up and stay there for days, which Florence had neither the time nor the inclination to do. If she had a limited amount of time to spend touring the state on suffrage business that summer, she wished to do it in the companionship of Abby Scott Baker. Reluctantly, Paul advised Winsor to focus her energies on persuading Governor Milliken and other key political leaders to schedule a special session as soon as possible.[405]

Since Paul at this time was reduced to advancing funds to the NWP from her personal account to cover its bills, she was exasperated with Florence and everyone else who seemed to be losing focus at this crucial time. She wrote as much to Winsor. "It seems indeed a catastrophe in the midst of ratification work to have to stop to give so much time to getting money, but apparently this is what we shall have to do. Perhaps you can induce Mrs. Florence to go with you to see some people in Portland for money. If she realizes how the whole ratification campaign is held up for lack of funds, she will probably be willing to give up a little time even if she is so occupied."

By the end of July, the exact situation with regard to Maine's ratification campaign was confusing, as two conflicting viewpoints were circulating. On the one hand, Florence was confident that the situation was well in hand and was resistant to Winsor's (and Paul's) urging to try to ratify immediately. "It is absolutely impossible to get a special session of the legislature before October," she insisted in a letter to Paul. "There cannot be a referendum on the Presidential Suffrage bill before November or December and the Gov has promised to call one for the ratification before the other if the other is inevitable so I do not think it is wise to push for any other session." Florence and Robert were about to set sail for Squirrel Island for their first real visit in two summers, evidence that Florence felt there was so little cause for alarm that she was prepared to take a brief vacation.[406]

Winsor had had some different intelligence and clearly thought Florence's information was suspect. Her informant was state Senator Willis A. Ricker of Castine, who was not too favorably inclined toward suffrage. Ricker assured Winsor that the suffrage referendum would be scheduled in September, since a special election had already been called at that time. In fact, according to Ricker, there was no other option. "The Governor is legally obliged to call on the election to be held within 30 days after the requisite number of names have been obtained," Winsor reported back to NWP headquarters in early August. She wrote further that Ricker believed the legislature's special session was now scheduled for October 8th, which meant that the presidential referendum vote would already have taken place by the time it occurred. If the voters rejected presidential suffrage in September, Ricker thought the legislature would be unlikely to ratify the Federal Amendment, exactly as Florence had been predicting. Winsor was a little miffed that Florence had preferred to work with Baker over her. "Mrs. Whitehouse seemed to think that it would be impossible [sic] to get up any meetings for me in Maine at this time of year and that the best results would be obtained if she took Mrs. Baker to see the Governor etc." As she closed her letter to Vernon, Winsor suggested that Florence was not on top of things and required some pushing from headquarters. "I should advise you to urge on Mrs. Whitehouse," was her parting shot.[407]

Naturally, Winsor's letter resulted in considerable alarm at NWP headquarters, and Paul promptly urged her to take command of the situation. "Possibly you can direct agitation from your part of the state, while you are taking your holiday," Paul suggested, oblivious to the fact that it would not be much of a holiday for Winsor if she were heading up a campaign—in an area of the state where there were virtually no active suffragists—to persuade the governor to call an emergency session for ratification. Furthermore, Winsor, though willing to help, was suffering from rheumatism that made movement painful and limited her mobility. Nevertheless, her call to alarm appeared justified when a clerk in the governor's office confirmed, in response to an inquiry from Paul, that the presidential suffrage bill would be voted on in September's special election. Paul immediately wrote to Governor Milliken directly to verify the scheduling and then fired off letters to NWP organizers Margaret Whittemore and Dora Lewis, asking for their help in what might be a very dicey campaign to get a special session called for ratification before the second Monday in September. Florence got a letter, too, with a copy of the letter from the governor's office to illustrate the peril in which Maine stood.[408,409]

In truth, their alarm was justified. While there had been an initial wave of ratifications, the campaigns in some states had bogged down, and it was clear that suffragists would be unlikely to secure all 36 states by the end of the year, let alone by September as Paul had briefly hoped. Virginia's legislature was just then meeting in special session to consider a road bill, but suffrage supporters had not been able to secure the votes they needed to bring up ratification, despite the fact that Paul had three of her most capable staff stationed there: Betty Gram, Mabel Vernon, and Anita Pollitzer. Alabama's legislature had rejected the Federal Amendment in its session, but there was some hope that it could be brought up for reconsideration before they adjourned. NAWSA had conceded defeat in that state and had withdrawn its organizers, but Paul was proposing to fight on; since Alabama's legislature met every four years, this might be the last chance they would have to get it through. Only one other governor, in Minnesota, had agreed to schedule a special ratification session that summer, with four others (including Maine) possible in the fall.[410]

By mid-August, 14 states had ratified and 22 more states would have to do so before woman suffrage could become part of the Constitution. Nine states were not scheduled to have a regular legislative session until sometime in 1920, and an additional 17 would have their next regular session in 1921. This meant that in most states, two campaigns would be required—one to persuade the governor to call a special session and a second to secure the necessary votes for ratification in the legislature. A number of governors were opposed to suffrage, so just getting a special session called represented a formidable obstacle in some states. Therefore it was critical, in a state like Maine where there was substantial political support for ratification, to prevent anything from derailing it.[411]

Florence wrote, too, from her vacation home on Squirrel Island, addressing her letter sweetly to "My Dear Governor," and telling him she thought there had been some mistake. "I shall greatly appreciate being set right upon this matter, and appeal to you to use your influence and power to get the F.A.

ratification firmly on the books before the Presidential suffrage bill goes to defeat, as it undoubtedly will if the people vote on it."[412]

For once, it appeared that Maine was in better shape than recent reports indicated; Florence had been right all along. While Governor Milliken was attending a conference out of state, one of his clerks had given out incorrect information regarding the timing of the presidential suffrage referendum. On his return, the governor personally wrote to Alice Paul to set the record straight. "The date of the referendum election on the presidential suffrage bill has not been determined and probably will not be determined until after the special session of the Maine legislature which will be held sometime in the fall...," he assured her. While this was a huge relief to everyone, Alice Paul was leaving nothing to chance. When Margaret Whittemore, then serving as the NWP's National Secretary, was vacationing in Maine later in August, Paul encouraged her to connect with Florence and interview the governor about the prospects of a special session. The governor agreed to see her, and Whittemore reported that he was sure the roads bond would pass on September 8th, making a special session inevitable. If for some reason it did not, he was committed to ensuring that Maine ratified in 1920 and would call a session for that purpose alone.[413,414]

Whittemore was unable to reach Florence, who was still at her summer home on Squirrel Island and far from a telephone. Paul had rerouted Abby Scott Baker from Maine to Salt Lake City in early August, where she was needed to lobby at a regional governors' conference being held there. As the NWP's Political Chairman, Baker had proven to be very effective working at high levels in all political parties to get language inserted in party planks, or resolutions passed. Her trip to Salt Lake City was fruitful: at her urging, the governors passed a resolution encouraging states to schedule special sessions for ratification in time for women to vote in the 1920 elections. From Salt Lake City, Baker traveled on to California, where the NWP was still working on Governor Stephens to call a special session. As he was still reluctant to do so, she expected to be there for some time, so once again her plans to work with Florence in Maine had to be postponed until at least September.[415]

Florence would have liked to have seen Baker, but must have secretly rejoiced a little at this turn of events, for it meant she could have a lengthy and badly needed vacation on Squirrel. Maine was behaving as it should with regard to suffrage, so there was no pressing need for Florence to be raising money or organizing meetings or interviewing politicians. She could walk the paths on the small island, sketch and paint, write, and visit with friends she had barely seen for the last two summers, as suffrage and war work had preempted her vacations.

Florence returned to Portland at the end of August much restored by her "summer outing," as she referred to it. On September 9th she wrote Mabel Vernon to report playfully that the special roads bill had gone through "with a flourish and now the Governor will call a session of the legislature to ratify 'somethin'.'" She was pondering what to do next about the ratification campaign, and, in the short term, she was busy nursing Bob, who was getting his tonsils out, and in visiting with Penn and Dorothy, who were staying with them in Portland until Penn started law school. After these domestic duties were discharged, she would be free to work for suffrage but wondered if that might prove to be counterproductive in the end. "It seems best to let things go as they are going, for if we try to make a fight we will stir up the antis…Advise me if you think differently."[416]

The NWP evidently agreed with Florence that the best strategy was one of watchful waiting, as there was little in the newspapers through September and October about the impending vote. Florence and Robert kept in touch with state legislative leaders, and in DC the national NWP staff did the same, but it appeared that the fight had gone out of the antis. The pro-suffrage forces got an extra boost when the California legislature ratified on November 1st, with a unanimous Senate vote and just two opposed in the House.

MWSA members were feeling quite confident of victory and behaving as if suffrage were an accomplished fact. They had spent much of 1919 preparing a booklet called "The Duty of Women Voters" and organizing county-level MWSA chapters throughout the state that could train women how to handle the vote responsibly. At NAWSA's request, they had also been writing a history of Maine's suffrage work, in which MWSA figured prominently and the NWP (and Florence's) contributions were pointedly ignored. At their annual meeting in October, MWSA officers all spoke as if ratification of the amendment was assured, and they had to be chided by the new president, Mabel Connor, to stay in the fight until the end. She reminded them that "nothing worth having was achieved without effort, reforms do not come automatically…It won't come unless we work for it."[417]

Thus the suffragists were shocked when, just days before the special session convened, the Maine Federation of Labor (MFL) issued a letter opposing ratification of the Federal Amendment on the grounds that "if the

Anthony Amendment is passed it absolutely kills the Referendum." MFL President C. P. Smith of Waterville and Secretary H. B. Brawn of Augusta co-signed the letter and sent it to every state lawmaker. It revealed the surprising statement that "The Referendum Act was fathered by the Labor Organizations; it is our own child. We cannot witness any attempt to nullify it, Directly or Indirectly, without offering a serious protest and opposing such action by every means in our power." Smith and Brawn insisted that they were not trying to influence the outcome of the ratification vote; they just believed that the legislature should not act until the people had had the chance to express their views on the presidential suffrage referendum. "The Labor organizations of Maine believe in law and order," they concluded. "They demand that in this case the spirit of the law be respected by the law-makers."[418]

National labor organizations understood the connection between woman voters and improved labor laws, and had actively supported suffrage for several years, so what was going on in Maine? It is true that Maine suffrage organizations had never joined forces as solidly with labor organizations as other states had; indeed, this failure contributed to the downfall of the 1917 referendum campaign. But there had been no hint from Maine's leading labor group of its intention to oppose ratification. Quite the contrary, it had passed several resolutions in recent years calling for Congress to pass the Federal Amendment. The pro-suffrage forces scrambled to find out what was behind this surprise announcement and to counter its effects. They had to respond quickly or ratification, which so recently had seemed to be a sure thing in Maine, could be in jeopardy. Florence sent a frantic telegram to Alice Paul early in the morning on October 29th, explaining the situation and asking for help.[419]

Paul took the threat seriously and marshaled a swift response. In a return telegram, she urged Florence to contact the Woman's Trade Union League in Boston to send up an organizer to reach out to women workers in Maine and put pressure on the MFL. The American section of the International Woman's Labor Congress happened to be meeting in Washington, DC, at that time, and Paul persuaded them to pass a resolution calling on Maine to ratify. The National Woman's Trade Union League paid to have a copy of this resolution sent to every member of the Maine legislature. The NWP also mailed each Maine legislator a copy of the resolution passed by the American Federation of Labor at its national convention urging suffrage ratification. Finally, NWP organizer Elizabeth Kalb was dispatched to Hagerstown, Maryland, where the

Farmers National Congress was in session, to urge them to call on Maine and other states to ratify the Federal Amendment. This they speedily agreed to do, and sent a copy of their resolution to every Maine state legislator.[420,421]

The American Federation of Labor (AFL) had passed a resolution in June urging state legislatures to ratify the Federal Amendment, and declared it would "do all in its power to aid in the speedy consummation of this last step in woman's enfranchisement, as it has ever aided throughout the long struggle." On hearing from Paul that the MFL was opposing ratification, Frank Morrison, the AFL secretary, wrote MFL Secretary Brawn to remind him of the national organization's position on this issue. He pointedly instructed Brawn what he ought to do: "Pursuant to the foregoing, your organization is requested to give all possible assistance in having the members of the Maine legislature vote for the ratification of the measure, when it is brought up. Hoping to receive a favorable reply...."[422,423]

Dora Lewis was already in Maine helping Florence with last-minute arrangements, and Alice Paul arrived in Maine a few days before the special session opened to take charge of the final lobbying effort. It was becoming abundantly clear that they could not depend on any state to ratify without a struggle, and the incident with the MFL demonstrated that the antis still had substantial strength in Maine.

The editor of the *Kennebec Journal*, Lewis Burleigh, was a vital source of aid to the suffragists during this difficult time. He and Florence were well acquainted, as he had also been born and grew up in Augusta. His father, Edwin C. Burleigh, had been governor of Maine from 1889 to 1893, had served in the US House of Representatives from 1897 to 1911, and was elected to the US Senate in 1913, dying in office in 1916. He had become the principal owner of the *Kennebec Journal* in the 1880s. Edwin's brother, Albert C., had served on the board of Florence's Suffrage Referendum League in 1917. While Lewis Burleigh could not avoid printing the antis' political advertisements, or news of the MFL's opposition to ratification, he very obligingly made the pro-suffrage ads and letters front-page news as well. He also wrote several editorials supporting suffrage. The NWP then placed copies of the newspaper on the desks of every member of the legislature.

On the eve of the special session, the Maine branch of the NWP held a great "Ratification Dinner" at the Congress Square Hotel in Portland. Once again, the purple, white, and gold banners of the NWP were brought out to decorate the walls, and huge bouquets of yellow flowers were placed at intervals around the room (in deference to the fact that it was November, these were chrysanthemums, not jonquils). There was a celebratory tone to the affair, whose official purpose was to honor the work of Alice Paul and the National Woman's Party. Louisine (Mrs. H. O.) Havermeyer traveled to Maine from New York to share in the honors. Havermeyer was a wealthy art collector and philanthropist who had donated substantial sums of money to the NWP and was a fearless and outspoken suffrage leader. She had been arrested and sentenced for five days in the DC jail at the final watch fire demonstration in February, which earned her a spot on the Prison Special that toured the country later that month. Every available seat was taken at the round tables that filled the dining room, by women and men who wished to pay tribute to Paul and the party she had created.[424]

Florence presided at the long head table with Alice Paul on her right and Louisine Havermeyer on her left. With them sat Dora Lewis, Lois Warren Shaw (chair of the New Hampshire branch), and Grace Hill and Mrs. Warren of the Maine branch. After the plates were removed from dinner, Florence rose to make a few remarks and to introduce the speakers. She touched on Maine's unusual situation of having to act on both the presidential suffrage bill and the federal suffrage amendment, just managing to refrain from blasting MWSA leaders too much for their foolishness in causing this predicament. She also spoke of the support the Federal Amendment enjoyed among the state's political leaders, and confidently predicted a favorable vote of 116 in the House and 20 in the Senate.

Dora Lewis spoke next, followed by Havermeyer, and then Paul made the final speech of the night. All three women spoke frankly of their activism, their arrests, and the time they had spent in prison. While this was generally a friendly crowd, many of the guests had been troubled by the NWP's picketing, burning of Wilson's speeches, and willingness to risk imprisonment. Many had condemned it, at least privately, and only Florence had been willing to defend it publicly. What did they make of these gentle, educated women, clad in elegant evening gowns, who showed not the least embarrassment at what they had done and insisted that their actions had been instrumental in bringing the suffrage campaign to a more rapid conclusion? These women were unafraid of public criticism and disgrace in their pursuit of justice. They knew how to work the crowd; they had them laughing at some amusing incident in one minute, and, in the next minute, soberly reflecting on the similarities between NWP activists and Joan of Arc, Galileo, and Abraham Lincoln. Alice

Paul even managed to imbue the speech-burning with a symbolic beauty and poetry: the president's words had not been consigned to flames on the sidewalk or in a rusty old trash can, but "in a beautiful Grecian urn in which a watch fire was burning day and night, in front of the White House." By the time Alice Paul got to the "money speech," her plea for funds to support the ratification work that remained, the listeners were completely won over. Within minutes, they had passed up to the front the staggering sum of $815, a remarkable achievement from a small group of people in conservative, tight-fisted Maine. It was a stirring tribute to the courage and tenacity of Alice Paul and her associates in the NWP.

Governor Milliken called Maine's legislature into special session on November 4th, a Tuesday. While the roads bill was a big item on the agenda, everyone knew that the most important business in front of the lawmakers was ratification, which would be brought up for debate on the first day of the session. Florence, Paul, Lewis, and several other suffragists from Portland traveled up to Augusta to monitor the proceedings. In his opening speech, Governor Milliken urged the legislators to ratify the Federal Amendment. It was simply the right thing to do, Milliken insisted. "[I]t is not a question of how many women are seeking the right of suffrage and…if only one woman in Maine wants the vote it should be granted her."[425]

The Senate was the first to act on the measure. Senator LeRoy R. Folsom of Somerset County introduced the resolve and moved that it be voted on with "yeas and nays." Opponents made a feeble attempt to derail this. Senator Alfred Ames from Washington County moved that the issue be referred to the regular session of the next legislature so that Maine men would have an opportunity to vote on the presidential suffrage bill first. Ames sided with those who believed it was underhanded for the legislature to ratify the Federal Amendment before the people had had their say. He saw no difference between the presidential suffrage bill and the Federal Amendment. "It matters not whether she is dressed in a hobble skirt or an evening gown, she is the same old girl," he quipped.[426]

Senator Folsom had no patience with Ames's position. Everyone was well acquainted with arguments for and against suffrage, he pointed out, and there was no point in discussing the merits of the issue any longer. It was time to get on with the vote. This they soon did and it sailed cleanly through the Senate on a vote of 24 to 5 with two members absent, an even better showing than Florence had predicted the night before.

The House proved more difficult, however. The last-minute opposition from the MFL had had the desired effect, and support for the Federal Amendment was eroding quickly. The suffragists had discovered that MFL Secretary Brawn was employed by one of Maine's most prominent anti leaders. His boss had encouraged him to issue the letter, which reflected Brawn's beliefs only; he had not consulted the general membership and they had not voted to publish the letter. On Tuesday afternoon following the successful Senate vote, with the House scheduled to consider ratification the next morning, Florence, Alice Paul, and Dora Lewis met with the MFL officers in an eleventh-hour effort to reverse the damage the letter had done.[427]

The meeting dragged on for hours. Secretary Brawn could not be present for the first part, and the women had to content themselves with persuading MFL's President Smith and Treasurer Fitzgerald to recant. The officers stubbornly resisted this, eventually going off to find Brawn and explain to him what they were being pressured to do. Brawn later claimed that when Fitzgerald absolutely refused to issue a letter supporting suffrage, the women gave up on him and concentrated their efforts on Smith and Brawn. When Brawn met with them, it appears that Florence took the gloves off, threatening that he should give up any political ambitions unless he reversed his stance on ratification. "I was told that already plans were being made in their vicinities to GET ME, and that in the end I would be placed in OBLIVION," he later complained. He refused to yield, and at last the exasperated women turned their attention back to President Smith, who, for whatever reason, was more malleable. Brawn was unsure exactly what arguments against Smith eventually triumphed. "The only reason that I can see to explain it was that he got cold feet, or his brain had a storm and refused to stand for his previous act." We will never know exactly what arm-twisting Florence and Paul employed, but at some point it must have become clear to Smith that these angry women were simply not going to accept no for an answer. When the meeting finally adjourned, Florence had a statement signed by Smith (that Brawn claimed she wrote out for him) placing all the blame for the previous letter squarely on Brawn's shoulders, and calling on the legislature to ratify the Federal Amendment *(see Figure 17)*. The following morning, as House members showed up for their session, each found a copy of the *Kennebec Journal* on his desk folded neatly to display a paid political announcement printed boldly in the lower left-hand corner of the newspaper's front page.[428,429,430]

The NWP had scored an impressive victory by getting Smith to sign

PRESIDENT MAINE FEDERATION
OF LABOR FAVORS RATIFICATION
FEDERAL SUFFRAGE AMENDMENT
BY THE MAINE LEGISLATURE

The National Woman's Party leaders in Augusta met in conference with President, Secretary and Treasurer of the Maine Federation of Labor Tuesday afternoon to talk over the letter which was published and sent to the members of the Legislature and signed by the Pres. C.P. Smith and the Secretary H.B. Brawn. It developed in the course of the conference that the letter was instigated and written by the secretary with no suggestion from the main body of the State Federation which has four times indorsed woman suffrage—and the other members of the Executive Board, three in number were telephoned and asked to stand for the sentiments therein expressed. President Smith made the following statement and signed his name to it, at the same time authorizing its publication.

"I believe the Legislature should ratify the Federal Suffrage Amendment at this session.

(Signed)   C.P. Smith"

FLORENCE BROOKS WHITEHOUSE
Chairman Maine Branch
Nat. Woman's Party

FIGURE 17 From the Kennebec Journal , November 5th, 1919.

this statement, but would it be enough to save ratification in Maine? The antis were in no way ready to concede the fight. Their hopes were pinned on Representative Sherman L. Berry of Waterville, who had led opposition to the suffrage referendum in 1917. When House Speaker Frank Farrington brought the session to order, Berry quickly rose to move that the ratification vote be delayed until the regular session of the next legislature, just as Ames had proposed in the Senate. He was a split second too late, however; Farrington first recognized Representative Percival Baxter from Portland, who moved that the Senate vote to ratify immediately. Berry persevered, pressing his motion and protesting that it was unfair to the people for the legislature to act first. "All through this great land of ours there is a spirit of unrest, and I think one reason for it is the forcing down throats of men what they do not want. Why this seeming haste to adopt the Susan B. Anthony amendment? Are the supporters of this afraid to trust the people at home?"[431]

Seeming haste? Susan B. Anthony had first introduced her amendment to Congress in 1878, more than 40 years before, and the Maine legislature had considered the issue on many occasions since. This was no rush to judgment; it was the culmination of decades of exhausting work by millions of suffrage supporters. The answer to Berry's final question was clearly yes—there was no faith that the voters would do the right thing and support ratification—but as in the Senate, the pro-suffrage forces had no intention of debating ratification endlessly. Baxter urged them to get on with the vote. Speaker Farrington ruled that Baxter's motion had precedence over Berry's and began calling the roll. By the time they were halfway through, so many votes were negative that the antis began to smile, anticipating victory. The suffragists watched helplessly as many men who had assured them of their support voted against ratification. It hardly seemed possible that they could get this close and lose, especially when victory had seemed such a sure thing just a week before. Toward the end, though, the "yeas" came more frequently, and the final tally was 72–68 in favor. Applause swept the room, lasting several minutes as the relieved suffragists celebrated the end of a very long journey. A watching reporter observed that the rejoicing practically "assumed the proportions of a demonstration" because it continued so long, perhaps a sly nudge at Alice Paul and the other NWP members who were among those celebrating.

Maine was the 19th state to ratify the 19th Amendment! Instantly the antis began calling for reconsideration of the vote, and for several tense hours it appeared that this might actually occur. The antis claimed they had lined up

10 House members who would change their votes. Suffragists countered that 14 members had said they would switch to "yea" if the vote were reconsidered, but they were understandably leery of putting this to the test, so they renewed their lobbying of House members to prevent it from happening. Fortunately, most legislators were weary of suffrage and accepted that its adoption was inevitable, so they agreed to let the results stand.

Two days after the vote, Florence passed Representative Berry in the lobby outside the House chambers. He gave her a brief nod as he went by and she smiled at him, half-nodding in return. He continued on a few paces, then wheeled around and came back, saying to her, "You have been in this legislature two years, Mrs. Whitehouse, and that is the first sign of recognition you have ever given me."

Florence was a little taken aback by this. "Why should I recognize you, Mr. Berry; I don't know you and I am not in the habit of speaking to men I don't know," she replied.

Berry pointed out that she certainly knew who he was, just as he knew her by sight, and that, in any case, her lobbying frequently required her to speak to men with whom she had no acquaintance.

Florence agreed that this was so, but noted that she had tried in those circumstances to have someone introduce her properly. But knowing that he was the leader of the opposition, "...there was no reason I should try to meet you."

Berry chose to take this personally. "I am not a bad sort of man, Mrs. Florence; in fact, some people think I am rather decent, but you have made me feel as though I have a black stripe down my back," he complained.

"Thank you, Mr. Berry," said Florence dryly, curtseying. "I did not know I had that much power." She reiterated that she had not bothered to approach him because she knew that he was an anti, and "...it would be a waste of time to go to you when you had spoken against the bill I was interested in and had led the fight against it."

Berry insisted that he might have been willing to change his mind, but then proceeded to list a string of reasons why he remained opposed to woman suffrage. Florence just listened, not bothering to argue as he ranted on. [432]

"You won in the House, Mrs. Florence, by a turn of the hand," he whined. "The Speaker recognized Mr. Baxter before he did me and we were on our feet at the same time. If he had recognized me, my motion to postpone would have won by ten votes."

"That is the fortune of war, Mr. Berry," replied Florence crisply, losing patience with him. "Time and again we have had anti Speakers in the House and lost." On this key vote, it had gone the suffragists' way, yet there had been so many times when backroom deals had brought defeats when they had thought victory was in their grasp. To Florence's delight, as other legislators walked back and forth through the hall, they correctly divined that Berry was whining to Florence about the vote. One after another, they stopped to clap Berry on the shoulder and advise him not to be a crybaby, to bear up like a man, and to accept that the suffragists had won in a clean fight. After some time, he grudgingly admitted the truth of this, and tried to leave the conversation on a more positive note, saying that he had respect for her sincerity and wished her no ill.

Victory was sweet, and Florence was more than willing to savor the antis' loss, particularly after they published an article in their weekly national newspaper, *The Woman Patriot*, attacking her methods of persuading President Smith to sign his pro-ratification statement. "Aren't they wretched losers?" she joked in a letter to Lewis Burleigh thanking him for coming to their aid in the recent session. "Their love of vituperative criticism of women in general and some women in particular is almost beyond belief, and makes one really wonder if it's safe to let such women participate in full citizenship...I am not going to write anything more about it for it is not worth noticing but it does exasperate one to have to deal even so slightly with such people."[433]

Florence could not resist one last broadside to the National Association Opposed to Woman Suffrage, however. She wrote them a scathing letter, and surprisingly, since it was decidedly uncomplimentary, they elected to publish some of it. Since many suffragists subscribed to *The Woman Patriot* to keep tabs on what the opposition was up to, they must have been delighted to read her strongly worded denunciation.

There is no money which I expend which I feel is so little worthwhile as the money which pays for your publication. There is no time which I feel is so nearly wasted as the time it takes to read that same sheet. After I have finished reading each edition of the paper I feel as if I had been reading the *Police Gazette* and need a mental and moral bath. How you women can be willing to be scavengers in a world which has so many beautiful things in it passes my comprehension, and incidentally your attitude toward women and toward life in general is the strongest argument I have ever seen for anti-suffrage...

You ask for my opinion of THE WOMAN PATRIOT. I believe, with the

New York Tribune, that it is an insult to the womanhood of America, that it is vulgar, vituperative, and unfair...Only cremation could improve the future of THE WOMAN PATRIOT.

****

On November 7th, Governor Milliken held a ceremony to sign the letter notifying the US Secretary of State that Maine had ratified the Susan B. Anthony Amendment. In recognition of this historic occasion, he invited six women to witness his signature. Florence stood directly behind the governor, with her good friend and vice chairman Grace Hill directly to her right *(see Figure 18)*. Representing MWSA were Mabel Connor, its current president; Katherine Reed Balentine, Legislative Committee chairman; and Gertrude McKenzie Pattangall, Corresponding Secretary. Also in the group was Anne Gannett, president of the Augusta Suffrage Association. A photograph of the event shows the six women standing around the desk, watching the governor as he signs. Florence's rather mannish hat is cocked at a jaunty angle, her hand rests casually on the back of the governor's chair, and she seems to be hiding a smile. The cause of this hidden amusement, perhaps, was the fact that the feathers of the quill the governor was using were dyed the purple, white, and gold of the National Woman's Party. This was a ceremonial pen the NWP national headquarters had commissioned specifically for ratification ceremonies, and it was sent from state to state as needed.[434]

Governor Milliken was surely aware of what the colors meant, and of MWSA's longstanding animosity toward the NWP. He used the pen anyway, and then added a twist of his own. Following the signing, he presented each woman with a souvenir: the four MWSA representatives and Grace Hill each received a pen made out of steel; to Florence, in recognition of her leadership and perhaps with a nod to her outlaw sympathies, the governor gave a pearl-handled gold pen.[435]

The newspapers reported these little distinctions factually without pursuing their meaning any further, and they were quickly forgotten. Certainly, MWSA leaders never admitted publicly that their radical sister organization deserved any credit for helping to win suffrage in Maine. Indeed, it was at this early date that they took steps to expunge the NWP almost entirely from Maine's written suffrage history. The history MWSA forwarded to NAWSA mentions the NWP branch only in passing, as an annoying and troublesome fringe group

FIGURE 18 Governor Carl Milliken signing the ratification of the 19th Amendment. From right to left standing behind him are Florence Brooks Whitehouse, Grace Hill, Mabel Connor, Mrs. Arthur T Balentine, Mrs. Guy (Anne) Gannett, and Mrs. William R. (Gertrude) Pattangall.
The Sewall-Belmont House Collection.

that did more harm than good. Florence's name was connected primarily to the NWP as a rabble-rouser, her early contributions to MWSA barely mentioned.

Nevertheless, the intense last-minute lobbying from the NWP almost certainly saved the day for the pro-ratification forces. While earlier polls had shown solid support among legislators for the Federal Amendment, the antis had quietly persuaded many legislators to change their positions. Public opposition from Maine's labor leaders just days before the session began, when it was almost too late to counteract it, very nearly lost them the House vote. Interestingly, while members of MWSA were present in Augusta during the special session, the newspaper accounts make no mention of MWSA activities at all. NAWSA sent no national organizers to help with the lobbying effort, and MWSA members were simply not up to employing the sort of tough tactics that the NWP used to deliver the ratification vote in Maine.

For her part, Alice Paul was more concerned with *making* history than recording it. After Maine ratified, there were 17 states remaining before the Federal Amendment would become part of the US Constitution, and winning the last few states turned out to be every bit as grueling as getting the last few votes in the US Senate had been. Only after the last state ratified did the NWP begin actively planning its future, looking ahead rather than examining its past. As a result, there was never a parallel pressure from the NWP on its state branches to record their histories, for their own sakes or for inclusion in an official history of the organization, although several of her top organizers wrote books about it. Paul took credit for maneuvering the Federal Amendment through Congress and through the state ratification process, but she and her supporters were already turning their attention to the next big challenge: persuading the country to recognize equal rights for women.

Ratification did not end the suffrage battles in Maine completely. Immediately following the vote, the antis had signaled that they would accept the outcome, but some weeks later they sued the state on the grounds that Maine's Constitution allowed ratification of federal constitutional amendments only via citizen referendum. Maine was one of six states where antis launched these suits after their legislatures had ratified the amendment, and eventually Ohio's case made its way to the United States Supreme Court. In June 1920, the Supreme Court justices ruled unanimously that the US Constitution provided for state legislatures, not citizen referendum campaigns, to ratify amendments, so all referenda organized for that purpose were invalid. Maine suffragists had to wait eight long months after their legislature had ratified while the case wound through the Supreme Court process, and during this time, they could not be confident that the results would stand. Since the issue was in the courts, there was little they could do to influence the outcome, but it also meant that they had to remain vigilant until the matter was decided.[436,437]

Only after the Supreme Court had ruled and full woman suffrage had become the law of the land did Maine finally get around to voting on its presidential suffrage referendum. Interestingly, the state's constitution had provisions for holding a referendum vote but not for canceling one; once it was on the ballot the voters had to have their say. In September 1920, women voters helped pass the measure easily with 88,080 in favor and 30,462 opposed. MWSA leaders were quick to claim the results showed strong support for suffrage, which, on the face of it, certainly seemed true. Yet the strength of the opposition vote was surprising. While it was lower than the 38,000 votes polled against suffrage in 1917, this was three years later and full suffrage was already an established fact. There were no exit polls or any other way of knowing how men and women had voted on this issue, but it seems clear that many Maine men still did not approve of woman suffrage. If men alone had voted on the presidential suffrage referendum, they might well have rejected it, ensuring the defeat of ratification by the legislature. Florence and the NWP had been right to insist that the legislature ratify before the presidential suffrage measure went to the voters.

X   The Great Adventure

Free at last from the disapproval that had accompanied the NWP's more controversial actions, and from her responsibilities at home and with the Red Cross, Florence traveled down to DC to take part in discussions the NWP held in January 1921 to consider its future. While there, she attended a ceremony at the Capitol organized by the NWP and other suffrage groups (although NAWSA stuffily refused to take part). The ceremony was designed to mark the end of the fight for woman suffrage, and had all the pageantry and symbolism typical of NWP events. It culminated in the presentation of a sculpture honoring Lucretia Mott, Elizabeth Cady Stanton, and Susan B. Anthony, the founding mothers of the movement. This was given to Congress to be displayed in the Capitol.

After the ceremony the NWP got down to the business of determining its future. There was no need for a name change since, as Maude Wood Park had once pointed out, the words "woman suffrage" had never been included in its title. The new mission and goals required careful thought, however. The executive committee, the National Advisory Council, and the state chairmen all met separately to develop separate recommendations. After this, the full NWP membership came together in a week-long conference to consider the recommendations from these earlier sessions. Florence presided over the third day of the conference proceedings, when the state chairmen reported their findings. At the end of the conference, the membership was united in their decision to change the focus of the NWP to working for women's rights, resolving that "this new organization stand for the equality of women and see that such equality be won and maintained in any association of nations that may be established, and that the immediate work of the new organization be the removal of legal disabilities of women."[438,439,440]

When Florence returned home, the Maine branch enthusiastically endorsed the NWP's new mission. Florence continued to serve as chairman of the Maine branch, lobbying the congressional delegation to support the new constitutional amendment Alice Paul was promoting to give women equal rights with men. She was one of a small group of women (about 22 in 1921) who agreed to serve on the NWP's National Council, and she was still serving as state chairman for Maine as late as 1938.[441]

NAWSA was going through its own reorganization. Even before ratification was complete, Carrie Chapman Catt had led NAWSA in a discussion about its future, which focused on the need to educate women on how to use their votes responsibly. At a national conference in the spring of 1919, the membership approved new language stipulating that, when the 36th state ratified, NAWSA would automatically dissolve and be reconstituted as the League of Women Voters. State branches were urged to follow suit, and so it was that shortly after Maine ratified woman suffrage, MWSA members held a big celebration tea at which they happily voted to change its name and purpose. Florence remained estranged from her former suffrage colleagues, however, and it was several years before she joined the League.

However, she wasted no time in putting her suffrage skills to work in new causes. Before Maine ratified, she had agreed to chair the Home Directorate of the newly organized Maine Chamber of Commerce and Agriculture. Florence was the only woman on the executive council of the statewide group, which included prominent men such as Maine Secretary of Labor Roscoe Eddy. The group was designed to have a broad reach, encompassing all aspects of work, home, and society. In this way, the Chamber could examine problems simultaneously from many different perspectives and come up with a balanced solution. The Chamber was heralded as an innovative approach to solving society's problems, and was thought to be something that many other states would emulate. Certainly, it was unusual for women's interests and the home to be considered on the same plane as transportation or business development, and Florence was thrilled to be part of it. In her new role, she spoke frequently at community clubs, regional conferences around the state, and at meetings of granges in Maine and New Hampshire.[442]

While anxious to better the conditions of women working within and outside of the home, and of families and children, Florence believed strongly that it was her duty as a voting woman to stay abreast of world events. She remained a pacifist and was deeply committed to developing strategies to prevent future wars. She advocated publicly for the proposed League of Nations and chaired Maine's branch of the Women's Committee on World Disarmament.

Added to these responsibilities were a wide range of other charitable, social, and artistic endeavors that kept her busy and engaged. The first years of the 1920s were a heady period; women had not only won the right to vote but had helped bring about national prohibition as well. They were running for public office, sitting on juries, and persuading local and state lawmakers to pass laws favorable to families and children. With suffrage behind them, women knew how to organize and could be confident that, even if they did not achieve all their goals immediately, hard work and unwavering focus would get them where they wanted to go. There were opportunities to be active in local, state, national, and international issues, and Florence found ways to participate in many of these.

It was not long, though, before family duties called her back. Robert was not well, the victim of a lingering illness that sapped his strength and left him unable to work. Concerned, Florence traveled with him to the Bahamas in 1921 and 1922, hoping that the sun and an extended rest would speed his recovery. She was in the Bahamas with Robert in 1922 when she received word that her beloved mother had died, hard enough for Florence to endure but even sadder for having been absent during her final days. This added to her grief as Robert slipped further into a decline from which he never recovered. He died of pneumonia in Portland in February 1924.

Florence was devastated by Robert's death. He had been a true soul mate; they had connected on a deep emotional level and he had steadfastly supported all of her activities in a way that few wives of that period could expect from their husbands. Throughout their marriage, they had collaborated on all their projects, from producing plays to raising children or promoting social welfare legislation. It was Robert who had pushed her to write and publish her first book. He had joined her fight for suffrage, founding and chairing the Men's Equal Suffrage League, and had generously written checks to cover the cost of mailings, organizers, and other campaign expenses. He was also an invaluable advisor, providing her with critical insights into how to influence legislators and other key decision makers. Even when he differed with the NWP over its more controversial tactics, he championed its goal of passing the Federal Amendment; at times he might have forbidden Florence to picket the White House, but he never demanded that she sever her ties to the NWP.

She missed him terribly. Their lives had been so intertwined that there was virtually no area in which his absence was not keenly felt. In the following poem she grieves for the life they had together and for her loss.

The Great Adventure

We called Life the Great Adventure you and I
That day when first we told our love
And gazed with starry eyes all down the years.
And when as man & wife we left the gathered throng
And faced the friendly dark
You held me close and whispered "Great Adventure" still.
The little tousled heads which came,
To break our treasured solitude
Brought each the thrill of untried paths
And charmedly we followed where they led.
The "Great Adventure"! All the lure uncharted seas
Hold to the sailor, all sails set were ours.
And then the greatest of them all you said
That last adventure—Death
But on it you fare forth alone dear heart
And I bereft kneel sobbing in the dark.[443]

It was some time before Florence found the strength to become active again, but when she was ready, she did so with her customary total commitment. In the late 1920s, she rededicated herself to the peace movement. Over the next ten years, she joined the National Council on Prevention of War, chaired the Government and International Cooperation Committee of the Maine League of Women Voters, served as the state Chairman of Government and International Cooperation for the Maine Federation of Churches, and represented the State Peace Commission on the World Unity Council. She did radio broadcasts on WGAN discussing peace and disarmament, and continued to promote the League of Nations. These activities assumed a new urgency as Hitler rose to power in Germany.

She stayed abreast of politics and current events, maintaining thick files of press clippings on topics including immigration, birth control, and illiteracy, as well as on music, art, and science, among many other subjects. She particularly

enjoyed political cartoons and clipped those regularly. In 1935 she accepted
a two-year term as Chair of the Department of Legislation for the Maine
Federation of Women's Clubs.

While Florence stayed busy with peace projects and other community work,
she also returned to her artistic roots and managed to have some fun besides.
Just after New Year's in 1930, she and her old friend Grace Hill drove across
the country to visit Florence's brother Percy out in California. They stayed
with friends when they could or in small hotels, sightseeing and taking their
time. Grace was also an accomplished artist, and they stopped to paint or
sketch whenever they saw an interesting subject. They were on the road almost
six months, returning to Maine in early June. Florence drove the entire way
except for a forty-minute stretch through the Mojave Desert, where the road
was so straight and flat that Grace felt she could take the wheel.[444]

Florence and Grace both joined the Haylofters, an artists' cooperative that
quite literally occupied space in a barn loft off of Congress Street in Portland.
Membership in the Haylofters was by invitation only, and it included a number
of other locally prominent artists, including Josiah L. Tubby. There was work
space in the loft and room for exhibitions as well. Florence often went on
painting excursions with friends, out into the countryside, to Monhegan Island,
and occasionally as far as the Gaspé Peninsula.

Painting came to be Florence's chief pastime after her community work. In
the early 1930s, she wrote another novel that she was unable to get published.
With the nation gripped by the Great Depression, her agent told her that the
publishing houses were only taking on "sure things," and her novel did not fit
the profile. Florence was deeply discouraged by her inability to get published
again and seems to have largely given up on her creative writing after that.

The Depression took its toll on the Whitehouse family fortunes as it did on
so many other people during that period, including her friends the Gannetts
(with whom she was now reconciled). In 1933 Florence was forced to sell the
great house on Vaughn Street and move in with Penn, who was then living
in a mansion he and his wife had built in Falmouth. When Penn's marriage
to Dorothy Case dissolved, the Falmouth house, too, was sold and Florence
moved back into Portland to live in a series of small apartments, including one
that was hardly more than a room attached to Penn's law offices. Through it all,
she was resolutely cheerful, declaring that she was happy not to have the care
of a large house so she could spend more time doing what she liked to do. One
of those things was going to the movies; Penn's offices were on the top floor of

the State Street Theatre on Congress Street, so when she lived there she could see movies whenever she pleased.

Penn eventually moved away, first to Michigan and then to California. Bob had married but divorced within a few years; he remained single after that and had no children. He started a paving business in Portland and lived nearby so he could help Florence out if she needed him, and when she went on painting expeditions with friends, he often served as the chauffeur. Brooks returned to Portland when he finished Harvard Law School. He married Anne Bradstreet Darling and they had three children, Priscilla, Anne, and Brooks. Having raised only sons, Florence was thrilled with her granddaughters and was particularly close to Priscilla. Brooks took to living out in Raymond at Camp Aqueni from April through November, so first Priscilla and later Anne lived with Florence in Portland while they attended Waynflete School.

As time wore on, the hectic suffrage years receded ever more into the background. Florence became known locally for her efforts to promote peace, for her art, and for her involvement with the State Street Church, where she taught Sunday school. Her involvement with the NWP officially ended around 1938, after 23 years of serving as chairman of the Maine branch. Her granddaughter Priscilla recalls many conversations about current events and world affairs, especially during those winters when she stayed with Florence in Portland. Florence appears not to have reminisced much about her suffrage work, though. She did tell Priscilla that she "lost a lot of friends" working for suffrage because they disagreed on how to go about it. She never seemed particularly bothered by this, merely remarking that friends like that had not been worth having in the first place. To her grandchildren, she was just a comfortable grandmother with a lively mind and a great sense of humor. They also knew her as a painter with an assortment of eccentric artist friends. From time to time, they heard reference to her suffrage activities, but they had no inkling of her leadership or level of activism. With WW II raging, everyone's attention was focused on that, and no one cared about a time more than 20 years in the past when women were denied the right to vote.

In the early 1940s, with the Depression over, her sons pooled their resources to buy Florence a lovely farm out in East Raymond. The house sat in the middle of a hundred acres of sloping fields and woods, with views of the White Mountains to the west, and it was less than a mile from Camp Aqueni on Panther Pond. It was part Christmas present, and part thank-you to her for having stoically endured her more straightened circumstances in the previous ten years. She was delighted with this gift and loved spending time out there in the summer, although she continued living in an apartment at 33 West Street in Portland during the winter.

One chilly January day in 1945 she called her daughter-in-law, Anne, to say that she felt ill. Anne was concerned and went over right away to find Florence in bed, resting and feeling a little weak. After chatting for a bit, Florence agreed a cup of tea would be nice, so Anne went off to the kitchen to put the kettle on. She thought she heard a cry and went back to the bedroom to investigate, only to find that Florence had suffered a heart attack. She died peacefully in her own bed with a minimum of fuss, which is no doubt just how she would have wanted it to be.

Florence died in the waning months of WW II. Eight months after she died, the first atomic bombs would be dropped on Hiroshima and Nagasaki, ushering in the nuclear age and the Cold War. The fight for women's rights took a backseat to the country's recovery, and woman suffrage history was generally forgotten. The 1960s revived interest in women's issues, and research uncovered the stories of Alice Paul and the National Woman's Party, and the National American Woman Suffrage Association as they fought to wrest voting rights from a reluctant nation. Yet the stories of women who led the suffrage battles at the local and state level have remained largely untold.

Florence was a remarkable woman of many talents who used them all in service to her family, her community, to women, and to the world at large. She deserves recognition for challenging the rigid bonds of social convention that held women to a lesser role, seeking to silence their voices and weaken their influence. She distinguished herself from her Maine peers by understanding from an early stage that the real fight was not just about suffrage, but about women's right to define themselves and to control their own destinies unfettered by what men and society at large thought they should be. Ironically, while this put her at odds with other Maine suffragists who thought her too radical, she came under equal pressure from Alice Paul and other NWP activists for not being radical enough. Through all of this, Florence stubbornly worked for what she believed, but did so in a way that allowed her to continue to function within her family and community.

Ultimately, Florence's story is a study in leadership. Alice Paul and her colleagues in the national office exhibited one type of leadership as they launched the unpopular picketing and willingly risked imprisonment, hunger strikes, and forced feedings, not to mention the wrath of NAWSA and a good chunk of society. Through a world war and a major influenza epidemic, among other challenges, they refused to be distracted from the goal of winning woman suffrage. They continued to work for women's rights long after suffrage was won, never achieving their aim of making the Equal Rights Amendment part of the US Constitution but helping to advance the cause nonetheless. They took enormous risks and richly deserve our admiration and thanks for what they accomplished.

Florence's allegiances were more varied and complex, demanding her leadership on a number of different levels. As a married woman with children, she had a responsibility to her family's health and welfare that she took seriously and refused to sacrifice for her other causes. When her children needed her, as when Brooks contracted polio and required operations as part of his recovery, they were her first priority. During WW I she turned from suffrage for long periods in order to devote herself to Red Cross work because she perceived that her community had the greatest need of her skills. Workers in every cause she dedicated herself to recognized her many strengths and elevated her to high-ranking positions. She never fully abandoned any of the causes she passionately supported, but simply juggled them so that each received her best effort when her influence was most needed and she could be most effective. Throughout, she remained true to the vision she recited to the Maine Judiciary Committee in 1917: "…the world is mine, as yours/ The pulsing strength and passion and heart of it;/ The work I set my hands to, women's work,/ Because I set my hand to it."

END NOTES

i   "Record Crowd Hears Debate on Suffrage," Daily Eastern Argus, February 2, 1917.

ii   Florence Brooks Whitehouse to Senator Jones, FBW Papers, Box 2 Folder 2, undated.

iii   National Woman's Party to Florence Brooks Whitehouse, FBW Papers, Box 2 Folder 2, January 1, 1919.

iv   Lucy Burns to Florence Brooks Whitehouse, November 6, 1917, FBW Papers, Box 2, Folder 5.

v   Agger, Lee, Women of Maine, Guy Gannett Publishing Co., Portland, ME, 1982.

1   "Hamlin Lecture Course held in the Congress Square Hotel," *Portland Sunday Telegram*, January 19, 1913. See also *Portland Sunday Telegram,* January 27, 1913.

2   Varney, Geo. J. *History of Augusta, Maine,* Boston, MA, B. B. Russell (1886).

3   Varney, Geo. J., *History of Augusta, Maine,* Boston, MA: B. B. Russell (1886).

4   Burt, Elizabeth V. *The Progressive Era Primary Documents on Events from 1890 to 1914,* Westport, CT, Greenwood Press, 2004.

5   Marquis, Albert N., ed. *Who's Who in New England*, 2nd ed. Chicago: A. N. Marquis & Company (1909).

6   Ibid.

7   "Timely Sketches of People Prominent in the Public Eye," *Portland Sunday Telegram,* April 23, 1905.

8   Unfortunately, her plays have not survived, probably lost in a house fire at Florence's East Raymond farmhouse in 1947.

9   "Florence B. Whitehouse, An Accomplished Maine Writer," *Lewiston Journal,* April 12, 1902.

10   Ibid. Eugene Scribe (1791–1861) was a famous French playwright. According to the Encyclopedia Britannica he is credited with the perfection of the "well-made play," which "called for complex and highly artificial plotting, a build-up of suspense, a climactic scene in which all problems are resolved, and a happy ending."

11   "Florence B. Whitehouse," *Book News*, Philadelphia, PA, June 1902.

12   "Florence B. Whitehouse, an Accomplished Maine Writer," *Lewiston Journal*, April 12, 1902; "The God of Things," *The New York Times*, May 17, 1902; "The God of Things," *The World*, Cleveland, OH, May 18, 1902.

13   Whitehouse, Florence Brooks. *The God of Things: A Novel of Modern Egypt*, Boston: Little, Brown and Company (1902).

14   Senator William P. Frye to Florence Brooks Whitehouse, June 2, 1902, Gass family private collection.

15   "Timely Sketches of Portland People Prominent in the Public Eye," *Portland Sunday Telegram*, April 23, 1905.

16   Whitehouse, Florence Brooks. *The Effendi: A Romance of the Soudan*, Boston: Little, Brown and Company (1904).

17   Interviews with Anne Whitehouse Gass and Priscilla Whitehouse Rand, Brooks's daughters.

18   Whitehouse, Florence Brooks. "By Way of Compensation", Gass Family Private Collection.

19   Marquis, Nelson. *Who's Who in New England: A Biographical Dictionary of Leading Living Men and Women*, Chicago: A. N. Marquis and Company (1915).

20   Solomon, Howard M. "Combating the 'Social Evil': Masculinity and Moral Reform in Portland, 1912–1914," *Maine History*, Volume 43, No. 3, January 2008, pp. 139–165.

21   Ibid.

22   Buechler, Steven M. *The Transformation of the Woman Suffrage Movement*, New Brunswick, NJ: Rutgers University Press (1986).

23   Harper, Ida Husted, ed. *The History of Woman Suffrage, Vol. 5*. National American Woman Suffrage Association (1922).

24   Irwin, Inez Hayes. *The Story of Alice Paul and the National Woman's Party*, Fairfax, VA: Denlinger's Publishers, LTD (1964).

25   "Call for a Woman Suffrage Convention," *Portland Daily Eastern Argus*, January 29, 1873. The other signers included John Neal, S. T. Pickard, Mrs. Olive Dennett, Mrs. Eleanor Neal, Chandler Beal, Wm. H. Libbey, Gtr. Selden Conbut, H. H. Hamlen, H. S. Osgood, Mrs. C. A. Quimby, Mrs. W. K. Lancey, Mrs. D. M. Waitt, Mrs. W. B. Lapham, Mrs. S. M. Barton (all from Portland), and J. J. Eveleth, Mayor of Augusta.

26   "Woman's Suffrage Association," *Portland Daily Eastern Argus*, January 31, 1873.

27   "Historical Sketch of the Maine Woman Suffrage Association," *Portland Daily Eastern Argus*, June 26, 1917.

28   Bacon, George F. *Portland [Me.], its Representative Business Men and its Points of Interest*, Newark NJ: Glenwood Publishing Co. (1891).

29   Agger, Lee. *Women of Maine*, Portland, ME: Guy Gannett Publishing Co. (1982).

30   Helen Bates to Ida Greenwood, November 10, 1913, Ida Greenwood Collection, University of Maine, Orono (hereafter known as the Ida Greenwood Collection).

31   "Equal Suffrage Program" news clipping, undated, FBW Papers Box 2, Folder 4.

32   "Answers Anti's: Mrs. R. T. Whitehouse Reads Paper on Woman Suffrage," *Portland Press Herald*, January 7, 1914.

33   Ibid.

34   "A Big Audience Hears Suffrage Debate," *Portland Evening Express & Advertiser*, March 17, 1914.

35   "Women's Advance Causing Panic in Saloon Ranks," *Portland Evening Express & Advertiser*, March 18, 1914.

36   "A Big Audience Hears Suffrage Debate," *Portland Evening Express & Advertiser*, March 17, 1914. The judges were Henry F. Merrill, Edmund T. Garland, and Edgar R. Payson.

37   Ibid.

38   "Women's Advance Causing Panic in Saloon Ranks," *Portland Evening Express & Advertiser*, March 18, 1914.

39   "A Big Audience Hears Suffrage Debate," *Portland Evening Express & Advertiser*, March 17, 1914.

40   Lucy Hobart Day to Ida Greenwood, March 11, 1914, Ida Greenwood Collection.

41   Florence was on good terms with Richards, and later in 1917 recruited her to contribute to a special suffrage edition of the *Argus* (see "How Women Helped in War Time," *Portland Daily Eastern Argus*, June 26, 1917). Then in her mid-sixties, however, and with an active writing career, Richards never took on a leadership role in Maine suffrage activity.

42   Helen Bates to Ida Greenwood, November 10, 1913, Ida Greenwood Collection.

43   Few records of the Junior Suffrage League survive, nor do the newspapers carry much report of its activity. Its initial purpose was to educate younger women about suffrage.

44   MWSA stationery used in correspondence from Helen Bates to Ida Greenwood, November 10, 1913, Ida Greenwood Collection. MWSA's officers at the time Florence first joined the board were as follows:

Miss Helen N. Bates, President: *65 Sherman Street, Portland*

Mrs. Hannah J. Bailey, Vice-President-at-Large: *Winthrop Center*

Mrs. Emma E. Knight, Vice-President: *5 Knight Street, Portland*

Miss Anna Burgess, Recording Secretary: *8 Whitney Street, Portland*

Mrs. Lucy Hobart Day, Corresponding Secretary: *655 Congress Street, Portland*

Mrs. Lizzie H. French, Treasurer: *90 High Street, Portland*

Miss Alice Blanchard, Auditor: *Preble House, Portland*

Miss Susan A. Clark, Supt. Literature: *21 E. Promenade, Portland*

Miss Margaret Laughlin, Supt. Enrollment: *18 Spring Street, Portland*

Miss Ella O. Woodman, Supt. Press Work: *492 Cumberland Avenue, Portland*

45   Lucy Hobart Day to Ida Greenwood, March 11, 1914, Ida Greenwood Collection.

46   Helen Bates to Ida Greenwood, November 10, 1913; Lucy Hobart Day to Ida Greenwood, February 6, 1914; Lucy Hobart Day to Ida Greenwood, March 11, 1914; Lucy Hobart Day to Ida Greenwood March 31, 1914; Lucy Hobart Day to Ida Greenwood, November 10, 1914: all from the Ida Greenwood Collection.

47   Lucy Hobart Day to Ida Greenwood, March 11, 1914; Sara Anthoine to Ida Greenwood, September 24, 1914: Ida Greenwood Collection.

48   Helen Bates to Ida Greenwood, March 3, 1914, Ida Greenwood Collection.

49   Literature distributed by the Men's Equal Suffrage League, FBW Papers, Box 2, Folder 5.

50   Ibid.

51   Portland newspaper clipping, undated; Private Collection. Vice-President positions were filled by Morrill N. Drew, C. S. Stetson, William R. Pattangall, and Ira G. Hersey. George Allan of Portland was Treasurer and Ralph O. Brewster, also of Portland, served as Secretary.

52   The Political Graveyard, www.politicalgraveyard.com.

53   Gregory, J. B. *Maine Register or State Year-book and Legislative Manual*, No. 45 (July 1914), page 221.

54   "Woman Suffrage Defeated After Interesting Debate Lacked Ten of Two-Thirds, *Daily Eastern Argus*, March 24, 1915. Other supporters included Representatives Thombs, Smith, Lawrence, and St. Clair.

55   Ibid.

56   Ibid.

57   "Equal Suffrage Defeated by Tory Democrats and Republicans in a Non-Representative Maine House," *Lewiston Journal,* March 24, 1915.

58   "Woman Suffrage Defeated After Interesting Debate Lacked Ten of Two-Thirds," *Daily Eastern Argus*, March 24, 1915.

59   Catt, Carrie Chapman, and Nettie Rogers Schuler. *Woman Suffrage and Politics: The Inner Story of the Suffrage Movement*, New York, C. Scribner's Sons (1923).

60   Whitehouse, Florence Brooks. "An Argument in favor of Votes for Women," Maine Woman Suffrage Association, Portland (1915).

61   Ibid.

62   Ibid.

63   Ibid.

64   Eisenstein, Sarah. *Give Us Bread But Give Us Roses: Working Women's Consciousness in the United States, 1890 to the First World War*, London: Routledge & Kegan Paul (1983).

65   Eddy, Roscoe, Maine Commissioner of Labor, to Florence Brooks White-house, August 27, 1915. Eddy said no data existed on the number of women employed outside manufacturing, but he believed 25,000 was a low estimate.

66   Wolman, Leo. "The Extent of Labor Organization in 1910 and 1920," Chapter 4 in *The Growth of American Trade Unions, 1880–1923*, National Bureau of Economic Research (1924), page 85.

67   For example, the Woman's Trade Union League was founded in 1903 when the American Federation of Labor made it clear that it had no intention of representing women. Encyclopedia Britannica, http://www.britannica.com/EB-checked/topic/647200/Womens-Trade-Union-League-WTUL.

68   Eisenstein, Sarah. *Give Us Bread But Give Us Roses: Working Women's Consciousness in the United States, 1890 to the First World War*, London: Routledge & Kegan Paul (1983).

69   Notes taken by Florence at a meeting she attended of the New England Committee on the Shorter Workday for Women and Minors, Boston MA, at the Women's Trade Union League, May 22, 1915, FBW Papers, Box 2, Folder 8.

70   Ibid.

71   Irwin, Inez Hayes. *The Story of Alice Paul and the National Woman's Party*, Fairfax, VA: Denlinger's Publishers, LTD (1964).

72 Flexner, Eleanor, and Ellen Fitzpatrick. *Century of Struggle: The Woman's Rights Movement in the United States*, Cambridge, MA: Belknap Press of Harvard University (1959), page 256.

73 Alice Paul's report to the NAWSA Annual Meeting, December 1913, 33/73, in The Papers of Carrie Chapman Catt, Library of Congress (hereafter referred to as the CCC Papers).

74 Ibid.

75 Lucy Burns to Anna Howard Shaw, December 23, 1913, 33/73, CCC Papers.

76 Alice Paul to Mary Ware Dennett, December 16, 1913, CCC Papers.

77 Ruth McCormick to Anna Howard Shaw, February 3, 1914, CCC Papers.

78 Ibid. According to wordsmith.org, the phrase "Kilkenny cat fight" refers to people who fight relentlessly until they destroy each other. It is based on an old limerick, as follows:

There wanst was two cats of Kilkenny
Each thought there was one cat too many
So they fought and they fit
And they scratched and they bit
'Til instead of two cats there weren't any.

79 Mary Ware Dennett to Alice Paul, February 10, 1914, 33/73, CCC Papers.

80 Antoinette Funk to Anna Howard Shaw, February 26, 1914; March 4, 1914; April 29, 1914: 33/73, CCC Papers.

81 Alice Paul to Mrs. Oakes Ames, March 17, 1915, 33/73, CCC Papers.

82 Helen Bates to Carrie Chapman Catt, January 6, 1916, 33/73, CCC Papers.

83 Ibid.

83A Lucy Burns to Florence Kelley, September 11, 1915, NWP Papers, Part 2, Series 1, Reel 19; Annie E. Porritt to Alice Paul, October 28, 1915, NWP Papers, Part 2, Series 1, Reel 20; Annie E. Porritt to Alice Paul, October 30, 1915, NWP Papers, Part 2, Series 1, Reel 20; and Alice Paul to Florence Brooks Whitehouse, November 12, 1915, NWP Papers, Part 2, Series 1, Reel 20.

Florence was not the NWP's first choice for the national advisory committee. They were considering Mrs. Morrill (Jessamine R.) Goddard, who was probably a summer resident. They also did not decide to invite Florence to serve as Chairman right away; two alternatives were Mrs. W. L. Hunt or Mrs. Frances B. Ayer, both of whom lived in Bangor. However, as another NWP organizer noted, "Distances and means of communication [in Bangor] are rather intimidating. Trains in winter are very rare, roads are terrible, and suffragists are few and far between." They also had no money. Portland was a better choice, and Kelley thought Florence the clear winner for the role.

84   "Congressional Union Meets," *Portland Evening Express*, September 2, 1915.

85   Adams, Katherine H., and Michael L. Keene. *Alice Paul and the American Suffrage Campaign*, Urbana and Chicago: University of Illinois Press (2008), pages 103–109.

86   Flexner. *Century of Struggle: The Woman's Rights Movement in the United States.*

87   "Hear Echoes of National Convention: Equal Suffragists Listen to Some Interesting Addresses," *Portland Daily Press*, December 22, 1915.

88   McCormick, Ruth Hanna (Mrs. Medill). "The Shafroth Suffrage Amendment," 59/73, CCC Papers, undated, circa 1915.

89   "Which Amendment Shall We Support?" Congressional Union for Woman Suffrage, Washington, DC, undated, circa summer of 1914.

90   Flexner. *Century of Struggle: The Woman's Rights Movement in the United States.*

91   Ibid.

92   Lunardini, Christine. *From Equal Suffrage to Equal Rights: Alice Paul and the National Woman's Party, 1910–1928*, San Jose, CA: toExcel, 1986.

93   Ibid.

94   Ibid.

95   Flexner. *Century of Struggle: The Woman's Rights Movement in the United States.*

96   Helen N. Bates to Carrie Chapman Catt, January 6, 1916, 33/73, CCC Papers. (In fact, Bates sent two letter to Catt that day; a first (typed) letter was sent regular mail, and a hastily scrawled second letter containing much the same complaints was sent special delivery because Bates feared Catts would not get the first one in time to respond before the MWSA Board meeting.)

97   Helen N. Bates to Carrie Chapman Catt, January 22, 1916, CCC Papers.

98   James, Edward T., Janet W. Ames, and Paul S. Boyer, ed, *Notable American Women, 1607–1950: A Biographical Dictionary, Volume 2*, Cambridge: Harvard University Press (1971), page 588.

99   "Program for the Suffrage Convention," *Portland Evening Express*, February 26, 1916.

100   *Portland Sunday Express*, March 17, 1916. Sykes's husband was president of Connecticut College.

101   List of officers of the Maine branch of the Congressional Union, April, 1916, National Woman's Party Papers, Library of Congress. These were as follows:

Chairman:	Florence Brooks Whitehouse, 42 Deering Street, Portland
1st Vice Chairman:	Mrs. Philip F. Chapman, 175 Spring Street, Portland
2nd Vice Chairman:	Mrs. Edward S. (Sarah) Anthoine, 87 Emery Street, Portland
3rd Vice Chairman:	Mrs. Frederick Ayer, 75 Ohio Street, Bangor
4th Vice Chairman:	Mrs. Isabel Whittier Greenwood, Farmington
5th Vice Chairman:	Mrs. Eva L. Bean, Old Orchard

102   Julia Emory to Alice Paul, February 24, 1918, National Woman's Party Papers, Library of Congress (hereafter referred to as the NWP Papers).

103   Florence Brooks Whitehouse to Elizabeth Elder, April 4, 1916, NWP Papers. The tour was of the "Suffrage Special," a train car carrying Union representatives bearing appeals from the disfranchised eastern states to their western sisters in pressuring Congress and the president to pass the Federal Amendment.

104   "Augusta Suffrage League Auxiliary to the State and National Organizations," *Portland Evening Express*, March 10, 1916.

105   Florence Brooks Whitehouse to Alice Paul, April 14, 1916, NWP Papers. Florence mentions that Senator C. F. Johnson remained opposed to suffrage ("the Negro problem is his problem"), and that Congressman D. J. McGillicuddy left before they could see him.

106   Ibid. The resolution Florence sent read: "The members & friends of the Maine Branch of the Congressional Union for Woman Suffrage do earnestly request the women of the enfranchised states to use to the utmost their direct influence upon Congress through their Senators and Congressmen to pass the Federal Amendment enfranchising women." This was adopted by MWSA leagues in Augusta, Bangor, Waterville, and Portland, as well as by the Maine branch of the CU.

107   Unknown person at Union headquarters to Florence Brooks Whitehouse, April 18, 1916, NWP Papers.

108   Alice Paul to Florence Brooks Whitehouse, April 18, 1916, NWP Papers. Paul was very appreciative and said she had shown the article to a number of people at headquarters.

109   "Resigns as President of Suffrage Ass'n," *Portland Evening Express*, March 30, 1916.

110   Florence Brooks Whitehouse to Alice Paul, July 4, 1916, NWP Papers.

111   Form letter sent to Maine legislators from Florence Brooks Whitehouse, May 1916, FBW Papers, Box 2, Folder 10.

112   Florence Brooks Whitehouse to Alice Paul, July 4, 1916, NWP Papers.

113   "Time Ripe to Present the Suffrage Question to People, Says Milliken,"
       Portland Evening Express, March 22, 1916.

114   Florence Brooks Whitehouse to Alice Paul, July 4, 1916, NWP Papers.

115   Alice Paul to Florence Brooks Whitehouse, July 8, 1916, NWP Papers. These
       words would come back to haunt Florence before suffrage was won. Paul
       demonstrated here the political prescience that made her such an effective
       leader, accurately predicting the very situation in which Maine would find
       itself in 1918.

116   Alice Paul to Mrs. Lawrence Lewis, July 8, 1916, NWP Papers.

117   Alice Paul to Dora Stevens, April 12, 1916, NWP Papers.

118   Lunardini. *From Equal Suffrage to Equal Rights.*

119   Flexner. *Century of Struggle: The Woman's Rights Movement in the United
       States.*

120   Flier for National Woman's Party Convention, June 6, 1916, NWP Papers.
       These included the Democratic, Progressive, Republican, Prohibition, and
       Socialist Parties.

121   *New York World*, June 7, 1916.

122   Ibid.

123   Stevens, Doris, and Carol O'Hare, ed. *Jailed for Freedom: American Women
       Win the Vote*, Troutdale, OR: NewSage Press (1995), page 51.

124   Lunardini. *From Equal Suffrage to Equal Rights.*

125   Alice Paul to Katherine Morey, telegram c. October 1916, NWP Papers.

126   "Woman Suffrage Department: Florence Brooks Whitehouse," *Lewiston
       Journal*, October 26, 1916.

127   Ford, Linda G. *Iron-Jawed Angels: The Suffrage Militancy of the National
       Woman's Party 1912–1920*, Lanham, MD: University Press of America (1991).

128   "Woman Suffrage Department: Florence Brooks Whitehouse," *Lewiston
       Journal*, October 26, 1916.

129   Ibid.

130   "Campaign for Woman Suffrage—Wyoming Women Enthusiastic in Cause
       and Ready to Help," *Lewiston Journal*, October 24, 1916.

131   "Says Republicans Unjustly Blame Women for Defeat," *Portland Sunday
       Telegram*, November 19, 1916.

132   Florence Brooks Whitehouse to Alice Paul, December 12, 1916, NWP Papers.

133   "Maine Suffragists Like Rip Van Winkle: Likelihood of State Referendum in 1916 Throws Consternation into Ranks!" *Lewiston Journal*, October 13, 1916.

134   "Maine Suffrage Convention Opens," *Bangor Daily News*, October 13, 1916; also "Maine Suffragists Vote to Work for Referendum After a Lively Meeting on Friday," *Kennebec Journal*, October 14, 1916.

135   As Speaker of the House, he became known as "Czar Reed" for his use of the Speaker's power in maneuvering the Republican agenda through the House, and imposed "Reed Rules" to change how the business of the House would be conducted. Many of these are still used in the House today.

136   "Maine Suffragists Vote to Work for Referendum After a Lively Meeting on Friday," *Kennebec Journal*, October 14, 1916, and "Suffrage School is a Success," *Daily Eastern Argus*, January 18, 1917.

       Other officers included Mrs. J. Frank Rich, Rockland, Recording Secretary; Mrs. Katie L. Luce, Old Orchard; Mrs. A. L. T. Cummings, Auditor. The congressional district chairmen were: 1st District—Mrs. F. E. Woodruff; 2nd District—Mrs. Obadiah Gardner, Rockland; 3rd District—Mrs. Henry Cobb, Augusta; 4th District—Mrs. Ralph Jones, Orono.

137   "Suffrage School is a Success," *Daily Eastern Argus*, January 18, 1917.

138   Harper, Ida H. *The History of Woman Suffrage, Vol. 6, 1900–1920.* New York: J. J. Little & Ives Company (1922).

139   Florence Brooks Whitehouse to Alice Paul, December 12, 1916, NWP Papers. All other quotes in this paragraph are from this letter.

140   Alice Paul to Florence Brooks Whitehouse, December 18, 1916, NWP Papers, Reel 36.

141   Ford. *Iron-Jawed Angels: The Suffrage Militancy of the National Woman's Party 1912–1920.* The five women were Elizabeth Selden Rogers, Anna Lowenburg, Caroline Spencer, Florence Bayard Hilles, and Mabel Vernon. They later lamented that the cords with which they held the banner were too long, so that it hung too low and was thus easier to reach. They had intended for it to hang longer.

142   Florence Brooks Whitehouse to Alice Paul, December 12, 1916, NWP Papers.

143   Stevens, Doris, and Carol O'Hare, ed. *Jailed for Freedom: American Women Win the Vote*, Troutdale, OR: NewSage Press (1995), page 51.

144   Alice Paul to Florence Brooks Whitehouse, December 18, 1916, NWP Papers, Reel 36.

145 *Daily Eastern Argus*, January 11, 1917, Portland, Maine, page 6.

146 "The White House Pickets," *Washington Herald*, January 11, 1917.

147 "'Mild Militancy' is Repudiated by President Maine Woman Suffrage," *Kennebec Journal*, January 15, 1917.

148 Ibid.

149 Anne Martin to Florence Brooks Whitehouse, December 30, 1917, NWP Papers. Martin was at that point serving as the NWP's legislative chairman.

150 Senator Bert W. Fernald to Florence Brooks Whitehouse, January 10, 1917, NWP Papers.

151 Rep. Wallace H. White, Jr., to Florence Brooks Whitehouse, January 12, 1917, NWP Papers.

152 "Inspirational Leaders Conduct Free Maine Suffrage School at Portland for Two Weeks—Political Methods Advised—Story of Opening Sessions," *Portland Evening Journal,* January 10, 1917.

153 Lister, Lynn. "Isabel W. Greenwood and the Women's Suffrage Movement," master's thesis, University of Maine at Farmington (1991).

154 Ibid.

155 "Large Suffrage Audience Addressed by Mrs. Cotman and Mrs. Justina L. Wilson," *Daily Eastern Argus*, January 12, 1917.

156 Legislative Record of the 78th Legislature of the State of Maine, Augusta: *Kennebec Journal*, 1917. It read: "Resolve proposing an amendment to the Constitution granting suffrage to women on equal terms with men."

157 "Suffragists and Antis Assemble in Augusta Today," *Daily Eastern Argus*, February 1, 1917.

158 "Record Crowd Hears Debate on Suffrage," *Daily Eastern Argus*, February 2, 1917.

159 Ibid.

160 Ibid.

161 Legislative Record of the 78th Legislature of the State of Maine, Augusta: *Kennebec Journal*, 1917. It is not clear from the record which of the three suffrage organizations was responsible for this stunt.

162 Ibid.

163 Ibid.

164   Ibid.

165   "Decisive Victory for Equal Suffrage in the Maine House," *Daily Eastern Argus*, February 22, 1917.

166   Legislative Record of the 78th Legislature of the State of Maine, Augusta: *Kennebec Journal,* 1917.

167   Copy of letterhead, FBW Papers, Box 2, Folder 7. The full board roster was as follows:

Officers

President: Mrs. Florence Brooks Whitehouse
Vice-President: Mrs. Guy P. Gannett
Secretary: Mr. George Burgess
Treasurer: Mr. Frederic W. Freeman

Executive Board Officers Ex Officio

Mr. Ralph O. Brewster
Mrs. Madeleine Louise Freeman
Mrs. Elizabeth Bates Keith
Mrs. Anna B. Stephens
Mr. John H. Walzer

Advisory Council

Androscoggin
Hon. Charles. S. Stetson, Greene
Aroostook
Hon. Albert A. Burleigh, Houlton

Cumberland
Miss Katrina Brewster, Portland
Mrs. Dorothy Bates Burgess, Portland
Mr. Harrie B. Coe, Portland
Miss Helen Coe, Portland
Hon. Howard Davies, Portland
Hon. Albert P. Gardner, Portland
Mrs. Augusta M. Hunt, Portland
Dr. Adam P. Leighton, Jr., Portland
Hon. William H. Looney, Portland
Mr. Edward F. Moody, Portland
Mrs. Jennie M. Moody
Mr. W. S. McGeoch, Portland
Mr. Stephen J. Richardson, Portland
Mrs. Sue M. Walzer, Portland
Hon. Robert Treat Whitehouse, Portland
Mrs. F. O. McDaniel, Portland
Mr. Henry C. Hunt, Brunswick
Rev. A. S. Bisbee, Woodfords

Franklin
Mrs. Frank W. Butler, Farmington
Hon. Elmer E. Richards, Farmington

Hancock
Mrs. Florence Kelley, Naskeag

Kennebec
Mr. Guy P. Gannett, Augusta
Mrs. Laura E. Richards, Gardiner

Lincoln
Mrs. Gertrude Leavett Coombs, Waldoboro

Oxford
Mrs. Rhima McDonald Sturtevant, Dixfield
Mrs. Edith H. Wheeler, So. Paris
Mrs. Bradford Andrews, Rumford

Penobscot
Mrs. Fred R. Ayer, Bangor
Mrs. Penelope P. Davis, Bangor
Mrs. Sylvia K. Ross, Bangor

Somerset
Hon. Wm. L. Walker, Skowhegan

Washington
Dr. Eliza Grady, Eastport
Rev. Robert Lee Russabarger, Lubec
Miss Helen N. Hanson, Calais

York
Hon. John P. Deeming, Saco
Mrs. David E. Doloff, Biddeford
Miss Edith B. Hunt, Springvale

168　　Florey, Ken. *Women's Suffrage Memorabilia: An Illustrated Historical Study*, Jefferson, NC: McFarland & Company, Inc., Publishers (2013).

169　　Costrell, Edwin. *How Maine Viewed the War, 1914–1917*, University of Maine Studies, Second Series, No. 49 (1940).

170　　Lunardini. *From Equal Suffrage to Equal Rights*.

171　　"Two Million Women Offer to Serve U.S.," *Washington Times*, February 25, 1917.

172　　Carrie Chapman Catt to Ethel Smith, August 3, 1917, CCC Papers.

173　　Ethel Smith to Carrie Chapman Catt, August 20, 1917, CCC Papers.

174 "Suffrage Workers to Unite Forces," *New York Times*, March 2, 1917.

175 Lunardini. *From Equal Suffrage to Equal Rights.*

176 Carrie Chapman Catt to Alice Paul, May 24, 1917, CCC Papers.

177 Ibid.

178 "Portland Boy Writes of Flights Among the Clouds," *Portland Sunday Telegram*, July 22, 1917.

179 "A Brief History of the American Red Cross," American Red Cross Museum website, http://www.redcross.org/about-us/history.

180 "Estimate Portland Total is $5,700,000 or $90 Per Capita," *Portland Evening Express*, June 15, 1917. Nationally, subscriptions of over $3 billion were predicted.

181 "Red Cross Fund Total in Portland is $102,985," *Portland Evening Express*, June 21, 1917; and "Portland Nears $150,000 in Red Cross Campaign, Goal is Now Set Higher," *Portland Evening Express*, June 22, 1917. The front-page article depicting the clock was surrounded by headlines trumpeting the arrest of suffragists at the White House gates, when the women first began holding banners quoting Wilson's speeches.

182 Laura Hughes Lunde Papers, University Library, University of Illinois at Chicago.

183 "Miss Laura Hughes Wins Her Audience on Friday Evening," *Kennebec Journal*, June 9, 1917.

184 Florence Brooks Whitehouse to Jane Addams, June 12, 1917, FBW Papers, Box 2, Folder 2.

185 Florence Brooks Whitehouse to Alice Stone Blackwell, June 13, 1917, FBW Papers, Box 2, Folder 2. Blackwell was the daughter of Lucy Stone, one of the suffrage pioneers who worked closely with Susan B. Anthony and Elizabeth Cady Stanton.

186 Will Ourcadie cartoons, FBW Papers, Box 5, Folder 1. In 1918 Freeman became a secondary source of cartoons for *The Suffragist*, which was the National Woman's Party weekly newspaper. See Editor, *The Suffragist* to Mr. F. Freeman, February 1, 1918, NWP Papers.

187 Florence Brooks Whitehouse to Carrie Chapman Catt, June 27, 1917, FBW Papers, Box 2, Folder 2.

188 Florence Brooks Whitehouse to Mrs. Frank J. Schuler, June 27, 1917, FBW Papers, Box 2, Folder 2.

189 Florence Brooks Whitehouse to Mrs. Frank J. Schuler, July 3, 1917, FBW Papers, Box 2, Folder 2.

190   Florence Brooks Whitehouse to Mrs. Veo. F. Small, July 3, 1917, FBW Papers, Box 2, Folder 2.

191   "Rotarians to Hear Suffrage Orator, Here," *Lewiston Journal*, April, 1917.

192   "Maine Woman Suffrage Assn. 37th Convention," *Kennebec Journal*, September 18, 1917.

193   Florence Brooks Whitehouse to Deborah Knox Livingston, FBW Papers, undated, c. August 1, 1917, Box 2, Folder 7.

194   "Anti-Militant: Mrs. Livingston Deplores D.C. Acts," *Kennebec Journal*, 1917, Series 1, Reel 54.

195   Ford. *Iron-Jawed Angels: The Suffrage Militancy of the National Woman's Party 1912–1920.*

196   Florence Brooks Whitehouse to Alice Paul, NWP Papers, Series 1, Reel 54.

197   Senator A. A. Jones to Mrs. Maud Wood Park, June 30, 1917, CCC Papers.

198   Park, Maud Wood. "Report on Press Situation," July 5, 1917, CCC Papers.

199   Ford. *Iron-Jawed Angels: The Suffrage Militancy of the National Woman's Party 1912–1920.* Ford also notes that the *Washington Post*'s coverage of the NWP dropped off substantially in the summer of 1917.

200   Maud Wood Park to J. P. Yoder, United Press Association, July 3, 1917, CCC Papers.

201   Ford. *Iron-Jawed Angels: The Suffrage Militancy of the National Woman's Party 1912–1920.*

202   Helena Hill Weed to Florence Brooks Whitehouse, March 18, 1917, FBW Papers, Box 2, Folder 1.

203   "Presidential Intercession on Appeal in Picketing Cases," *Kennebec Journal*, July 19, 1917. Eight of the women were married, and some had young children. The KJ also reported that the husbands were most anxious to bail them out of jail. It appears that this did not happen, however; all of the women left the prison at the same time.

204   Ibid. Alice Paul, now back on the picket line, reportedly had her neck gashed in one of these incidents.

205   "Inactive State Chairmen Do Not Respond When Called Upon to Work," NWP Papers, Series 1, Reel 54. The list in this report included the chairmen of over 20 other states.

206   "Miss Trax of Baltimore is Now in Maine," *Kennebec Journal*, July 11, 1917. Margaret Brent was the first woman suffragist in the United States; Susan B. was named for Susan B. Anthony.

207 "Mrs. Carrie Chapman Catt Opens Suffrage Campaign With Big Augusta Rally," *Kennebec Journal*, July 25, 1917. Actually, Mrs. Gannett never made it to the tea she was supposed to be hosting. She was "unavoidably detained" outside the city, and Mrs. Roy H. Bodman presided in her absence.

208 Ibid.

209 Florence Brooks Whitehouse to Deborah Knox Livingston, undated, c. August 1, 1917, FBW Papers, Box 2, Folder 7.

210 Florence Brooks Whitehouse to Miss Thirza Davis, August 3, 1917, FBW Papers, Box 2, Folder 4.

211 Florence Brooks Whitehouse to Captain Williams, August 8, 1917, FBW Papers, Box 2, Folder 4.

212 Florence Brooks Whitehouse to Miss Helen Maxey, August 20, 1917, FBW Papers, Box 2, Folder 4.

213 Florence Brooks Whitehouse to Mrs. George Bingham, August 20, 1917, FBW Papers, Box 2, Folder 4.

214 "Unfair Methods," *Portland Evening Express*, September 6, 1917.

215 "Who is John B. Mailing?" *Portland Evening Express*, September 1, 1917.

216 Catt, Carrie Chapman, and Nettie Rogers Shuler, *Woman Suffrage and Politics: The Inner Story of the Suffrage Movement*, New York: Charles Scribner's Sons (1926).

217 "Pine Tree State Rejects Suffrage," *New Britain Connecticut Herald*, September 13, 2017.

218 Chief Justice Walter Clark to Florence Brooks Whitehouse, August 16, 1917, FBW Papers, Box 2, Folder 4.

219 Florence Brooks Whitehouse to Chief Justice Walter Clark, August 20, 1917, FBW Papers Box 2, Folder 4.

220 Florence Brooks Whitehouse to Deborah Knox Livingston, August 20, 1917, FBW Papers, Box 2, Folder 4.

221 Ibid.

222 Ibid.

223 Florence Brooks Whitehouse to advertisers, August 27, 1917, FBW Papers, Box 2, Folder 4.

224 Charles E. Gurney to Florence Brooks Whitehouse, August 30, 1917, FBW Papers, Box 2, Folder 4.

225 Lucy Burns to "Fellow-member," August 25, 1917, NWP Papers, Box 2, Folder 4.

226 "Governor Milliken to Speak Tonight with Mrs. Catt," *Daily Eastern Argus*, September 8, 1917. The leagues were the Portland Equal Franchise League, MWSA, the Men's Equal Suffrage League, and the Equal Suffrage Referendum League.

227 "Large Audience Cheers Speakers at Suffrage Rally," *Portland Sunday Telegram*, September 8, 1917. Chandler's Band was established in 1833 and is believed to be the country's second oldest professional band in continuous service; www.chandlersband.com.

228 "Suffrage 19,428, Opposed 36,713," *Portland Evening Express*, September 12, 1917.

229 "The Vote in Portland," *Daily Eastern Argus*, September 11, 1917; and "Suffrage Beaten Badly in Bangor," *Bangor Daily News*, September 11, 1917.

230 "The Result: Contributory Causes," *Portland Evening Express*, September 11, 1917.

231 "The Time is Not Ripe for National Suffrage," *Daily Eastern Argus*, September 12, 1917.

232 "Praises Women Who Picket White House, But Says They Defeated Suffrage in Maine," *Portland Sunday Telegram*, September 15, 1917.

233 "The Suffrage Defeat in Maine," *New York World*, reprinted in the *Daily Eastern Argus*, September 13, 1917.

234 "Miss Connor New President of Maine Suffrage," *Kennebec Journal*, September 18, 1917.

235 "Suffragists of State in Convention Today," *Portland Evening Express*, September 18, 1917.

236 "Senate Committee Favorably Reports Suffrage Amendment," *Daily Eastern Argus*, September 14, 1917.

237 "Suffragists are Elated, Now Plan Vigorous Contest," *Portland Evening Express*, September 25, 1917; and "A Committee on Suffrage is Created," *Daily Eastern Argus*, September 25, 1917.

238 Florence Brooks Whitehouse to Alice Paul, September 24, 1917, NWP Papers.

239 Abby Scott Baker to Florence Brooks Whitehouse, October 18, 1917, FBW Papers, Box 2, Folder 5. In the end, Doris Stevens became gravely ill and Abby Scott Baker came in her place.

240 Florence Brooks Whitehouse to Berthe Arnold, NWP Papers, undated, Series 1, Reel 54.

241 Lunardini. *From Equal Suffrage to Equal Rights*; and Ford. *Iron-Jawed Angels: The Suffrage Militancy of the National Woman's Party 1912–1920*.

242 Lucy Burns to member of "Women in Jail Garb Rouse Suffragists"; news article, source and date unknown; CCC Papers.

243 Lucy Burns to Florence Brooks Whitehouse, November 6, 1917, FBW Papers, Box 2, Folder 5.

244 "Endorsement of Woman Suffrage," *Daily Eastern Argus*, November 2, 1917. The cabinet members were Josephus Daniels, Secretary of the Navy; Franklin K. Lane, Secretary of the Interior; David F. Houston, Secretary of Agriculture; William G. McAdoo, Secretary of the Treasury (and the president's son-in-law); and William C. Redfield, Secretary of Commerce.

245 "Social Gossip," *Portland Evening Express & Advertiser*, November 7, 1917.

246 "The Letter Box: American Women," *Portland Evening Express & Advertiser*, October 20, 1917.

247 Curiously, in later years family myth had it that Florence was arrested, jailed, and bailed out by her son Bob. This almost certainly never occurred. In early January 1918, Florence publicly admitted to picketing, but she never claimed to have been arrested or jailed. The NWP's records do not show her as one of those subjected to that treatment. On occasion, families did bail out pickets, but usually only if they became gravely ill, and even then over the prisoners' strong protests. Paul recruited pickets with the understanding that if sentenced they would do their time as political prisoners.

248 Whitehouse, Florence Brooks. Notes of a telephone conversation with Mrs. Bates, undated, c. 1917 or early 1918, FBW Papers, Box 3, Folder 9.

249 "The Confessions of a Picketeer," *Daily Eastern Argus*, January 7, 1918.

250 "Correspondence," *Daily Eastern Argus*, January 8, 1918.

251 "President for the Anthony Amendment," *Daily Eastern Argus*, January 10, 1917.

252 Alice Stone Blackwell to Ruth Pickering in *Pearson's Magazine*, January 14, 1918, NWP Papers, Series 1, Reel 55.

253 "Portland Suffrage Leaders Are Of Course Delighted With Action," *Daily Eastern Argus*, January 11, 1918.

254 Representative Ira Hersey to Miss Ella A. Clarke, February 11, 1918, FBW Papers, Box 2, Folder 5.

255 Whitehouse, Florence Brooks, Notes from meeting with Senator Frederick Hale, February 12, 1918, FBW Papers, Box 3, Folder 9.

256 Florence Brooks Whitehouse to Senator Frederick Hale, February 13, 1918, FBW Papers, Box 2, Folder 5.

257   Frederick Hale to Florence Brooks Whitehouse, February 16, 1918, FBW Papers Box 2, Folder 5.

258   Telegram from Florence Brooks Whitehouse to Alice Paul, January 23, 1918, NWP Papers, Series 1, Reel 56.

259   Florence Brooks Whitehouse to Alice Paul, February 7, 1918, and Florence Brooks Whitehouse to Doris Stevens, February 12, 1918, NWP Papers, Series 1, Reel 56.

260   Julia Emory to Alice Paul, February 16, 1918, NWP Papers, Series 1, Reel 56.

261   Julia Emory to Alice Paul, February 24, 1918, NWP Papers, Series 1, Reel 56.

262   Ibid.

263   Ibid.

264   Anne M. Gannett to Florence Brooks Whitehouse, October 19, 1917, FBW Papers, Box 2, Folder 5.

265   Nettie Rogers Shuler to Florence Brooks Whitehouse, January 28, 1918, Box 2, Folder 5.

266   Julia Emory to Alice Paul, March 5, 1918, NWP Papers.

267   Leonard, John William. *Woman's Who's Who of America: A Biographical Dictionary of Contemporary Women of the United States and Canada, 1914–1915*, New York, American Commonwealth Co. (1914). Peaslee, some 20 years Florence's senior, was another of the older generation of suffrage workers. She had testified several times on behalf of suffrage at the Maine legislature and once in front of the US Senate.

268   Florence Brooks Whitehouse to Alice Paul, March 7, 1918, NWP Papers.

269   Julia Emory to Alice Paul, March 5, 1918, NWP Papers, Series 1, Reel 58 .

270   Membership Chairman to Florence Brooks Whitehouse, March 1, 1918, NWP Papers. The new members were Miss Susie P. Clement (Portland), Mrs. Frank Weddell (Cape Elizabeth), and Mrs. George A. Weyer (Portland).

271   Helen M. Leonard to Mrs. Mary G. Fendall, March 7, 1918, NWP Papers.

272   Alice Paul to Julia Emory, March 8, 1918, NWP Papers.

273   Julia Emory to Alice Paul, March 5, 1918, NWP Papers.

274   Florence Brooks Whitehouse to Alice Paul, March 7, 1918, NWP Papers.

275   Orsdel, Josiah A. Van, Associate Justice. *In the Court of Appeals in the District of Columbia, No. 3121,* NWP Papers, Series 1, Reel 58.

276   Florence Brooks Whitehouse to Alice Paul, March 7, 1918, NWP Papers.

277   "Senator Gallinger Declares Votes for Women," *Kennebec Journal,* March 1, 1918.

278   Alice Paul to Florence Brooks Whitehouse, March 13, 1918, NWP Papers.

279   Julia Emory to Alice Paul, March 14, 1918, NWP Papers, Series 1, Reel 14.

280   Ibid. Suspicion of German sympathizers was common in Portland in this period. A fire that burned the top story and annex of the Press building on March 7th, for example, was followed by speculation in the papers that it had been set by German sympathizers angry with statements the newspaper had published. Why anyone would believe the Germans were funding the NWP is unclear; perhaps it was intended to encourage distractions from winning the war.

281   Beulah Amidon to "Family" at NWP Headquarters, March 16, 1918, NWP Papers.

282   "Is Gunning After Senator Fred Hale: Beulah Amidon the Picket," *Daily Eastern Argus,* March 14, 1918.

283   Beulah Amidon to Alice Paul, March 14, 1918, NWP Papers.

284   Beulah Amidon to "Family" at NWP Headquarters, March 16, 1918, NWP Papers. "Maidedness" is Amidon's term for the "state of having a maid."

285   Entry in "Society," *Portland Sunday Telegram,* March 17, 1918.

286   Julia Emory to Alice Paul, March 11, 1918, NWP Papers.

287   Florence Boeckel to Julia Emory, March 22, 1918, and Julia Emory to Alice Paul, March 19, 1918.

288   Robert Whitehouse, Jr., to Sen. Frederick Hale, March 29, 1918. The "third gigantic loan" referred to here was the third Liberty loan; at $3.6 billion, it was a staggering sum to raise in 1918.

289   "Heroes of the Air," *Daily Eastern Argus,* March 12, 1918.

290   Penn Whitehouse to parents, March 22, 1918, papers held by the Gass family.

291   "Anne Martin is Coming to Speak in Portland," *Daily Eastern Argus,* March 23, 1918.

292   Julia Emory to Alice Paul, March 23, 1918, NWP Papers.

293   "Raised Purse for Conversion of Senator Hale: Suffragists Are After Him,"
      Daily Eastern Argus, March 26, 1918.

294   *Portland Sunday Telegram*, March 24, 1918.

295   "Raised Purse for Conversion of Senator Hale: Suffragists Are After Him,"
      Daily Eastern Argus, March 26, 1918.

296   "Mr. Malone's Address," *Kennebec Journal*, March 28, 1918.

297   Florence Brooks Whitehouse to Alice Paul, March 30, 1918, NWP Papers,
      Series 1, Reel 58, and Julia Emory to Alice Paul, March 28, 1918, NWP Pa-
      pers.

298   "Delegates Arriving in Portland Republican State Convention...Some Night
      Before," *Kennebec Journal*, March 28, 1918.

299   Florence Brooks Whitehouse to Alice Paul, March 30, 1918, NWP Papers,
      Series 1, Reel 58.

300   Julia Emory to Alice Paul, March 31, 1918, NWP Papers, Series 1, Reel 58.

301   Florence Brooks Whitehouse to Alice Paul, April 2, 1918, NWP Papers, Se-
      ries 1, Reel 58.

302   Hourwich, Rebecca. Weekly Report, May 27 to June 2, 1918, NWP Papers,
      Series 1, Reel 61.

303   Telegram sent by Doris Stevens to "Attached List," [state Chairmen and
      other key supporters], May 8, 1918, NWP Papers, Series 1, Reel 60.

304   Doris Stevens to State, Legislative, & Congressional District Chairmen, May
      16, 1918, NWP Papers, Series 1, Reel 61.

305   Sue White to Alice Paul, May 30, 1918, NWP Papers, Series 1, Reel 61.

306   Doris Stevens to Anne Martin, June 14, 1918, NWP Papers, Series 1, Reel 62.

307   "History of the Portland Chapter, American Red Cross, May 1st, 1919,"
      American Red Cross, Hazel Braugh Records Center.

308   "Information Service Bureau of Red Cross Does Important Work," *Portland
      Evening Express*, November 6, 1919.

309   NWP Press Chairman to Mr. Lawrence, May 25, 1918, NWP Papers, Series
      1, Reel 61.

310   Doris Stevens to Anne Martin, June 14, 1918; NWP Papers, Series 1, Reel 62.

311   Telegram from Florence Brooks Whitehouse to NWP headquarters, June 26,
      1918, Series 1, Reel 62.

312   Alice Paul to Alice Henkle, June 29, 1918; NWP Papers, Series 1, Reel 62.

313   Abby Scott Baker to Florence Brooks Whitehouse, July 3, 1918, NWP Papers, Series 1, Reel 62.

314   Alice Paul to Florence Brooks Whitehouse, July 7, 1918, NWP Papers, Series 1, Reel 62.

315   Telegram from Florence Brooks Whitehouse to Alice Paul, July 8, 1918, and Florence Brooks Whitehouse to Alice Paul, July 10, 1918; NWP Papers, Series 1, Reel 62.

316   Alice Paul to Florence Brooks Whitehouse, July 15, 1918, NWP Papers, Series 1, Reel 63.

317   Alison Turnbull Hopkins to Alice Paul, July 23, 1918, NWP Papers, Series 1, Reel 63.

318   Alice Paul to Mrs. O. H. P. Belmont, July 18, 1918, NWP Papers, Series 1, Reel 63.

319   Alice Paul to Mrs. Toscan Bennett, July 23, 1918, NWP Papers, Series 1, Reel 63.

320   Alice Paul to Florence Brooks Whitehouse, August 2, 1918, NWP Papers, Series 1, Reel 63.

321   Florence Brooks Whitehouse to Alice Paul, August 2, 1918, NWP Papers, Series 1, Reel 63.

322   Alice Paul to Florence Brooks Whitehouse, August 8, 1918, NWP Papers, Series 1, Reel 63.

323   Alice Paul to Rebecca Hourwich, August 8, 1918, NWP Papers, Series 1, Reel 63.

324   Alice Paul to "Attached List," August 9, 1918, NWP Papers, Series 1, Reel 63.

325   Alison Turnbull Hopkins to Alice Paul, August 1, 1918, and Mrs. O. H. P. Belmont, September 9, 1918, NWP Papers Series 1, Reel 63.

326   Press Department to Miss Catherine Flanagan, August 12, 1918, NWP Papers, Series 1, Reel 63.

327   Stevens, Doris, and Carol O'Hare, ed. *Jailed for Freedom: American Women Win the Vote,* Troutdale, OR: NewSage Press (1995).

328   Alice Paul to "Suffragist," September 5, 1918, NWP Papers, Series 1, Reel 64.

329   Alice Paul to Mrs. Lawrence Lewis, September 4, 1918, NWP Papers, Series 1, Reel 64.

330   Alice Paul to Elsie Hill, September 18, 1918; NWP Papers, Series 1, Reel 64.

331   As quoted in Stevens, Doris, and Carol O'Hare, ed. *Jailed for Freedom: American Women Win the Vote*, Troutdale, OR: NewSage Press (1995).

332   Alice Paul to Margaret Whittemore, October 7, 1918, NWP Papers, Series 1, Reel 64.

333   Alice Paul to "Suffragist," October 12, 1918, NWP Papers, Series 1, Reel 64.

334   "The Forgotten Plague of 1918," *Maine Sunday Telegram*, September 27, 1998.

335   Alice Paul to Mrs. J. A. H. Hopkins, October 16, 1918, NWP Papers, Series 1, Reel 65.

336   Alice Paul to Florence Brooks Whitehouse, October 16, 1918, NWP Papers, Series 1, Reel 65.

337   Alice Paul to Miss Vida Milholland, October 16, 1918, NWP Papers, Series 1, Reel 65.

338   Alice Paul to Florence Brooks Whitehouse, October 21, 1918, NWP Papers, Series 1, Reel 65.

339   Florence Brooks Whitehouse to Alice Paul, October 22, 1918, NWP Papers, Series 1, Reel 65.

340   Lambert, David A., MD, Elenis Giannouli, MD, and Brian J. Schmidt, MD. "Postpolio Syndrome and Anesthesia," in *Anesthesiology* (Vol. 103, No. 3, pp. 638–644), Winnipeg, Canada: The University of Manitoba; also Richard L. Bruno, "Preventing Complications in Polio Survivors Undergoing Surgery," Greater Boston Post-Polio Association website, www.gbppa.org.

341   Telegram from Alice Paul to Margaret Whittemore, October 7, 1918; NWP Papers, Series 1, Reel 64.

342   Alice Paul to Margaret Whittemore, November 14, 1918, NWP Papers, Series 1, Reel 65.

343   Elizabeth Selden Rogers to members of the National Advisory Council and State Chairmen, November 19, 1918, and Alice Paul to State Chairmen, November 19, 1918, NWP Papers, Series 1, Reel 65. [Paul's letter contained a typo; instead of asking each state to raise $1,000 in the next month, as she probably intended, she asked them to raise $100,000 each.]

344   Alice Paul to Florence Brooks Whitehouse, November 26, 1918, NWP Papers, Series 1, Reel 65.

345   Lucy Burns to Florence Brooks Whitehouse, December 3, 1918, NWP Papers, Series 1, Reel 66.

346   Florence Brooks Whitehouse to Mrs. Lawrence Lewis, December 3, 1918, NWP Papers, Series 1, Reel 66.

347   Alice Paul to Florence Brooks Whitehouse, December 7, 1918, NWP Papers, Series 1, Reel 66.

348   Florence Brooks Whitehouse to Dora Lewis, December 7, 1918, NWP Papers, Series 1, Reel 66.

349   Florence Brooks Whitehouse to Dora Lewis, December 10, 1918; December 7, 1918, NWP Papers, Series 1, Reel 66.

350   Florence Brooks Whitehouse to Alice Paul, December 11, 1918, NWP Papers, NWP Series 1, Reel 66.

351   National Woman's Party to Florence Brooks Whitehouse, January 1, 1919, FBW Papers, Box 2, Folder 6.

352   Mabel Vernon to Florence Brooks Whitehouse, January 6, 1919, FBW Papers, Box 2, Folder 6.

353   Lucy Burns to Doris Stevens, January 8, 1919, NWP Papers, Series 1, Reel 67.

354   Maud Younger to Percival Baxter, January 4, 1919, NWP Papers, Series 1, Reel 67.

355   Betty Gram to Maud Younger, January 20, 1919, NWP Papers, Series 1, Reel 67.

356   Betty Gram to Alice Paul, January 24, 1919, NWP Papers, Series 1, Reel 68.

357   Maud Younger to Percival Baxter, January 23, 1919, NWP Papers, Series 1, Reel 68.

358   Betty Gram to Alice Paul, January 31, 1919, NWP Papers, Series 1, Reel 68.

359   Betty Gram to Mary Gertrude Fendall, February 1, 1919, NWP Papers, Series 1, Reel 68.

360   Florence Brooks Whitehouse to Alice Paul, January 31, 1919, NWP Papers, Series 1, Reel 68.

361   Alice Paul to Florence Brooks Whitehouse, January 18, 1919, NWP Papers, Series 1, Reel 67.

362   Betty Gram to Maud Younger, January 20, 1919, NWP Papers, Series 1, Reel 67.

363   Ibid.

364   "Woman's Party Holds a Rally," Newspaper clipping circa December, 1918 [Maine NWP]; and "Suffragists Hear Talk on War Work, Newspaper clipping circa December, 1918 [Portland Equal Franchise League], FBW Papers, Box 2, Folder 7.

365   Betty Gram to Maud Younger, February 3, 1919, NWP Papers, Series 1, Reel 68.

366   Lucy Burns to Miss L. J. C. Daniels, February 4, 1919, NWP Papers, Series 1, Reel 68.

367   National Woman's Party press release, February 8, 1914, CCC Papers, 33/73.

368   Park, Maud Wood. "Congressional Work for Nineteenth Amendment: Supplementary Notes," CCC Papers, 33/73.

369   Stevens, Doris. *Jailed for Freedom: American Women Win the Vote*, Troutdale, OR: NewSage Press (1995).

370   Alice Paul to Betty Gram, February 12, 1919, NWP Papers, Series 1, Reel 69.

371   Elsie Hill to Alice Paul, February 24, 1919, NWP Papers, Series 1, Reel 69.

372   "The Letter Box: Suffragists in Boston," letter to the editor from Florence Brooks Whitehouse, *Portland Evening Express*, February 27, 1919. The two speakers arrested were Elsie Hill and Mrs. Warren; the latter was released the same day.

373   Ibid.

374   "Suffs Start a Hunger Strike: Militants Absolutely Refuse to Touch Prison Fare," *Portland Evening Express*, February 26, 1919.

375   "Suff Lifted Bodily Into Patrol Wagon; 22 Arrested in Front of State House," *Portland Evening Express*, February 24, 1919.

376   "The Letter Box: Suffragists in Boston," letter to the editor from Florence Brooks Whitehouse, *Portland Evening Express*, February 27, 1919.

377   Alice Paul to Florence Brooks Whitehouse, March 1, 1919, NWP Papers, Series 1, Reel 69.

378   Alice Paul to Florence Brooks Whitehouse, February 14, 1919, NWP Papers, Series 1, Reel 69.

379   "Proposes That Suffrage Measure be Submitted to Vote of the People," *Portland Evening Express*, February 27, 1919.

380   Florence Brooks Whitehouse to Alice Paul, April 16, 1919, NWP Papers, Series 1, Reel 70.

381 Florence Brooks Whitehouse to Alice Paul, April 16, 1919, NWP Papers, Series 1, Reel 70. The dashes and parentheses used in place of periods are due to the fact that the period key on Florence's old typewriter had ceased functioning.

382 Press Department to Florence Brooks Whitehouse, April 23, 1919, NWP Papers, Series 1, Reel 70.

383 Alice Paul to Helen Hunt, April 21, 1919, NWP Papers, Series 1, Reel 70.

384 Alice Paul to Emma Wold, April 16, 1919, NWP Papers, Series 1, Reel 70.

385 Press Department to Florence Brooks Whitehouse, May 4, 1919, NWP Papers, Series 1, Reel 70.

386 "Suffs Certain of Victory at Extra Session," *Portland Evening Express*, May 9, 1919. President Wilson won Harris's favorable vote after meeting with him in Paris at the peace talks.

387 "Will Take 25 Years to Pay Off War Debt," *Portland Evening Express*, February 25, 1919, and "Make This Town Blossom with Buttons," *Portland Daily Eastern Argus*, April 25, 1919.

388 Florence Brooks Whitehouse to Anita Pollitzer, May 21, 1919, NWP Papers, Series 1, Reel 71.

389 Maud Wood Park to Congressional Chairman, May 23, 1919, CCC Papers, 32/73.

390 Maud Younger to Alice Paul, May 29, 1919, NWP Papers, Series 1, Reel 71.

391 "Suffrage Wins in Senate; Now Goes to States," *New York Times*, June 5, 1919, and "Expect Vote Later Today on Suffrage," *Daily Eastern Argus*, June 4, 1919.

392 Ibid.

393 Florence Brooks Whitehouse to Alice Paul, June 5, 1919, NWP Papers, Series 1, Reel 71.

394 Alice Paul to Florence Brooks Whitehouse, June 5, 1919, NWP Papers, Series 1, Reel 71.

395 Florence Brooks Whitehouse to Mabel Vernon, June 7, 1919, NWP Papers, Series 1, Reel 71.

396 Whitehouse, Florence Brooks. Notes taken from a *Portland Evening Express* interview, undated (c. July 1919).

397 Maud Younger to Florence Brooks Whitehouse, June 23, 1919, NWP Papers, Series 1, Reel 72.

398   Vivian Pierce to Mabel Vernon, July 1, 1919, NWP Papers, Series 1, Reel 72.

399   Legislative Record of the Maine State Senate, February 27, 1919, page 348.
       Maine State Archives.

400   Legislative Record of the Maine State Senate, March 11, 1919, page 480.
       Maine State Archives.

401   "Governor Milliken Refers Referendum Problem to Court," *Portland Eve-
       ning Express*, July 10, 1919.

402   Florence Brooks Whitehouse to Abby Scott Baker, July 11, 1919, NWP Pa-
       pers, Series 1, Reel 72.

403   Florence Brooks Whitehouse to Mabel Vernon, June 7, 1919, NWP Papers,
       Series 1, Reel 71.

404   Florence Brooks Whitehouse to Abby Scott Baker, July 11, 1919, NWP Pa-
       pers, Series 1, Reel 72.

405   Mary Winsor to Alice Paul, July 13, 1919, and Alice Paul to Mary Winsor,
       July 17, 1919, NWP Papers, Series 1, Reel 72.

406   Florence Brooks Whitehouse to Mary Winsor, August 2, 1919, NWP Papers,
       Series 1, Reel 73.

407   Mary Winsor to Mabel Vernon, August 8, 1919, NWP Papers, Series 1, Reel
       73.

408   Alice Paul to Mary Winsor, August 12, 1919, NWP Papers, Series 1, Reel 73.

409   Lelia E. Teaton to Mary Winsor, August 11, 1919, FBW Papers, Box 2,
       Folder 6.

410   Alice Paul to Dora Lewis, August 13, 1919, NWP Papers, Series 1, Reel 73.

411   Ratification Schedule, August 16, 1919, NWP Papers, Series 1, Reel 73.

412   Florence Brooks Whitehouse to Governor Carl Milliken, August 17, 1919,
       FBW Papers, Box 2, Folder 6.

413   Governor Carl Milliken to Alice Paul, August 18, 1919, NWP Papers, Series
       1, Reel 73.

414   Margaret Whittemore to Alice Paul, August 28, 1919, and Margaret Whitte-
       more to Florence Brooks Whitehouse, September 2, 1919, NWP Papers Series
       1, Reel 73.

415   Mabel Vernon to Dora Lewis, August 29, 1919, NWP Papers, Series 1, Reel
       73.

416   Florence Brooks Whitehouse to Mabel Vernon, September 9, 1919, NWP Papers, Series 1, Reel 73.

417   "State Officers of Suffragists Elected Today," *Portland Evening Express*, October 17, 1919.

418   C. P. Smith and H. B. Brawn to "Dear Sir," October 27, 1919, NWP Papers, Series 1, Reel 74.

419   Florence Brooks Whitehouse to Alice Paul, October 29, 1919, NWP Papers, Series 1, Reel 74.

420   Alice Paul to Florence Brooks Whitehouse, October 29, 1919, NWP Papers, Series 1, Reel 74.

421   Elizabeth Kalb to Mabel Vernon, October 30, 1919, NWP Papers, Series 1, Reel 74.

422   Copy of resolution passed by the American Federation of Labor, June 1917, FBW Papers, Box 2, Folder 2.

423   Frank Morrison to H.B. Brawn, October 30, 1919, FBW Papers, Box 2, Folder 6.

424   "Ratification Dinner Served Last Evening in Honor of Two Well Known Suffragists," *Daily Eastern Argus*, November 4, 1919.

425   "If But One Maine Woman Wants to Vote She Should Have Chance Says Governor," *Portland Evening Express*, November 4, 1919.

426   "Maine Senators Vote to Ratify Suffrage 24–5," *Portland Evening Express*, November 4, 1919.

427   Mabel Vernon to Caroline Katzenstein, November 11, 1919, NWP Papers, Series 1, Reel 74.

428   "An Illustration of Suffrage Methods and Mendacity," *The Woman Patriot*, November 29, 1919.

429   Mabel Vernon to Caroline Katzenstein, November 11, 1919, NWP Papers, Series 1, Reel 74.

430   Political Advertisement: "President Maine Federation of Labor Favors Ratification Federal Suffrage Amendment by the Maine Legislature," in *Kennebec Journal*, November 5, 1919.

431   "Suffrage Wins in Maine House," *Portland Evening Express*, November 5, 1919.

432   Whitehouse, Florence Brooks. Notes from her conversation with Representative Sherman L. Berry, November 7, 1919, FBW Papers, Box 2, Folder 8.

433   Florence Brooks Whitehouse to Lewis Burleigh, November 3, 1919, FBW Papers, Box 2, Folder 6.

434   "Governor Milliken Signing Letter Notifying Sec. Lansing that Maine had Ratified Federal Suffrage Amendment," *Portland Evening Express*, November 13, 1919.

435   "Notification of Suffrage Vote is Sent to Lansing," *Portland Evening Express*, November 7, 1919.

436   "Says Suffragists are Afraid to Await Vote of People," *Portland Evening Express*, November 5, 1919.

437   Flexner. *Century of Struggle: The Woman's Rights Movement in the United States.* The other states were Massachusetts, Missouri, Texas, Oklahoma, and Ohio.

438   "To Preside One Session: Mrs. Whitehouse to Attend National Convention of Woman's Party," *Portland Daily Press*, January 8, 1921.

439   "Reorganize Branch of the Woman's Party, To Work for Equality of Opportunity Now," Newspaper clipping circa January, 1921, FBW Papers, Folder 4.

440   Beginning in 1923, the NWP introduced an amendment reading "Men and women shall have Equal Rights throughout the United States and every place subject to its jurisdiction. Congress shall have power to enforce this article by appropriate legislation."

441   Doris Stevens Papers, MC 546, Box 45, Folder Reel 5, Schlesinger Library, Radcliffe College.

442   "Maine Will be Pioneer State in this Work: Clearinghouse Formed for All State Activities," *Daily Eastern Argus*, December 4, 1919. The new organization was the result of a merger between the State Board of Trade and the Agricultural and Industrial League.

443   Florence Brooks Whitehouse, private diary, 1924; Gass family collection.

444   Grace Hill, private journal; Hill family collection.

INDEX

Acknowledgements

I am indebted to the wonderful staff of the Maine Historical Society (MHS) whose encouragement throughout the lengthy process of researching and writing this book kept me returning to it despite (repeated) long absences from it. MHS also holds the Florence Brooks Whitehouse's papers and I spent many happy hours in their lovely reading room getting to know my great-grandmother.

I'm also grateful to the Portland Public Library, through which I could arrange to have research materials from all over the country sent on microfiche. During the countless hours I spent in the library the staff was always unfailingly courteous and kind, not just to me but to the many less fortunate people who sometimes take refuge there. What a gem of an institution.

It was a delight to end this journey supported by my talented nephew, Sam Brooks Walker, who offered his skills as a designer for the book. His eye for detail made the book more attractive and readable.

Finally, thanks to the many others who prodded me to return to this project when I got discouraged, or was distracted by other interests and obligations. Chief among these was my mother, Anne Whitehouse Gass, and my aunt, Priscilla Whitehouse Rand. I regret not being able to place a finished copy in their hands. My sister Vicki opened my eyes to the NWP' collection at the Library of Congress, and to Florence's labor interests. My husband, Rick Leavitt, and my children, Silas and Emma, also encouraged me to finish this book, and their belief in me and the value of this research helped give me the strength to do it.

About the Author

Anne B. Gass is Florence Brooks Whitehouse's great-granddaughter. She is the author of *Voting Down the Rose: Florence Brooks Whitehouse and Maine's Fight for Woman Suffrage*, published in 2014. Her article, "Florence Brooks Whitehouse and Maine's Vote to Ratify Women's Suffrage in 1919," appeared in the Maine History Journal in 2012. Gass lectures regularly on Florence Brooks Whitehouse and Maine suffrage history at conferences, historical societies, libraries, and other events.

In her professional life, Gass has continued her great-grandmother's activist tradition. She is the founder and principal of ABG Consulting, a small business devoted to supporting nonprofits, local and state governments, and foundations in their efforts to help people in need build stable, productive lives. Her clients create affordable housing and provide services that help people who are low income, homeless, are refugees, have mental illness, or incarcerated.

Working both in Maine and nationally Gass has written over $150 million in successful federal grants since founding her business in 1993. She has also completed numerous other special projects. Gass received her BA degree from Reed College in 1982 and a MA from the University of Maryland in 1987.